Portrait of Burkewood Welbourn
– an Engineer

Rh.

Portrait of Burkewood Welbourn
– an Engineer

D. B. Welbourn, F.Eng.

The Pentland Press Limited
Edinburgh • Cambridge • Durham • USA

First published in 1996 by
The Pentland Press Ltd.
1 Hutton Close
South Church
Bishop Auckland
Durham

British Library Cataloguing in Publication Data.
A catalogue record for this book is available
from the British Library.

ISBN 1 85821 389 4

Typeset by CBS, Felixstowe, Suffolk
Printed and bound by Antony Rowe Ltd., Chippenham

PREFACE

When my mother and father were separated from one another, they wrote to each other every day if it were humanly possible. They kept all these letters until they left their last house to live with their daughter, when they decided that they were too personal to leave for other people's eyes, and destroyed them, with the exception of those which my father had written when travelling abroad on business. These travels took him to Canada in 1907, to Moscow in 1908, to St Petersburg in 1909, to Constantinople (twice) in 1912 which he visited again in 1913. The last are from the USA and Canada in 1922.

Professor F.J. West, F.R.Hist.S., F.A.H.A., read them and suggested that they should be published. At my request, he has written an historical background, while at his suggestion I have written a memoir of my father, to accompany the letters.

My principal sources have been the few papers which my father left; picture postcard albums belonging to my late sister Edith and my eldest brother Tom; the proceedings of the Institution of Electrical Engineers; a draft copy of the history of the BICC plc by R.M. Morgan, to whom I am deeply indebted; the archives of the BICC which are deposited in the archives of the National Museums and Galleries of Merseyside, whose curator, Mr D. Le Mare, could not have been more helpful; and, above all, my own memory. My younger brother, Professor R.B. Welbourn FRCS, has also contributed. Our family home in Rainhill was only two miles from the BI works in Prescot (it was known locally as the BI or the wireworks), and in the holidays and vacations I frequently walked to work with my father in the morning, or walked home with him in the evening, when he would talk about what he had been doing that day. I think that this was partly to help to educate a budding engineer, partly to clear his own mind. Unfortunately, I have left writing this memoir until my memory is failing, and much that I once knew has gone. It has, however, been jogged and helped by many people in the British Standards Institution, the Cable Makers Association, and old associates of my father, who have written to me over the years.

I hope and believe that what I have written is factually accurate; the obituary published in *The Times*, written in haste by me, contained numerous errors, which are corrected here. I do not think that any of the stories are *ben trovato*, but they might well be. While I have never worked in the cable industry, I have spent my life as an engineer and cannot remember a time when I had not been in the BI works in Prescot, to which I have vague memories of first being taken one Sunday when I was about six years of age. Now almost as old as my father was when he died, I think that I can understand what he must have been feeling at the different points in his career.

CONTENTS

A **Memoir** by his son, D.B. Welbourn F.Eng., Fellow of Selwyn College, Cambridge

The **Historical Background** by Emeritus Professor Francis West, F.R.Hist.S., F.A.H.A., Professor of History and Government, Deakin University, Australia

The **Letters**, annotated and edited by D.B. Welbourn F.Eng., F.I.Mech.E., FIEE

NB: The letters printed here are printed in full, as are also two letters from Mr N.K. Bunn, who succeeded my father as Contracts Manager (pp. 253-256). A few letters, the only ones to survive, are also printed (pp. 294-298) to show what his normal flow of correspondence with his wife was like.

Burkewood Welbourn Hon.M.Eng.(Liverpool), AKC, MIEE

Born: 13 December 1875, died 1 July 1961.

Married: 29 July 1901 to Edith Annie Appleyard, born 10 July 1879, died 25 February 1969, daughter of Joseph Appleyard, founder with his father of Johnson and Appleyards, Furniture makers, of Rotherham and Sheffield.

Their children were:

Edith Burkewood Welbourn	b. 30 Aug 1902, d. 14 June 1986
Joseph Thomas (Tom) Burkewood Welbourn	b. 30 Aug 1905, d. 3 August 1988
Frederick (Fred) Burkewood Welbourn	b. 12 Oct 1912, d. 6 July 1986
Donald Burkewood Welbourn	b. 11 Feb 1916 (the writer)
Richard (Dick) Burkewood Welbourn	b. 1 May 1919

They lived at Ingleton, Prescot Road, St Helens, Lancashire, from 1901 to 28 July 1904. (In a letter my father refers to their first home at the Toll Bar, which is between Prescot and St Helens.) From 1904 to 1908 at Clarach, Warrington Road, Rainhill, Lancashire, the end house just to the West of the War memorial; from 26 March 1908 to 1924 at Craven Lodge, Craven Road, Rainhill, and from 23 October 1924 to 18 October 1950 at The Croft, St James Road, Rainhill, which they built. From 18 October 1950 to 1958 at Homecroft, 7 Eddisbury Road, West Kirby, Wirral; and from 1958 until his death at their daughter's home, St John's Vicarage, Caterham. My mother died in the Royal Hammersmith Hospital.

Chapter 1

THE FIRST 21 YEARS

Burkewood Welbourn's ancestry can be traced back to a labourer who married in the charming church, part Norman, part Gothic, of North Witham in 1695. The village is near Colsterworth, about 8 miles south of Grantham. His great-grandfather was a labourer of Long Sutton in Lincolnshire, whose elder son Thomas, born on 30 November 1814, moved to London. On his marriage certificate, dated 8 June 1840, he is described as a carpenter, of 106 Drummond Street. This house is one of a fine row of three-storied stone houses to the west of Euston Station. His wife was Louisa Chatfield, a servant, daughter of Robert Chatfield, shoemaker, of Lewes. By the time that his son Frederick Burkwood (*sic*) Welbourn, born 19 March 1843, was married on 4 January 1873 at St John's Church, Hampstead, he describes himself as a builder in the firm of T. & F. Welbourn, his son Frederick being the partner. At the time of his death in 1881 he was a wealthy man, owning about 50 houses in the St Johns Wood area of London as well as building land in Barnet. In 1902, after some had been sold, his estate still possessed 41 houses, 3 stables, and a studio producing an income from rents of £3,675 p.a. against which had to be offset ground rents of £529 and mortgage interest at between 4½% and 5% on £28,223. This gave a net income of about £1,500 p.a. The property probably had a market value just under £40,000. (For 1994 values, multiply by 50 or more.)

Frederick married Clara McLatchie on 29 March 1878; she was born on 23 December 1852, the daughter of a Scotsman who, according to his Army papers, was born at Abbey in Renfrew. However, no record of his birth can be found in the parish register. He served from 1843 to 1864 as a Private in the 2nd Fusilier Battalion Scots Guards, and at the age of 39 took an honourable discharge. He then vanished, possibly going back to Montreal where his regiment had been stationed for the previous four years. According to his marriage certificate, his father, too, had been a soldier. He married a Miss Harriet Jones, probably from Kington in Herefordshire or Knighton in Radnor who, according to family tradition, was housekeeper for the Earl of Powis. Her father was a farmer, Edward Jones. Frederick and Clara married just a week after her twenty-first birthday; no member of either of their families signed the register.

Frederick and Clara Welbourn's first child, Edith, was born on 13 May 1874, and died on 19 December 1875, just six days after the birth of their son, Burkewood, on 13 December 1875. Within a fortnight the father, who was consumptive, had to go off to the south of France for the sake of his health. Both children had been born at 8 Bernard Street, a cul-de-sac off Regent's Park Road, London NW. The street had been renamed or vanished before 1948.

In letters to his wife from France in early 1876, Frederick refers to their infant son as Burkewood Thomas Welbourn Esq., but for some reason the Thomas was dropped when Burkewood was christened. As a young man, Frederick Welbourn had spent several winters in Hyères and other places in the south of France because of his consumption; in letters which survive, he records visiting the galleys in Toulon. When she was about 95, with her memory far gone, Clara Welbourn once talked to the writer about Paris before the war, which turned out to be the Franco-Prussian War of 1870. She was then only 17. Did Frederick meet her there? If so, how did she come to be there, daughter of a private in the Scots Guards? Was perhaps her mother lady's maid to the Countess of Powis? In his letters after the birth of their son he assumes that she understands French. In a birthday book which belonged to the father of his wife's second husband, he is referred to as 'Frederick Welbourn, London and Paris'. He died on 29 March 1878 when his son was only two years three months old. Family tradition has it that he caught pneumonia on a railway station when in pursuit of his sister Emily, a much beloved aunt of Burkewood, who had run away with her paramour, Hunter John Dodds by whom she had one son. She later married Henry Gregory, a farmer of Pinner, by whom she had ten children. Romantic as this story may be, the dates fit and it appears to be true, despite the fact that it conflicts with what Welbourn wrote many years later. He had said that his father's health had been weakened as a result of catching pneumonia at the age of 20 when travelling by train to Doncaster, to see what he could do for his uncle, Robert Welbourn of Cowbit, who was in the workhouse, having 'gone wrong' after an unsuccessful second marriage. As a boy, Burkewood had once visited him in Cowbit, and it is clear from papers left by his mother's father-in-law by her second marriage, that the tale about Robert cannot be true, since the dates do not fit. In 1863, when my grandfather was 20, Robert was farming successfully in Cowbit, and fathering children, one of whom emigrated to Hamilton in Canada. One of his sons became a brigadier, another a major in the Salvation Army.

Welbourn's relatives had emigrated to Australia, and the Hon. Tom Playford, 'Honest Tom', Premier of South Australia, used to visit him when in England.

Burkewood's father Frederick died on 29 March 1878, predeceasing his grandfather, Thomas Welbourn, who died on 26 September 1881, shortly after his daughter-in-law Clara Welbourn had remarried on 1 March 1881 her first husband's second cousin, William Thomas Welbourn, and moved with her son to her husband's farm at Weston St Mary near Spalding in Lincolnshire. They lived at Chestnut House, Broadgate, of which Burkewood made a pencil drawing in 1894. According to the 1881 Census, William had 20 acres, given to him by father, while his father, John Welbourn, living nearby had 50 acres, and lived in a house with three resident maids. John Welbourn, cousin of Welbourn's father, had started his career as a cottager owning 3 acres, and had prospered. Unwisely, he went on buying land at about £100 per acre on borrowed money after the onset of the agricultural depression of 1872. After his death in 1882 his son William inherited all the property, but had to sell up in 1900 or 1901, shortly after Burkewood had started work in industry. He became weighman at the coal depot at Peakirk railway station. He was a nice, quiet man in his later years, but showed no signs of the ability which his father must have possessed, and can hardly have been a source of inspiration to his step-son, Burkewood.

Chestnut House is about a mile south of Weston St Mary on slightly higher ground. There Welbourn grew up, riding his pony to Moulton Grammar School from 1881 until the end of 1890. On 31 July 1885, he was awarded as a prize 'for good conduct and improvement', G.A. Henty's *Facing Death – a tale of the coal mines*; forty years later his children were still reading Henty for pleasure; but not this one! On 2 April 1891 he received a formal testimonial from the headmaster.

The headmaster's comments on his school reports are typically, 'Work and Conduct and Progress very good', but in July 1886 he writes, 'Excellent conduct. The most intelligent and promising pupil in the form. Is very attentive and good'. His marks were fairly consistently high, with the exception of those for Euclid, which rather surprisingly, in view of his very logical mind, caused him trouble throughout his school days.

In view of his later career in electrical engineering, a certificate from the Department of Science and Art of the Committee of her Majesty's Most Honourable Privy Council on Education is of interest. At the examination in electricity and magnetism held on 15 May 1889, for which 12,463 candidates presented themselves, he obtained 2nd Class Honours in the Elementary Stage. The school must have been progressive in its outlook.

A photograph, which might be from about 1885, shows the headmaster, the Revd Frederick Hart MA, in academic dress, with what appear to be two masters wearing billycock hats, two boys of uncertain standing wearing MA caps, and 18 other boys, most of them wearing a round peakless cap, but Welbourn is in a tam-o-shanter.

Toward the end of his life, he saw a granddaughter's pony for the first time, and accurately summed up her points. He had never shown any interest in horseflesh, and in reply to an amazed comment that he was so well informed, he remarked that he had ridden to school daily for nine years. While at school his pony was stabled in one of the pubs to which the farmers from roundabout rode on quiet nags in the evening. At the end of it, the farmer's reins would, if necessary, be knotted, the owner hoisted into the saddle, and the mount given a good slap on its quarters to start it on its way home into the Fens.

In an obituary notice which he wrote of Mr William Watson Fisher of Moulton, (b. 23 January 1824, d. 18 February 1906) who had married an Elizabeth Welbourn, Burkewood Welbourn recalls how at the age of six he was picked up one day from Moulton Grammar school by Mr Fisher, who had lost his only son, and taken home to midday dinner and to his cosy fireside. There he enjoyed his daily dinner until he left the school, and from him Burkewood picked up his Conservative politics; the Home Rule Bill for Ireland of 1885 was hotly debated. Mr Fisher had been in North America in his younger days; he interested him in the architecture of Weston St Mary, a small Early English church, and of Moulton, a Decorated church.

Welbourn was confirmed in Spalding on 17 November 1890, just before his fifteenth birthday, and took his first communion on 23 November 1890 at St Mary's, Weston. He remained a practising Christian, with deep-seated belief, all his life. After his marriage, he and his wife knelt together in prayer by their bedside every night of their long lives.

According to his wife, in his younger days Welbourn had felt neglected, since his mother was busy producing eleven further children between 1881 and 1896 (she died on 28 August 1950 at the age of 97). She might have had more time for him had not the country been in the depths of a long lasting agricultural depression which had started about 1872. The Chestnuts can scarcely have been large enough to hold them. When he was almost 73 he wrote, 'I cannot remember my father at all, but I still have the sense of loss of not knowing him, and having his guiding hand'. He never mentioned any of his school companions in later life. He had a gun, which he sold soon after getting married, although there must have been rough shooting to be had around Rainhill; and he certainly skated on the fens, using the 'fen runners' which had a long blade turned up at the front, mounted in wood, with a screw in the heel to screw into normal working boots, and a strap to fasten over the toes. After his marriage he had half a dozen pairs in various sizes, and his children all learned to skate using them. When he was diagnosed as having a 'weak' heart is uncertain; when mustered in the 1914–18 war, he was graded medically 'B', although no reasons are given on the medical certificate. Rheumatic fever was however common in his young days. He also claimed to have weak ankles, and wore boots all his life; his wife was always amused that the first thing that he noticed about a woman was her shoes.

On the death of Welbourn's father, Richard Hackworth had been appointed

4

as his guardian and trustee, together with Mr John Hoggard Hanson (d. 1913 aged 80). His children never heard him speak of the latter, but Mr Hackworth he loved and revered. It was probably he who recommended that Welbourn be sent to Framlingham College, which he attended from January 1891 until December 1892. A testimonial from the Headmaster of Framlingham dated 3 December 1893 is formal.

Richard Hackworth (b. 27 October 1815, d. 9 July 1910) came from Lincolnshire to St John's Wood in London in 1853 and went into partnership with Welbourn's grandfather in his building business; why he retired from this in 1873 is not clear, but obviously he remained on the best of terms with the family. Possibly it was to make room for Henry Gregory to join the business. In 1861 he became a member of the Hampstead Vestry, and served on it until its duties were taken over by the borough council, when he was presented with a gold watch by his fellow vestrymen on 31 May 1886 to commemorate 25 years of service. Through his work for the Vestry he had become acquainted with Mr (later Sir William) W.H. Preece AKC, Chief Engineer of the Post Office and founder of the well-known consulting firm of Preece, Cardew and Rider. Later in life Welbourn recorded that Mr Preece advised both Mr Hackworth and him that he should read electrical engineering at King's College, London, under John Hopkinson. The electrical engineering profession was the thing of the future, but in order to understand it, a proper theoretical education in it was essential.

However, an undated letter written by Mr Hackworth on holiday in Margate says (*sic* is omitted throughout!):

'My son Alfred has forwarded your letter to me & as you seem to have a desire to terminate your connections with Framlingham, & as I assume that your Mother and Father are in accord with such a desire, individually I can have no objection. When does your next term commence? Shall I be home before it is necessary to give notice? You ask am I satisfied with the progress you have made at College; well I fear I am scarcely qualified to give an opinion, my own education been of so very limited a character, but I should think you have done wonderfully well & I sincerely hope you may do equaly well in all your future undertakings. As to your choice of a Profession I think it is best you should follow the bent of your own Inclination whatever it may be your superior education will give you an imense advantage over your less educated compeers. I fell in my own mind there is one Profession especially that is rapidly coming to the front & which is destined to have a great future, that is the electrical Engineering it is as yet only in its Infancy, but it is applicable to so many purposes hardly yet thought of that it must prosper. Faithfully Yours, R. Hackworth.'

The reason for Welbourn wishing to leave Framlingham may well have been that it could teach him no more. He was already in the top form, was a sub-prefect, and had won the Packard Prize for Science, for which he received a leather-bound and tooled three volume *Life and Letters of Charles Darwin*.

He studied electrical engineering at King's College, London from January 1893 to July 1895, (eight terms), the fees averaging about £18. 10s. 0d. a term, about £1 per term more than at Framlingham. After initial kitting out, the account book for his father's estate shows that he received an allowance of £10 a month; a skilled man at that time earned about £1 a week. His grandfather had provided an annuity of £52 p.a. to pay for his education, so he was well off. He probably lived with the family of his much-loved Aunt Emily (Mrs Henry Gregory) in St John's Wood.

A certificate issued by Walter Smith, Secretary of King's College, on 8 February 1898 states that 'Burkewood Welbourn was a student in the Faculty of Sciences (Engineering Division) of this College during eight terms from January 1893 to July 1895 and that he gained Prizes in Practical Physics and Workshop, also Certificates in Mathematics, Chemistry, Mechanical Engineering, Drawing, &c, &c; he was appointed a Student Demonstrator in the Electrical Laboratory in October 1895, and was elected an Associate of the College in January 1896.' It is curious that no mention is made of electrical subjects. He was presumably made a Student Demonstrator to allow him to stay an extra term, since he had started in January 1893. As a Student Demonstrator, he worked for John Hopkinson not merely in the laboratory, but in his private practice as a consulting engineer, and used to dine at his home. From the bottom of the table would come the stentorian command from Hopkinson's wife, 'Now, no shop tonight, dearest.' He frequently lunched at Dow's in the Strand with Ernest Wilson, who succeeded Hopkinson as Professor, and who really ran the department.

A report for his work for the Easter Term 1895 shows the number of lectures given and the number attended. He attended all four Divinity lectures, and chapel on 32 out of 45 occasions. He only missed 3 out of 135 lectures and labs, his knowledge and progress ranging from 'Very Fair' in mechanics to 'Excellent' in electrical engineering, given by John Hopkinson. In mathematics the lecturer comments, 'Good enough to warrant continued work in the subject.'

A good caricature of a British tourist on the bottom of a scrap of working paper from an exam has on it, 'A souvenir of the King's Coll. Scholarship Examinations October 94', but is unfortunately unsigned. Welbourn did not get a scholarship. He was however a prizeman in practical physics and engineering, and won the Bishop Barry Divinity Prize. He attended chapel most mornings, and in later life expressed his gratitude for the possibility to do so.

Welbourn bought a fine set of drawing instruments, housed in a fitted mahogany case, from Stanley, Great Turnstile, Holborn, which his sons Tom

6

and Donald were also to use. It contains ivory scales which are very far from being the modern standard lengths.

In order to obtain his AKC, Welbourn had to attend lectures in theology on Saturday mornings, and to pass an examination in the subject. On the occasion of the visit of the Shah of Persia to London the whole class played truant, and the following Saturday the lecturer, Professor Wace, began by commenting that on the previous Saturday it had preferred the study of an Eastern Potentate to that of an Eastern God.

Apart from work, Welbourn had a bicycle, a penny farthing, bought in January 1893 for £10. 0s. 0d. He also sang, having a fine baritone voice, and in 1895 had two volumes of drawing-room ballads bound; the first ballad had been bought on 13 February 1893, perhaps the date on which he started to take singing lessons. He was a frequenter of 'the Gods' at Covent Garden; in the 1950s, not long before his death, he commented that the contemporary singers such as Joan Sutherland, Isobel Bailey and Kathleen Ferrier were every bit as good as the famous names such as Patti and Melba whom he had heard in his youth. He greatly admired the de Rezke brothers. The big difference between the opera of his early and his later days was that the orchestras in his youth had been miserable, and only the coming of the gramophone, allowing listeners to compare orchestras at home, had brought up performing standards. This view clashes with the accepted one that it was Sir Henry Wood and the Promenade Concerts which did the trick.

He was elected Treasurer of the King's College Engineering Society on 29 March 1895, and in the Michaelmas Term 1895 became President, with Magnus Mowat, for many years Secretary of the I.Mech.E., as Secretary. The presidential address on 18 October 1895, by Mr Welbourn Stud.I.C.E., was on 'Electrical Distribution'. On 22 February 1894 he had read a paper on 'File Cutting', which received notices in *The Engineer* and also in *Engineering*, both high-class journals. The interest in 'File Cutting' was probably that it gave him a sound excuse to visit Sheffield, where lived his future wife, whom he first met on 14 March 1893. At the King's College Engineering Society First Annual Dinner on 3 December 1894, for which he had been on the committee, he sat next to Professor Capper, who gave him advice on not mixing his drinks. In the first part of the entertainment he sang *Friars in Orders Grey*, just before Mr S. Joyce Thomas, a law student and future Puisne Judge in the West Indies, later to be best man at his wedding, proposed 'The Engineering Society and Officers'. In the second half he sang that rousing song *Mandalay* by Rudyard Kipling. He was one of two accompanists. On 29 November 1895 he was elected an Honorary Member of the King's College Engineering Society to which he had read two papers, and of which he had been both Treasurer and President. The faded certificate is still impressive.

In the *King's College Gazette* for 1895 he gives an account of two months spent during the previous long vacations sailing on a tramp to the Black Sea and back to Hull. The skipper of the boat, to whom a friend had recommended him, had started life as a medical student. He enjoyed the stories he heard from officers and crew, including one man who had won the VC (tantalisingly no more is said about him), learned something about marine engineering and navigation, as well as seeing Constantinople for the first time. Probably from this period came two of his favourite stories: 'It was a dark and stormy night, and the rain came down in torrents; the captain, the cook and the mate stood on the bridge, and the captain said to the mate, "Mate, tell us a story". So the mate began as follows; "It was a dark and stormy night . . ."' The other was of the captain, mate and passenger eating their Sunday dinner, when a roly-poly pudding appeared on the table. 'Do you prefer end or middle, Mr Jones?', says the captain, waving his knife. 'Well, captain, I prefer middle.' 'Well, Mr Jones, me and my mate prefers ends,' and cuts the pudding in two.

A curious aspect of this article is that he does not mention that he was accompanied on the trip by his uncle Henry Gregory, husband of his favourite Aunt Emily. On his marriage, Henry Gregory had joined his father-in-law's firm of builders in St John's Wood. A letter dated (Friday) 31 August 1894 from Henry to his brother James Gregory, who farmed in Pinner, is written from Iaganrof on the Black Sea. 'We arrived here on Monday last, and Burke and I came on shore on Wednesday. The sea of Azov is shallow, and in some parts fresh. This is close to the entrance to the Don and is in the Cossack Country. Our ship is now in the roads 20 miles away, and we hear that a steam lighter is now discharging into her about 500 tons, we take about 3000 tons to fill.' This is surprising in view of a bad drawing of her by Welbourn in his sketch book, which suggests a much smaller vessel. 'There are about 30 ships at anchor, some coming and going daily, most for England. The tonnage now here represents 100,000 tons of corn. This place is about 50,000 inhabitants, has very wide streets with trees planted both sides, mostly acacia. There are a great lot of official people here and in most towns the men are very fine grown and on the average above ours in height; there are no end of drosky drivers and traps. Nearly all the houses have quite a farmyard at the back, keep fowls, goats, cows, pigs etc. The band plays in the Public Garden at nights when all the town turn out. The entrance at evening is 7 copecks, about 1½d. On passing we had a few hours at Constantinople; this is most beautiful from the sea, but very dirty on shore. We went over St Sophia and the bazaar etc., and saw some of the effects of the earthquake. We were at Genoa a week, and I shall never forget the lovely palaces and places there, and on our voyage we passed Etna and saw Stromboli, the volcanic mountains. We also passed a few miles off Balaclava heights in coming through the Black Sea.' The sketchbook also records Stromboli and Etna.

A photograph shows that during the summer of 1895 he visited the Black

Forest with his uncle Henry Gregory and his cousin Elsie, later to become an artist who exhibited regularly at the Royal Academy. They were a good-looking trio. Welbourn was about 5' 8" (173 cm) tall, with darkish skin, and curved little fingers, a sign of ? syndrome, which some of his children inherited. According to Elsie's younger sister Doris, writing in 1971, Welbourn spent a great deal of his time as a boy in their home, and was treated like a son.

Welbourn's account book makes no mention of payment for digs. or food while at King's College, so he probably lived when in London either with the family of his guardian, Mr Hackworth, or with the Gregory family.

After Welbourn had been his assistant for six months or so, John Hopkinson recommended that he should gain some practical experience, and arranged for him to go to Willans and Robinson, the famous makers of reciprocating steam engines, at Thames Ditton, as a pupil at £25. 0s. 0d. per quarter. The firm issued monthly certificates of his behaviour and time-keeping to his guardian. A letter from the firm's Rugby office (later to become part of EECo. and now GEC) dated 10 February 1897 certifies that he was a pupil from 15 April 1896 to 28 November 1896. He had to pay a fee of £12. 10s. 0d. when he broke off his pupillage. Work from Monday to Friday was from 6 a.m. to 6 p.m. with breaks for breakfast and lunch, while on Saturdays it was from 6 a.m. to 12 noon. Willans and Robinson was one of the foremost firms of its day; Willans, who died in his early forties, was scientifically minded: steam turbine designers know the 'Willans Line' for steam consumption, but he also called in a mathematician from one of the London engineering colleges to investigate the problem of the hunting of engine-driven alternators.

Chapter 2

FIRST PAID EMPLOYMENT

John Hopkinson wrote on 9 November 1896 to Welbourn, shortly before the latter's 21st birthday, saying that he 'had been asked to recommend someone to act as electrician and chemist to a company for manufacturing caustic soda and bleach from salt by electrolysis. Their works are in St Helens in Lancashire. You will understand that the job is not in my gift; I am merely asked to suggest a name. Would the job suit? . . . I am writing in similar terms to Evans.'

On 27 November 1896, J. Leith, Secretary and Manager of the Electro Chemical Company Ltd., of St Helens, writes:

'Dear Sir:-
    I got a resolution passed yesterday to appoint you as assistant at these Works at a salary of £2 per week. Before any engagement is made we should want you to come for a month on trial. If you are agreeable to this, kindly let me know by return, as we should want you to come as soon as you can conveniently arrange.'

Welbourn was paid his first cheque by the company on 2 January 1897, presumably having worked for a week before Christmas.

He found very good digs. with a Mrs Jackson at 5 Moxon Street, St Helens; the house is (1994) one of a terrace of solidly-built small houses. Mr Jackson was the engineman responsible for the steam beam pumping engine at Whiston, which was still at work in the 1920s.

On 2 July 1897 he was paid £12. 10s. 0d., and continued to be so on a monthly basis at a rate of £150 p.a. An extract from Colonel Holland's letter of 3 July 1897 (Holland was an active director of the company) says:

'MR WELBOURN – You will see the resolution passed by the Board sanctioning increase of salary from 1st ultimo. Please tell Mr Welbourn from me that I was very pleased to have the opportunity of laying the matter before the Board, and of informing the Directors that I personally was so well satisfied with the care and attention given by Mr Welbourn to his duties, that I had personally taken upon myself the responsibility of granting the increase of salary suggested.'

Welbourn once said that on one occasion he almost lost his life when a fitting on a boiler under steam blew out, and whistled past his head. The only papers which he left from this period are reports for Mr J. Slater Lewis of P.R. Jackson and Co. Ltd., Salford Rolling Mills, Manchester, concerned with an efficiency test which was made on 25 August 1897 on Yates and Thom's Engine and Dynamo supplied by P.R. Jackson. The cost of power generated was 0.35*d*. per BTU with a load factor of 81.9% when due allowance had been made for standing charges, management, depreciation etc. Mr Slater Lewis was apparently going to use the figures in a paper, but Welbourn, writing on 17 December 1898, when he was already employed by the British Insulated Wire Co. Ltd., says that his name was not be used in connection with the data, since Colonel Holland has given instructions that the figures were not to be given officially. However, he hopes that his name might be brought in somewhere, 'since an Institution advertisement is worth having'. He signs his letter Student ICE. He had, in his student days, joined the Institution of Civil Engineers, which covered civil, as opposed to military, engineering, and published many of the early papers on electrical engineering; but in 1897 he had compounded his subscription as an Associate Member of the Institution of Electrical Engineers.

How soon he became disillusioned with the Electro Chemical Co. is not clear, but possibly he had already become friendly with Hollingsworth, an engineer with the Castner Kellner (late ICI) company in Widnes, and through him had become aware of the Gossage process for the manufacture of caustic soda without electricity; he may have had doubts about the future for the electrolytic process which the ECC was using. Certainly, when A.P. Lawrie wrote to him on 31 October 1900, two years after he had left the firm, saying that he had been appointed to Heriot Watt College, and that the directors had asked him to sound Welbourn as to whether he would like to succeed him as Manager, he had no difficulty in refusing.

Aunt Emily's husband, Henry Gregory, wrote to him saying that from time to time some of his father's old friends enquired after him, and in particular a Mr Gerstley was interested in how he was doing. He and his sons had a chemical firm in Liverpool needing a new General Manager, but although he probably had inadequate experience, one of the sons might call on him, 'and it will cost nothing to be in contact with them. There can be no harm in keeping in touch, and the Germans are rare people for enterprise in this country.'

On 20 December 1897, John Hopkinson wrote to him saying, 'I should certainly be very glad to have you engaged on the St Helens Tramways. The appointment, when it is made, will no doubt be made by the St Helens

Committee and not by myself.' On 11 February 1898 Mr Slater Lewis wrote him a glowing testimonial, and on 5 and 12 February respectively, Professor Capper and Assistant Professor Ernest Wilson wrote others. The Town Clerk of St Helens invited him to an interview on 24 February, but he did not get the job. Welbourn had a high regard for Ernest Wilson who did all the teaching in electrical engineering at King's College, while Hopkinson lent his illustrious name as head of the department, and used the laboratories for research.

On 22 March 1898 Welbourn received a letter from G.H. Nisbett, Chief Engineer of British Insulated Wire Co. Ltd. appointing him to his staff; this is followed by a slightly curious handwritten letter from Colonel Trevenen Holland on the letterhead of C. Townsend Hook & Co. Ltd., Snodland, Kent dated 25 March 1898.

'Dear Sir,

I submitted to the Board yesterday your letter of the 22nd instant and accept your resignation. Your engagement is now a yearly one subject to termination at a month's notice, to be given on the 1st day of any month, but as you are I believe suffering from ill-health and wish to leave St Helens, I am willing to accept the termination of your engagement from the date you name, and am very sorry that you are leaving us and especially for the cause.

I have throughout been very pleased with the attention and ability you have given to your work and duties; the only fault I have ever had to find with you has been in regard to your applying for other situations while in our service and keeping your applications and intention to leave us secret. This, however, was, as I have already said, probably due to inexperience. I have expressed my opinion about it before – all the other directors agreeing fully with me – so shall not refer to that subject again and shall have much pleasure in giving you a testimonial of the excellent manner in which you have carried out your duties with us.

I am, Dear Sir, Yours Faithfully,'

On 4 April 1898, Robert Shaw, Secretary, Electro Chemical Company, sent him a first-class testimonial with the approval of the Board.

Judging from his and his wife's practice in later life, he almost certainly kept a detailed account book showing all his expenditure and income. Unfortunately, all these account books were destroyed by them when they also destroyed most of the letters which he had written to her when he was away from home. Of the three account books which he left, the first starts as an account book for the Frederick Burkewood Welbourn estate which, however, contains the income from his employment and also miscellaneous items of expenditure, the basis for which is not clear. For instance, he is paying himself an average sum of about

£10 per month during this period, but also notes in it on 2 March 1897: 'Bicycle £15. 15s. 0d.' (was this his first 'modern' bicycle?) and on 1 December: 'Cash (Sale of bicycle) £8. 15s. 0d.' Was this his penny farthing?

On 29 June 97 there is an entry 'Dr. W. Heath Strange £2. 2s. 0d.' which is tantalising – was this the 'ill-health' mentioned by Colonel Holland? – since a little later comes the first reference to Dr. Herbert Knowles, who was to become a close family friend.

NB: To those used to decimal currency, the sums above, which are in £sd, may look odd. £1 = 20 shillings = 240 pence (*denarii*). The sum of £2. 2s. 0d. above was in fact two guineas. The guinea was the usual sum for professional fees (the change to the decimal coinage cost the writer 5% on his professional fees!). Tailors also charged in guineas, but if you paid cash, this was reduced to pounds. Sums such as 6/8d. and 13/4d. will be recognised as being one-third and two-thirds of a pound respectively, while one-twelfth of a pound was 1/8d.

St. Helens Tramway 1899.
Welbourn is in the middle wearing 'boater'.

Chapter 3

THE BRITISH INSULATED WIRE COMPANY LTD:

EARLY YEARS

On 18 March 1898 John Forster, Engineer, etc., St Helens, Lancashire, Telephone 56, writes to Welbourn (the grammar is a bit odd):

'Dear Sir,

I chatting with Mr Highfield this morning I learned you were seeking a change so as to gain experience in Lighting and Traction and offered to speak to the Electrical Manager of The British Insulated Wire Co. if he thought you would like me. As you were out of town & I was going to see Mr Nesbit (*sic*) today we both thought it would be well to speak to him.

I have done so, and he is quite favourably disposed to engage you, if you would like that kind of duties he thinks will give you the necessary experience so that if you entertain the idea & will see me I will take you to Mr Nesbit to introduce you & leave you to make your own arrangements. Yours truly'. (*sic*)

The British Insulated Wire Co. Ltd. made paper insulated cables, having acquired an American license for the process. It had been formed at a meeting in the home of Mr Joseph Musson in Rainhill early in 1890, and had commenced building its factory in Prescot early in 1891. The business had expanded rapidly.

On 22 March 1898 Mr G.H. Nisbett, aged 32, Chief Engineer of the BI since 1894 wrote, in his own hand, a letter confirming their conversation of that afternoon and his appointment as a superintendent on the staff of his company at a salary of 30*s*. per week and outside allowance of 30*s*. per week for expenses. He would join the firm in about a month. In fact he received his first pay on 13 May for 3 weeks. Writing some notes in July 1931 on the history of the BI, Welbourn records 'having my breath taken away by being given a higher salary than I was getting at the Electro Chemical Co.' In fact it was only £6, or 4%, more, per annum.

'I was sent as an assistant to J.E. Dodds (now in Australia) at Blackpool where, to fit the Season, most of the work had to be done at night round the

Tower. In those days we had all our own clerical work to do, using our digs. as an office. Everything had to be done in longhand and there was no such luxury as a typewriter or a clerk.

'After about a month's experience I was pulled out to go to Tandaragee Castle in Northern Ireland, to find a cable fault – without prior experience, and in much trepidation. Fortunately my own and the BI luck was in and I found the fault in a wet end in the first 5 minutes – and then had an extremely interesting week-end in the country: my first contact with the real green of Ireland's countryside.

'After this I was kept in Belfast for a short time to start the Harbour Board staff in the laying of cable for their Dock Lighting Scheme. The cable was unarmoured and, in our inexperience, it was pulled out in long lengths from the end, with the result that, on one occasion, the copper was found at least 16 ft. inside the end of the lead sheathing without any apparent harm being done to the cable. A similar experience was noted by G.K. Chambers with the work referred to in the next paragraph.

'In the early days, the contract work was coming in at such a rate that superintendents had to be sent out to take charge of work with very little experience, and had either to sink or swim.

'After a few months with the Company I had to take over the Ashton-under-Lyne Corporation and the Oldham-Ashton and Hyde Tramway Cable Contracts, and shortly afterwards had Wakefield Corporation added. I had to look after Wakefield myself during the week, leaving an assistant (R.G. Mercer – an amusing and most energetic Irishman) at Ashton, and had to spend most week-ends with him. Much experience was gained at Ashton-under-Lyne, where we were closely in touch with R.W. Blackwell and Co., who erected the tramway overhead equipment and got into several difficulties which gave us an insight in the pitfalls connected with this type of work.

'At that time (1898) we quoted the St Helens Corporation for the lighting and tramway cables in connection with the New Croppers Hill Power Station, and for the erection of 20 odd miles of overhead equipment for the electric tramways. The orders were obtained, and this gave us our first start in the overhead equipment business of any kind. I had the good fortune to be put in charge of it. Everything in the equipment went well and we were ready in time for the first trial runs which took place at night and were attended by Mr Nisbett as well as by Messrs. J.B. and J. Atherton, on whose instructions I was sent, within a few days, a cheque for £25 and instructions to clear off for a fortnight's holiday. I think that it was probably known that, before the trials, I had been working for about 55 hours with only one hour's sleep.' The brothers Atherton had been the driving force in the founding of the BI; they were aged about 40 and 42 at this time. J.B. Atherton was, at the time, Managing Director of the company, but had to retire due to a law-suit, while Jacob Atherton, although never a director of the company, had been very active in getting orders for it.

This story is supported by a letter from Mr Nisbett dated 5 July 1899 writing to acknowledge a letter from Welbourn, but saying that they cannot recognise overtime by superintendents as such. However, as soon as the Prescot and Denton's Green sections have been completed, he will send him a cheque for £20, and would give him a fortnight's holiday in which to spend the money. As he has recently had a rise in salary, his salary will be reconsidered at the end of the year.

Welbourn took himself off to Aberystwyth, where the Appleyard family were on holiday, and on 14 August 1899 he got engaged to Edith Annie Appleyard at Clarach.

An undated newspaper cutting tells how, one Friday evening sometime later, Mr B. Welbourn, 'one of the electricians employed by BI', was made the subject of a presentation by Mr I.F. Cuttler, Manager of the Tramway Company, accompanied by, among others, Mr S. Forster, Mr W.H. Lancaster, and Mr Jeffries. He received a solid-silver cruet and a solid-silver fish carver and fork in a case. After the presentation and speeches, a social evening was spent, songs &c. being given. Since the work Mr Welbourn had recently been appointed to one of the departments of the Wire Works at Prescot'.

At the end of the year he received a Christmas Bonus of £5, and from 1 January 1900 his salary was increased to £2 per week, with his allowance remaining the same at £1. 10s. 0d. An undated telegram addressed to Lyon House, Laurel Road, St Helens, with the Thatto Heath Post Office stamp for delivery on it, says, 'Salary will be £200 per annum. Insulator.' His account book shows the first monthly payment on 31 August 1900. The address and also his accounts show that he had moved his digs. about the beginning of December 1899 to this address, where he was looked after by Miss A.F. Windus. The digs. to which he had moved were only a couple of hundred yards from his first digs. in Moxon Street, which is at right angles to Laurel Road. The house was half of a pair of red sandstone semi-detached houses; Miss Windus seems to have mothered him and, until her death, remained friends both with him and his wife. A letter from one of his travels suggests that he may also have been in digs. for a while in 1898 at 45 Denton's Green Lane. Welbourn refers to her on various occasions as 'Miss' Windus; but what the ' ' imply is not entirely clear!

On 4 July 1900 the Guardian Life Insurance paid him £13. 10s. 0d. (knee claim). His claims for expenses show that he had been in Dundee, Bangor, Glasgow, South Shields, Birmingham and Newcastle in the course of the year. Despite this he had continued to pay his subscription to the St Helens Tennis Club, of which Dr. Fred Knowles appears to have been the secretary.

At the end of the year he received a Christmas Bonus of 4% (£8); the bonuses, in the form of a little pile of golden sovereigns, were handed out by the directors at Christmas parties, which he much enjoyed.

He summarised his expenditure during the year. To his mother and grandmother McLatchie he had given £95. 1s. 0d., his personal expenditure had been £163. 7s. 6d., he had paid out £31. 6s. 11d. in insurance, and he had bought a piano, a clock, and the 10th edition of the Encyclopaedia Britannica, all for £98. 15s. 0d. The piano was a fine upright rosewood Bechstein with brass candlesticks, the clock an ornate Chinese one with a brass or bronze case with monkeys climbing all over it, and a face inscribed with Chinese characters for the hours. For the Encyclopaedia Britannica he had a fumed-oak book-case built, with cupboard under it, by Johnson and Appleyards. He also noted that he had invested £442. 15s. 0d. in the course of the year. He had started to invest in BI shares within months of joining the company, and was soon not merely buying more of those, but also shares in other electrical concerns.

Early in 1901 he was brought to Prescot as Assistant to the Contract Manager, G.K. Chambers, and from 1 July his salary increased to £25 per month. When Chambers 'left to join the Westinghouse Company in charge of their Birmingham office', Mr Nisbett appointed him 'Contract Manager to the Company' from 1 December 1901; but his salary was not increased.

In the meantime, on 29 July 1901, he had married Edith Annie Appleyard, and been involved in expenditure for a wedding ring £1. 12s. 6d., Kodak etc. £2. 10s. 5d., Honeymoon £40. He had also bought, from Johnson and Appleyards Ltd., for £9. 12s. 6d., the fumed-oak desk at which this memoir has been drafted. He had continued to invest in electricals.

Chapter 4

COURTSHIP, MARRIAGE, AND FAMILY LIFE

Mrs Sarah Atkin (née Flint) of Decoy Farm, Cowbit, lying on the west side of the road leading north from Moulton chapel, near Spalding, was a cousin of Sarah Flint Appleyard, wife of Joseph Appleyard of Sheffield. The farm is in the flat and featureless fen, four or five miles from Chestnut House, Moulton, where Welbourn lived. The Atkin's eldest son Jack was born the same month as Welbourn, and both went to Moulton Grammar school. Jack had a sister Florrie, about a year older than himself, and an understanding developed that when Welbourn was twenty-one he would become engaged to Florrie.

Mrs Atkin, 'Cousin Atkin' as she was known to the Appleyard children, and her daughter Florrie, were welcome guests in Sheffield. The Appleyard boys used to visit Decoy Farm and also the Clayton's farm at Welland House, Saracen's Head near Holbeach, a few miles away, where another Flint cousin lived. Presumably during this time Welbourn got to know the oldest Appleyard boy Harry who, when Welbourn went up to King's College, was gaining experience in a firm in London.

On 14 March 1893, both Harry and Welbourn went down from London to stay the week-end with the Atkins in Cowbit, and there found Harry's younger sister Edith, staying for a change of air. At the dining-table Edith, only fifteen years nine months old, looked at his lovely brown eyes, and fell in love with him. Later that year, or early in 1894, Welbourn stayed at the Appleyard home in Park Grange, Sheffield, on the Fulwood side of the city, presumably at the invitation of Harry, in order to write his paper on 'File Manufacture' for the King's College Engineering Society. How soon after this Welbourn jilted Florrie and decided that he wanted to marry Edith is uncertain; but it led to a rupture between the Atkin and Appleyard families, much deplored by the other Appleyard children. Edith and Welbourn were forbidden to write to one another, so instead they wrote to Harry, who duly passed on their letters. While in Canada in 1907, Welbourn refers in a letter to an eventful visit to Park Grange, Sheffield, Edith's family home: but in what year was this?

On 5 November 1897 Mr Joseph Appleyard gave a banquet, to which Welbourn was invited, to the employees of Johnson and Appleyards Ltd. in the

Channing Hall, Sheffield, for Harry's coming of age. It was a grand occasion, with six courses and eight speeches listed on the menu. At that time Harry appears to have had his own home in Sheffield, and around the time of the banquet Welbourn, wrote to him asking whether he might come to stay, as he had to be there on business (for the Electro Chemical Co. – an unlikely story!) and would he invite his sister Edith to meet him. Soon afterwards he stayed at Park Grange, and asked her father, Joseph Appleyard, for her hand in marriage. The reply was that she was too young, and that they must wait until she was twenty.

Edith did not write to my father for his birthday in December 1898, fearing that it might look like encouragement. In 1899 he joined the Appleyard family on holiday at Clarach, near Aberystwyth, and on 14 August they became engaged.

Edith Annie Appleyard, born 10 July 1879 at Rotherham, was the third of seven children. Harry, her eldest brother, was born in 1876. Her great-grandfather, also Joseph Appleyard(1), was a joiner when his eldest children were christened, but a cabinet-maker by the time my great-grandfather, Joseph Appleyard(2) was born on 19 April 1819 at Conisborough. In his youth he had run away to sea, or had been press-ganged, and family tradition has it that he fought at Trafalgar. Joseph Appleyard(2) specialised in cases for grandfather-clocks, 'as essential to a newly wedded's home as a bed', to quote his obituary, but he (or perhaps my great-great-grandfather) made a superb folding chess-table inlaid in walnut and satin-wood as his wedding present to his wife, and he also made a beautiful mahogany dining-table with leaves, chairs and two carvers, for their own home. They are mistaken for Sheraton by the *conoscenti*. Clearly he was something of an entrepreneur, since he had the eldest of his three sons apprenticed as an upholsterer so that he could have the whole of a furniture-making business in the family. He was obviously a fairly wealthy man when he died, since he left '32 messuages or houses'. He first started a firm in Rotherham and then, together with his three sons and also financial help from Mr Laurence Simpson Friend, bought the firm of William Johnson in Sheffield in the 1870s, and founded the firm of Johnson and Appleyards. By 1890, when Joseph Appleyard(2) died, the firm, under Royal Patronage, employed several hundred people in Rotherham and Sheffield, and also had a branch, The Midlands Furnishing Company, in Melbourne, Australia.

His eldest son, Joseph Appleyard(3), b. 26 January 1848 in Conisborough, was Edith's father. He built the premises, which still (1994) stand on the corner of Leopold Street opposite the cathedral, and rented them to the firm. The middle son Walther, who became Lord Mayor of Sheffield in 1916, appears to have played little or no part in the business. The youngest son Frank ran the Rotherham branch of the business. Joseph(3) died on 10 February 1909 on board ship in Kobe Harbour in Japan when on his third journey round the

Parents Wedding 1901.

Back Row: Elsie Gregory, Joseph Appleyard, Edith Annie and Burkewood Welbourn, Joyce Thomas, Mr and Mrs Walter Appleyard

Front Row: Mrs J. Appleyard, Madge Appleyard, Mary Appleyard, Mrs Emily Gregory

21

world with his younger brother Frank. On a previous journey round the world in 1888 he had founded a branch of the firm in Melbourne, Australia. This branch is mentioned when, following the death of Joseph(2), Johnson and Appleyards was turned into a limited liability company. After Joseph Appleyard(3)'s death, the firm was run by Mr Friends's son as secretary and by an inadequate managing director. It finally ceased to trade during World War Two. Before World War One it had made superb furniture for the wealthy professional classes of Sheffield and further afield (it won a medal at the Paris exhibition in 1900), but after the end of the war, it failed to adapt to the new market conditions, and went bankrupt. As early as 1880 it had had a 'Royal Appointment to the Prince of Wales'.

On 17 May 1873 Edith's father married Sarah Flint Stokes, (b. 1 May 1850 in March, Cambridgeshire), the daughter of Thomas Stokes who owned and ran a successful school there. Her mother, née Flint, claimed descent both from the family of Wilberforce, famous for his work for the ending of slavery, and also from Admiral Lord Anson; a silver spoon with an 'A' on it is the only possible evidence for these claims.

Edith, to whom I shall now refer as Mother, was sent to school at the Sheffield High School for girls, run for the Girls Public Day Schools Trust by the formidable Mrs E. Woodhouse who, between 1878 and 1890, increased the numbers of girls in it from 40 to 400. *The Times* obituary compared her with Miss Beale and Miss Buss, saying that she was 'slight, bright-eyed, quick-witted, humorous, kindly, sapient and brave souled'. She left a permanent impression on Mother, and was often quoted by her. She also clearly impressed her father, who agreed to let her sit the Newnham College, Cambridge, entrance examination, which she passed. She spent one glorious night in Newnham when the candidates sat together in someone's room drinking cocoa and pretending that they were undergraduates. Since, however, she had got engaged immediately after being accepted, her father told her that she must stay at home and learn how to run a home and to cook. Perhaps he was glad to escape all the teasing which he would have had to endure from his business colleagues. When in due course her children all proceeded to universities, they regarded the lost opportunity as being tragic.

During this period she became not merely a first-class plain cook, but taught in a Sunday school and also learned a great deal about cabinet-making. When in 1924 my parents built The Croft, St James Road, Rainhill, the painters were startled to be instructed in the craft of doing an egg-shell finish for the panels on the doors, something they had never met. The Appleyard family were Unitarians, but had allowed a maid to take Mother to Evensong at the local Church of England church, a service which she much preferred to the somewhat arid Unitarian services of the period. Presumably for this reason, and also because Father belonged to the Church of England, they married on 29 July

1901 in the Sheffield Parish Church of St Peters, now the cathedral, with Sam Joyce Thomas as best man, and her younger sisters Mary and Madge as bridesmaids. The register was signed by Mother's parents, Joyce Thomas, and Father's cousin Elsie Gregory. His colleagues in the BI sent a canteen of cutlery as a wedding present.

An intriguing few loose and partially undated pages remain of a diary which Father kept on his honeymoon. During the wedding service, '"Thine for ever" was sung, *principally by ourselves.*' On one page, apparently describing their journey to London from Sheffield by train, they 'continued conversation at considerable length and arrived at mutual agreement on many weighty points'; and apparently after their wedding night, 'Conversation which cleared up many points satisfactorily and happily'. Presumably there were things which might not be discussed until after you were married. They stayed in Room 237 of the Great Central Railway Hotel, and on their wedding night, 'Everything passed off as smoothly as possible. Had a most happy time. Night was very hot. Hotel band played until about 11 p.m., and noise of cats went on considerably later'. They then went on honeymoon to Dieppe, Rouen, Paris, and Brussels, and thoroughly enjoyed themselves.

Father and Mother formed a loving and working partnership which lasted until his death. She provided the rock-solid background against which he could develop his career. Mr Noel Bunn, for many years his deputy and then successor as Contracts Manager, once said to Mother in my hearing that Father had only had two loves in his life, one being his family, the other the BI, and he was never certain which was the more important to him.

When they married she was perhaps an over serious, perhaps even prim girl much under the influence of Mrs Woodhouse. Two surviving letters to my Father speak of her high ideals both for him and for her, and how she had doubted whether she would ever find any man up to her standards. He wrote a limerick about her, probably in 1900:

> There is fair lassie named Appleyard
> Who's devoted to playing at tennis hard
> She walks and she cycles
> Won't talk about trifles
> In fact she's a 'brick' is Miss Appleyard.

Mother knew of his love of silly rhymes, and sent him a book of them for his birthday in 1899, in default of something more suitable. Father was not a great reader, and most of what he read had been read first by his wife. He was certainly pleased when detective stories became fashionable in the 1920s.

She danced, played hockey and tennis, and was indeed the first girl in Sheffield to serve overarm. The family had a tennis court at Park Grange, and

Honeymoon, Paris August 1901.

probably it was there that Father learned to play. When serving, she raised her upper arm level with the shoulder, and then gave the ball a sharp blow; it landed within inches of where she had intended in the service court, and did not rise much; good players found it testing. Later in life, when they owned their own lawn tennis court at The Croft, tennis parties were a great feature of Saturday afternoons in the summer, warmly recollected by many of their friends. In their early married years they both played tennis at the St Helens Tennis Club run by Dr. Fred Knowles, brother of Dr. Herbert Knowles who delivered their first child. Once they moved to Rainhill they also played on the dozen or so private lawn-tennis courts in the village. (The first hard court was only built in the village around 1936). Mother also played hockey. She had skated as a girl in the hard winters of the 1890s, and when she was fifty was still skating with her children, wearing fen runners, in the hard winter of 1929. On Saturday afternoons she walked the Yorkshire moors with her four brothers, Hathersage, some nine or ten miles away, being a popular place to have a high tea before walking home again.

She was an extremely good looking – even beautiful – girl, as a portrait, costing £50, painted in 1903 by Father's cousin, Elsie Gregory demonstrates. Elsie had been hung for the previous few years in the Royal Academy.

When they were first married, living at Ingleton, Prescot Road, St Helens, they had a resident cook-general maid, (was this Lizzie?) and when they felt like entertaining, they would hire a second girl to wait at table; including a bottle of wine, the whole evening would cost one golden sovereign.

Soon after their move to Rainhill in 1904 they both became teetotallers, or very nearly so. Father had always been a light drinker, never caring for undergraduate beer-drinking. The reason for their decision to become teetotal resulted from an experience when they were to go on holiday to Goathland, on the moors near Whitby, taking with them a young doctor in the village with whom they were friendly. He had taken to the bottle, but appeared to have mastered himself, and the holiday was to help him in his recovery. He did not appear at the station in the morning in time for the train, and so they had to go without him. It later turned out that he had been invited out to dinner the previous evening, and the wine at table had awoken his desire for alcohol; he had gone home and drunk a bottle of whisky. Mother said that they themselves must never lead anyone into temptation. On holiday on the continent they would, however, drink wine, as being safer than the water, and occasionally Mother would give Father a bottle of stout with his lunch if he were out of sorts. But another reason for becoming teetotal was that, every so often, her own mother took to the bottle, and when he came home, her father would desperately search the house to find where she had hidden it. However, Mother always kept whisky in the house when her elder brother, Lieutenant-colonel Wilfred Appleyard, came to stay.

One problem which they met was Father's need for enormous quantities of sleep, which led to them going to bed ver̶ ̶ ̶ ̶ ̶ ̶eing serenaded on warm summer nights by their friends who could not understand it! Later in life he learned to cat-nap, and after lunch at home would say after his coffee in the drawing-room, 'Now, I'm going to sleep for ten minutes'. Within half a minute he was sound asleep, and ten minutes later to the second he woke up again refreshed. For many years in later life he frequently went up to London and back to Rainhill the same day, going up on the breakfast train, to which Barnes, the BI driver drove him, coming back on the diner in the evening. There, too, he would settle into a corner and sleep until the steward came and summoned people to their dinners. He joined and left the train at Mossley Hill, since in those days all trains on the London line out of Liverpool had to stop there, a concession forced by the Rector from the railway company when the line was built.

Their first child, Edith Burkewood Welbourn, (Welbourn's great-grandfather had married a Miss Barkwood), was born on 30 August 1902, and their second, Joseph Thomas Burkewood Welbourn (Tom) on 30 August 1905, Dr.Knowles having advised them that three years apart was the ideal spacing for children! There was then a long gap until Frederick Burkewood Welbourn was born on 12 October 1912, and there is more than a suggestion that Mother had some sort of nervous breakdown during this period. It may well have been an anxiety neurosis brought on by her perfectionism. However, in a book on sex which she gave to me when I was an undergraduate, the advice was given that *coitus interruptus* could lead to nervous problems; in the margin was an underscored 'NO!' in her clear and upright handwriting. Perhaps it could. Donald Burkewood Welbourn was born 11 February 1916, and Richard Burkewood Welbourn on 1 May 1919. All were born at home, as was usual in those days.

Mother's younger sister Mary had been at a convent school in France, and there she met a German girl, Barbara Elizabeth Roth from Bamberg, who wanted to come to England to learn English. She came in 1907, was a great success, and stayed until 1914. When war broke out, all her friends in the village said, '*Frau*, we like you; the war will be over by Christmas, and there is no need to go home.' But Father, who by then had travelled throughout much of Europe, foresaw a long war, and escorted her personally to the ship in Dover which repatriated German women and children. She remembered this until her dying day as an example of his practical Christianity. Unfortunately they failed to find a similar post for '*Fräu*'s' sister; had they done so, she might not have married the Nazi Jew-baiter, Julius Streicher.

Both Mother and Father were staunch Christians, although when we all wanted, as undergraduates will, to argue about their beliefs, they were incapable of doing so. Father's Christianity had been part of his attraction for Mother –

as had been his wonderful singing in church! Mother ran the Mothers' Union in the village for many years, and also acted as an unofficial curate, before the ministry of women was thought of. Father was for many years Vicar's warden at St Ann's Church in Rainhill and a member of the Church Council. On holiday, if no Church of England service was available, they would go to wherever was accessible; the Wee Frees in Arran, where the sermon lasted a whole terrible hour, or in Belgium and France to the local Roman Catholic church. They were middle of the road in their preference for services; they insisted that the maids went to evensong on Sundays. They normally went to communion service before breakfast on Sunday mornings, and then to mattins at 11 a.m., when Father would read the lessons. Every night they knelt beside their bedside to pray, and if they had had any differences, to beg God's help in resolving them.

Between breakfast and going to mattins on Sundays, he would sit at his desk and write an individual letter to each of his children who was away from home; and when he himself was away from home, he would try to write every day to Mother. She kept all his letters, and he kept hers. When, however, they left their home in West Kirby, they destroyed all but the series to be found in this volume. When away from the children, they sent them a continuous stream of picture postcards, and the albums of these kept by Edith and Tom have provided quite a lot of information about their travels. Mother too wrote to all the children mid-week in a wonderful clear handwriting which she could write even in the train between Rainhill and Liverpool. Later, when she was about fifty, she bought a typewriter, to enable her to send us all copies of a letter to which she appended personal notes.

Politically they both voted Conservative all their lives, but they preached and practised Christian Socialism without realising it, and were much disturbed when all of their children, with the exception of Tom, tried to follow their thinking to its logical conclusion.

Father had bought a 'Swift' bicycle for Mother in April 1903, perhaps with a view to a cycling holiday, perhaps with a view to making it easier to get to the tennis and hockey club in St Helens. In 1911 he bought a Humber motorcycle with big wicker-work sidecar, but sold this to the BI in 1915, having spent many hours by the roadside mending it. He did not have a car until 1929, when he bought a Rover 16, with real leather upholstery and a trunk-rack at the back. This was followed in 1934 by a Rover 14, the first of the 'modern' Rovers. His last car, bought about 1952, was a Morris Minor. He was a safe driver, and had very few accidents.

Holidays played a large part in their lives, and were carefully planned well in advance. They appear to have gone to Goathland in 1902. In 1903 they went to Ingleton in Lancashire, and in 1904 they had clearly found someone, perhaps Nurse Booth, to look after their daughter Edith (who for many years they called Baba) while they went off in June on a cycling holiday which cost £12. 10s. 0d. At the end of October 1906 they left the two babies and went on a cycling holiday which included cycling in one day from Darley Dale in the Peak District, to Leicester, about 50 miles. Roads in those days were primitive by modern standards, and all cyclists carried repair kits for their tyres. In July 1907 they visited Welbeck Abbey, Sheffield and Sherwood Forest; and for Father's birthday in 1908 they were at Ingleton. The roads would have been macadamised, but not all of them tarred.

In 1909 they made a never-to-be-forgotten journey via Rotterdam to spend a week at Sobernheim in the Pfalz, coming back down the Rhine, and seeing many small towns as well as Cologne; this was probably organised for them by Fräulein Roth, who lived with them as a mother's help from 1907–1914.

In 1910, the year that Father was in St Petersburg, they took a fortnight's cycling holiday at the end of October and early November, first cycling from Leamington via Warwick to Stratford-upon-Avon, where they spent a wet week, and then round Sheffield.

In 1913, picture postcards to the children, addressed to Hoylake on the Wirral, were written from Kingston in Eire, to which Mother seems to have accompanied Father on business, not for the first time.

Immediately after the 1914–18 war they took their holidays at Meols, hiring a girls' school to house family, maids, cousins and friends; but they then decided on a policy of arranging their holidays to educate their children in geography. This was an extension of the education Mother had given to all of them until they went to school at the age of nine, using teaching materials provided by the Parents National Educational Union. She also taught for a time, and was paid for teaching, together with her son Fred, Margaret Thorpe, the daughter of a neighbour.

If before the war they had been happy to take their holidays inland, after the war they were all by the sea. Father was not interested in sailing, but he was a keen, if poor, swimmer who would swim in the sea with us all before breakfast, lunch and supper until over the age of 60. He was also a master of the art of building sand-castles and draining beaches, which contained a lot of instruction in the angles of repose of sand, and getting the right fall into his canals. Tennis was also played, and as the children grew older there was walking. If possible, rooms were taken with a piano so that we could all sing round it in the evening. For some years Mother took our own Bechstein piano on a works lorry to Criccieth and invited her niece Joan Beavis, who was a fine pianist, to stay!

In 1923, the family had a wet fortnight at Brodick on the Isle of Arran, and in 1924 at Duinbergen, not far from Zeebrugge in Belgium, with expeditions to see the remains of the famous raid on Zeebrugge, and also into Holland. The first holiday in Criccieth was in 1925, staying with 'Mr Jones the Shoemaker', whose brother was head of the NPL. This was followed by Tenby in 1926. In

1928 the family went for a most successful hot holiday on the Brittany coast near St Malo, and this was to have been the start of regular foreign holidays. However, the great depression came, and people were being urged not to spend currency abroad; so Welbourn and his wife dutifully, and characteristically, stayed in Britain.

In 1929, the first year in which they had a car, a Rover 16, the family went to Mortehoe in Cornwall, but with Mother driving the car ended in a ditch halfway there. In her fiftieth year she had determined to learn to drive, but never really mastered the art. One of the reasons for going to Mortehoe was that it was not far from Morwenstowe, where the author of *And shall Trelawney die* had been vicar; he belonged to the Hawker family, with one of whom their daughter Edith was in love.

1930 saw us at Filey, on the Yorkshire coast, where a lot of fishermen's boats were wrecked in a storm. Father had been outraged that evening when they failed to pull the boats as high up the beach as his landlubber's eye deemed to be necessary; and even *more* outraged when an appeal was launched in *The Times* to help them.

Bude was chosen in 1931 and again in 1933; nearby, Father was fascinated to discover the tomb of, and a memorial to, Goldsworthy Gurney, the builder of one of the first steam carriages and inventor of the limelight. Criccieth was chosen again in 1932 and then from 1934 to the outbreak of war in 1939.

Whereas in summer tennis filled the evenings, in winter, before World War One, musical evenings were common, with Father much in demand. On one occasion, at supper in the middle of such an evening, he heard the lady behind him say, 'My dear, its most *unusual* for a professional to have supper with the guests!' Shakespeare readings were also common. This pattern was upset by the coming of the wireless, but also perhaps by the fact that voices were getting tired, ruined by the fumes from the Castner-Kellner works in Widnes. In the early days of wireless, guests often brought their own loudspeakers to see whether they might have better reception than their hosts, in days when impedance matching was not properly understood.

Dances too were popular; by clearing the drawing-room at The Croft, twelve couples could dance to the gramophone, and invitations to these evenings, although no alcohol was served, were much sought-after, as indeed they were at their neighbours, the Thorpes. Mr Thorpe was Greenall Whitley's Brewer, and both the parents and their two daughters played tennis at county level. One woman remembers how 'your Father was not above dancing with a fat girl who was a continual wallflower at dances, and how grateful I was he could not guess.' She goes on to say: 'Your Mother's practical Christianity was an inspiration I shall never forget.'

During the winter holidays card games were played most evenings, firstly whist and then bridge (not auction bridge, which Mother thought too difficult), and also rummy and others, on the principle that in whatever society we found ourselves, we ought to be able to take part in its activities. For the same reason the children learned to swim and to ride. Father was a keen cribbage player, a game which he learned in his youth, and which still remained popular in the pubs until World War Two. The great evenings, however, were Saturday and Sunday, when between tea and supper we would gather round the piano and, to Father's playing, sing in unison songs from *Gaudeamus*, the *Harrow School Song Book*, and the *Scottish Students Song Book*. On Sunday, too, Moody and Sankey produced some boisterous singing.

Education was never far from the surface in the family. Asked for the weight of a railway engine, Father got me to make an estimate of the volume of the box which would contain it, and then of the proportion of the box which it would fill. Going on from there, we all knew very early that 'a pint of pure water weighs a pound and a quarter', and he supplied the weight of water per cubic foot. Then he made me guess how much heavier than water steel might be, and introduced the idea of specific gravity. And so, slowly, we homed onto the answer.

The eldest child, Edith, went to Roedean, where she was in No. 4 house, run by Miss A.L. Hyde, who was probably a girlhood friend of Mother, and in due course became my godmother. From there she became a Home Student at Oxford, having failed to get into Cambridge. All the sons went first to The Leas School, Hoylake and from there to Rugby. Tom, the eldest, then accepted a scholarship given by the Warwickshire Mine Owners, to go to Birmingham University to read mining engineering, while the remaining three went to Emmanuel College, Cambridge, on the advice of E.F. Bonhote, one of their mathematics masters, himself a Wrangler. Their youngest son Dick caused them much concern in his schooldays, being very backward compared with his elder brothers; later in life he had a worldwide reputation as a pioneering endocrine surgeon.

The outbreak of war in 1939 put an end to family holidays, and their own tended to pivot around frequent visits to Droitwich where the brine baths were beneficial to Mother's arthritis. After the war they had one great holiday in 1952 visiting their daughter, who was in Germany with her husband, a chaplain in the Control Commission, and seeing the Passion Play in Oberammergau.

Gardening was an art learned during World War One, when food was in short supply. Father became a skilled vegetable gardener, although not much interested in it; but through this he developed an interest in flower gardening, and became an expert with roses and dahlias, and above all, the grass on the tennis-court. He had been helped in the garden during the war by Mr Monks, a turner at Robey's Brass Foundry, whose kindly red-headed wife came as a daily to help in the house; after the war Mr Monks, and later his three boys, continued to work in the garden in return for flowers and vegetables, and also cast-off clothing. When, however, Robey's closed due to the depression, Father took him on full-time at the wage that he had been getting as a turner, 59s. 11½d., far higher than a gardener got at that time; but he also did the boots, and many another useful jobs. The three boys all went into the BI. Robey's Brass Foundry, the Liverpool side of the railway line from the station in Rainhill, had specialised in ships scuttles (the brass round the porthole). For two years no ship was built on Merseyside, and the firm closed. The colliers from the surrounding pits, squatting on their haunches, and the men from Robey's could be heard in the village square saying that it had been better in the trenches in 1916, when they knew at least that their wives had enough to eat.

Father was loved by all his children, although in later years his childless daughter felt that he discriminated against her because she was a woman. Whereas under his will he had left the sons their shares of his estate outright, he had left his daughter's share in trust, since he was afraid, and rightly, that she would give the money away. He and his wife had always given ten per cent of their income, a tithe, to charity, and did not wish what they had saved to go the same way. We all admired and respected Mother, but she tried to run our lives, and as a result we all tried to get away from home as much as possible, which was why the writer went to EECo. in Stafford rather than into the BI as his Father had hoped. Mother and Father succeeded, though, in giving their family a model of service to their fellow men.

Chapter 5

THE BRITISH INSULATED WIRE CO. LTD.

THE BRITISH INSULATED AND HELSBY CABLE CO. LTD.

1901–1914

Welbourn was appointed Contracts Manager on 1 December 1901, just before his twenty-sixth birthday, and was to hold that job for almost exactly twenty-six years. From 1 January 1902 his salary was increased from £250 to £300 p.a. He was instructed to satisfy the firm's customers, and to make the department pay: 'Strenuous efforts were made to turn the Department into a profit-making one, with some success'. The scale of his responsibilities may be judged from the fact that in 1902 one of his superintendents had 600 men working for him on a single contract in Dublin.

'In 1902 a Mr Ewart of Warrington was brought in to investigate the Contracts Department, but nothing eventuated from this'.

In 1902, as a result of the retirement of J.B. Atherton, the daily running of the firm was in the hands of the Works Committee consisting of two directors, together with the Company Secretary, Mr Kerfoot, and Mr Nisbett. When in that year Mr Dane Sinclair was brought in from a telephone company as General Manager, the Works Manager, Colonel (T.A.) Bates, the Sales Manager, Mr Doudney, and Welbourn were the only four managers summoned to attend the meeting of the committee at which he was presented to the Company. Mr Nisbett, who had been General Manager as well as Chief Engineer, now became Chief Engineer to BI. Over the years he made a great reputation for his shrewdness in buying copper, not very obviously the concern of the Chief Engineer!

Welbourn's nominal job was responsibility for the installation of all cable, whether power or telephone, supplied by the company, in so far as the customer did not wish to do the work himself; and, in addition, to supervise the building and erection of the overhead wiring for railways, tramways and power-lines. In some cases it also laid the tramway tracks. In his early married days, many nights were spent supervising tramway installation when the work could not be done by day, due to interference with the traffic – mostly horse-drawn.

The work, however, brought him into close personal contact with the managers and engineers not merely of the tramways, which were largely owned by the town councils, but also of the power distribution companies, many of which were also owned by town councils. Most of them were young, and he made many firm friends among the men who, like himself, were to become the leaders of their profession – men such as Charles Merz of Merz and Maclellan, and his colleague J.R. Beard, who succeeded him as head of the firm when Merz and his son were killed by a bomb during World War Two. John M. Donaldson, at that time Assistant Chief Engineer of the North Metropolitan Power Supply Company, became a close personal friend, and later godfather to the writer. Merz, Donaldson and Beard were all to become Presidents of the IEE. They were all engaged in exciting innovative work, with no one senior to tell them that things could not be done. They largely came from King's College, London, the City and Guilds, or Finsbury Technical College. Common sense, with which all were well endowed, was no substitute for a sound knowledge of the theory of alternating current problems.

During installation he would discuss with the power companies their future needs and, although particularly in the case of municipally owned companies, most new work would have to go out to tender, the specifications could be framed to meet the BI's interests. Even more important was the information which could be gathered as to how the minds of the engineers were working about future technical developments, and in particular the voltages which they envisaged.

In one of his letters from Moscow in 1908 he comments on the inability of the General Manager of BI, Dane Sinclair, to do his own estimating; clearly Welbourn had early learned to estimate for jobs, although this was not officially part of his remit, and was actively functioning as a salesman alongside his official duties. In the letters from Moscow are some expletive ones about how a telegram from the London office threatened to destroy weeks of negotiation. Perhaps it may be surmised that London had not liked his estimates prepared on the spot. Sadly, the records do not exist.

What is certain is that his enterprise and entrepreneurial outlook, together with his friendship with C.H. Merz, meant that in 1905 the BI got the first order for a 20,000 volt cable placed in the UK. He has left an account.

'We tendered to the Newcastle Electric Supply Company, in the summer of 1905, for about 15 miles of 20,000 volt 3-core belted type cable. Some weeks after doing so we withdrew our tender. Knowing all the facts, and being in Newcastle one day in August 1905 – and being much less cautious perhaps than now – I called to see Mr Merz and discussed the situation with him, with the result that I sent a long telegram on a Thursday to the General Manager, Mr Dane Sinclair (in the absence of Mr Nisbett on holiday). On arriving back at Prescot on Saturday morning,' (the firm worked a 5½ day week), 'Mr Sinclair asked me to take the first train back to Newcastle to hold the fort until Mr Nisbett could arrive. L.R. Morshead had been sent with my telegram to Mr Nisbett at the seaside, with the request that he would join me in Newcastle – which he did about 1.30 a.m. on Sunday, not too pleased about his interrupted holiday. As a result of the week-end negotiations with Mr Merz and the N.E.S. Company, we were given, on Monday morning, our first order for 3 miles of 20,000 v. cable, but the biggest part of the work went to the German AEG, who never got another order after the serious mess they made of their jointing! Elated with the order, Mr Nisbett sent me back to Prescot with a message to Mr Sinclair requesting an extra week's holiday, and this was forthcoming without demur. As some compensation for the big order going to AEG, we were also given a considerable order for 6,000 volt cables. From that time on we have done at least 80% of the 20kV work on the North-East coast, and that work led directly to the really big orders for the Melbourne Suburban Electrification and . . .'

What this account does not reveal is that he was in Newcastle by mistake on purpose!

The reference to AEG is interesting. Of the other great German cable firms Siemens had a works on the Thames, with underwater telephone cables as its speciality, while Felten & Guilleaume had been among the initial shareholders in BI. When later Welbourn was negotiating in Turkey, he would certainly have been competing with Siemens if not the others also.

The idea that he became much more cautious with advancing years is dubious. One of his staff commented, when he retired from being Chief Engineer to the company, that he may have been 20 years older physically than his successor, but he was 20 years younger mentally.

Another example of 'Welbourn selling' is recorded by F.J. Clements in some notes which he wrote on the history of BI. On 14 June 1906 Welbourn was visiting Northmet, just north of London, where J.M. Donaldson was, and discovered that the company urgently needed 9¼ miles of 11,000 v. 3-core cable, together with 4 5/8 miles of 8 core telephone cable, both to be installed by the end of July. He was given a free hand to telegraph(!) to Prescot, and as a result of this both cables were manufactured and installed by the required date. This involved employing 230 men; where they came from is not recorded. This job taught him the economies which may be obtained by doing jobs at one fell swoop.

The scale of Welbourn's job was also increasing; by the time that he went to Canada in 1907 he was certainly employing 4,000 men worldwide (he once said 10,000) as compared with less than 2,000 employed in the Prescot works of BI. A high proportion were unskilled casual labour, digging trenches and laying cables by hand; an advertisement from the 1920s entitled 'Seats of the Mighty' shows the backsides of a gang in the foreground, with the Houses of Parliament in the background. 1907 was the first year in which cable drums were shipped from the Prescot works on lorries, probably mostly steam ones made by Sentinel or Foden, although Welbourn recalled using one with an internal-combustion engine in that year.

In 1907 the BI had become worried about its Canadian Market, and sent Welbourn to investigate the situation. On his return to Prescot, he recommended in a brief but pithy report, that the BI should come to a marketing agreement with the General Electric Company of Schenectady and that it should send over an engineer as its resident manager. He found that a letter, written at his instigation by the GEC, had already arrived, and to it drafted and sent a reply. He also put forward the names of two possible men for the job of Manager, of which one was accepted. The result was that the BI captured the 11,000 v. cable business in Canada for many years.

In 1908 Welbourn went to Moscow with the BI's General Manager, Mr Dane Sinclair, both to obtain a contract for tramways in conjunction with the firm of Dick Kerr of Preston, and also to start negotiations to build a cable factory in Russia. Sinclair was a telephone man by background. The tramway contract was successfully landed: whereas the negotiations with regard to making cables in Russia, which started in a promising manner, later foundered.

The following year, 1909, he went on his own to St Petersburg to obtain a tramways contract, in which he was successful, but only after many of the frustrations which he had suffered under in Moscow.

Sometime, possibly in 1910, he was in Spain, but no records of this trip exist, except for a passing reference in a letter comparing the Spanish railway with the one on which he was travelling at the time. However, greetings cards for the New Year 1907 sent by his mother- and father-in-law from the Algarve might have been the result of him having been there on business first.

Mr Dane Sinclair had visited Turkey in 1909 to negotiate, together with the National Telephone Co., a contract with the Ottoman Telephone Company for a telephone system for Constantinople. In 1912 Welbourn followed this up, when he visited Constantinople, and finalised a contract to supply 80 miles of underground, and 70 miles of aerial, cables. He seems both to have completed all the contractual work, and also to have negotiated the contracts for laying the cables in the course of two visits with three weeks in England in between. However a picture postcard to his son Tom, dated 30 March 1912 suggests that work on at least one part of the contract was fairly well advanced. The picture shows a castle at Roumeli-Hissar, and on the card he wrote: 'Roumeli means European. There is also Anatolie-Hissar (meaning Asiatic Hissar) across the Bosphorus. The submarine telegraph cables are laid between the two villages and start from the foot of King Darius' tower which you see on the p.p.c. At this point the current is very swift and is always in one direction from the Black Sea to the Sea of Marmora, the Dardanelles, and then to the Mediterranean. There are lots of porpoises in it. Much love from Father.'

35

On the second trip he was accompanied by one of his staff, Noel K. Bunn, ten years younger than himself, who was to become his deputy the following year, and his successor as Contracts Manager in 1927. For his trip, Bunn had obtained a passport signed personally by Sir Edward Grey, the Foreign Minister, which consisted of a single sheet of paper about 15" x 11" (41 x 27 cm); presumably Welbourn had one too, but he does not mention it, although he does mention getting one in 1913.

He returned in 1913, together with Mr N.K. Bunn who was to be the site engineer, to get him started and to make sure that everything was proceeding smoothly. He travelled out via Bulgaria, to try to get some telephone business there for Mr Sinclair, and had an exciting time due to the Balkan wars which were threatening. His letters should be read for an account of his experiences.

Between his two journeys to Turkey, on 12 October 1912, seven years after the birth of his eldest son Tom, his son Fred had been born at home, as was usual in those days. The letters show that for some years his wife's health had been causing him worry, and possibly this is reflected in the fact that both he, his wife and also their one-month-old son went to stay in a hotel in Colwyn Bay in November, leaving Fräu in charge of the older two children. From Colwyn Bay daily picture post-cards were sent to them. As my Mother was able to breast-feed all of her children, the problems of being away from home would have been minimal.

His salary had increased steadily to £450 p.a. in 1908, in which year he was given a bonus of £100 for his successful work when accompanying Mr Sinclair to Moscow. However, in 1909, despite the success of his visit to St Petersburg, he did not get a rise, and perhaps it was this which led him to have serious thoughts about emigrating to Australia. BI were doing a lot of work there, and as early as about 1888 his father-in-law had founded an Australian branch of his furniture-making business in Melbourne (Johnson and Appleyards of Sheffield and Rotherham). In fact Welbourn made up his mind against it, possibly because his father-in-law died unexpectedly in 1909, and his wife felt that her siblings would not give her mother adequate support. On the other hand, it may have been a note from Mr Nisbett which made him restless. On 7 April 1911 Mr Nisbett informs him that the Directors have approved an increase in his salary from £450 to £500 p.a., but adds a personal note to say that 'I think it is right to tell you that, when sanctioning this increase, the Directors were of the opinion this should be the limit of the salary for the position you hold.' This seems slightly surprising in view of the fact that Nisbett himself was being paid £1,500 p.a. in 1900 when he was 34. Whatever the case may have been, Welbourn did not get a rise in 1912, but got £25 p.a. in 1913 and 1914, so that on the outbreak of war he was receiving £550 p.a.

The situation seems to be curious. Writing in December 1956 about the history of the company, when his mind was completely clear, he says that 'I was Contracts Manager for many years and combined with it for a long time the cultivation of schemes and the obtaining of orders for cables and other products and thus laid the foundation on which the company's business was built up on a wider basis than just cablemaking'. He then lists ten major schemes, and goes on to say that his trip to Canada in 1907 led to BI capturing the Canadian market for 11 kV cables for many years. 'The other trip [in 1912] was to Constantinople in connection with the promotion of the scheme for a complete telephone system. I was there twice in three weeks, and the order came off.' Dane Sinclair had first visited Constantinople in 1909 to discuss the matter with the Turkish government.

In addition to this he had, in 1911, reported on the supply of electricity to the Helsby factory, which had been generating its own, and had arranged a contract with the Mersey Power Company under which it would supply electric power to the works for 15 years, but that for a similar period it would buy all its power cables from the BI. This included an order for the first 33kV three-core belted type cable. Quite clearly Welbourn's activities covered areas which might well have been the function of the Chief Engineer, as well as those of the sales organisation. Indeed it seems probable that Nisbett, the Chief Engineer, was devolving the purely engineering side of his job to Welbourn, while devoting himself more and more to the affairs of companies such as the Midlands Electric Company, Thos. Bolton, Connollys etc. which BI were taking over; and also to the buying of copper, at which he was renowned for his skill.

To a generation used to inflation, the fact that the price-index for consumer goods and services stood at 94.0 in 1901 and 97.4 in 1910 may come as a surprise. It rose to 100.4 in 1912, but went back to 100 in 1913 and 99.7 in 1914.

Surprise may also be aroused by the fact that the company paid basic Income Tax – only 2%! – on all salaries. It stopped paying a Christmas Bonus in 1900, but as from 1 January 1913 introduced a Bonus Scheme. 'When in any year the dividend paid to the shareholders exceeds 10%, each staff member will receive for that year a bonus, free of income tax, calculated at the rate of 1% on the salary or wages paid to him for every ½% of dividend paid beyond the before-mentioned 10%.' In 1914 he received a bonus of £55, the BI having paid a dividend of 15%.

Welbourn might have been more restless had he depended entirely on his salary, but his income under his father's and grandfather's wills, and from wise investing, was far in excess of his income from the BI right up to the beginning of World War One. His wife too had brought a dowry of £300 p.a., which however was to vanish between 1914 and 1947 due to mismanagement of Johnson and Appleyards Ltd.

In 1909, the first year in which he did not get an increase, he did some private consulting at week-ends for the South Heath and Lee Green Colliery for which he was paid a fee of £25; this paid for a new drawing-room carpet. This work brought not merely an order for this pit for the BI, but also paved the way for much of the electrification of the SW Lancashire coalfield.

One of the problems facing the BI during this period was that Mr Sinclair, the General Manager, who had been a fecund inventor in his younger days, did not believe in research, and told Welbourn that it was simply money thrown down the drain. However, he was partially circumvented by the appointment in 1910 of Dr F.J. Brislee as Works Chemist to take responsibility for the testing of materials. Brislee was a first-class metallurgist, who had done research work in Germany. A good musician, with wide interests in microscopy and biology, he had the same attitude to women as had Welbourn, regarding them as equals, and was a congenial colleague. Under cover of his official activity he carried on a lot of more fundamental work. One series of experiments, carried out at the instigation of Welbourn, was on the properties of copper wire, which in due course led to an IEE paper. In one series of experiments, which Welbourn fondly recalled, they took rods of cold drawn copper, and by turning them down by varying amounts, were able to show that the increase of tensile stress due to drawing depended largely on the change in properties of the outer layers.

Welbourn was a good listener, and used to emphasise the importance of doing so by a story of how Thomas Bolton, the major supplier of copper rod, tube and sheet, in which the BI had a major stake, got into trouble with leaking boiler tubes supplied by them for use in locomotives. How Welbourn got involved is not clear, but he visited a boiler shop to discuss the matter. One of the boiler makers said that copper wasn't what it used to be. Welbourn pricked up his ears, and got hold of some samples of old copper, which had allegedly been satisfactory. On analysis the copper was shown to contain small quantities of gold and silver, which radically altered its coefficient of thermal expansion. Electrolytic refining of copper to produce copper of the highest possible conductivity resulted in the gold and silver being eliminated, and indeed, in being deposited in the vats as sludge, the recovery and sale of which paid for the process.

He had noticed, when wages were being paid, that old silver coins quite frequently appeared, and he got the pay department to collect them for him; these included some Queen Elizabeth I sixpences, but no rarities. At one point he got mildly interested in penny coins, and had one for each year from the beginning of the reign of Queen Victoria, with the exception of the one or two which were very rare and valuable.

Over these years Welbourn had contributed a number of articles to the engineering press, and in 1913 gave the first of his four major papers to professional institutions. He had also been a member of various British Engineering Standards Institution (later BSI) committees, jobs which again would have appeared to lie within the remit of the Chief Engineer. These activities deserve a separate chapter.

By about 1909 he was spending so much time in London that he joined the Constitutional Club in Northumberland Avenue, a Conservative club. Welbourn was not a 'clubbable' man, but it provided him with a central base, and somewhere to invite people more especially for business meals. He frequently spent a night or two a week there over long periods. At one point, possibly at the time after the end of World War One when he built his own house in Rainhill, he and his wife seriously debated as to whether it might not be better for them to live near London and for him to commute as necessary to Prescot. He travelled so much between his home and London that he had a season ticket from Liverpool to London. He knew most of the guards and stewards on the morning and evening trains, and would often chat with them about their families.

Chapter 6

PROFESSIONAL INSTITUTIONS, TECHNICAL

COMMITTEES AND PAPERS

Mr Nisbett took a keen personal interest in the engineering institutions, in particular in the Institution of Electrical Engineers, and encouraged his staff to do the same. Welbourn had become a Student Member of the Institution of Civil Engineers during his undergraduate days, doubtless under the influence of Professor John Hopkinson who read his first papers to it – 'Civil' meant 'civilian' – and continued to pay his subscription until 1901. However, on 11 February 1897 he became an Associate of the Institution of Electrical Engineers, and compounded his subscription for life for £14. In 1902 he was elected an Associate Member, AMIEE, (equivalent to MIEE in 1994) and in 1907 was elected a full member, MIEE (equivalent to FIEE).

When he first joined the IEE, his local centre was in Manchester; meetings could be attended conveniently by taking the train from Rainhill, using the Liverpool–Manchester railway built by George Stephenson. He first became a member of the Manchester Centre Committee in 1911 and was re-elected in 1912; for 27 years he was rarely, if ever, off either a centre committee or Council of the IEE. For 1915/16 he was Chairman of the Manchester Centre, which brought him *ex officio* onto Council, which promptly made him a member of the papers committee. He then served on Council from 1919/22 as an ordinary member.

After the end of World War One he was one of the founding members of the Liverpool Sub-centre, and wearing various hats was on its Committee from 1919 to 1938; he was its Chairman in 1922/23; when it became the Mersey and North Wales Centre, he was its Chairman in 1933/34. From 1929/32 he was Vice-President of the Institution, and on Council for two separate years as Sub-centre Chairman and Centre Chairman.

His great friends, Professor E.W. Marchant of Liverpool (President 1932/33) and J.M. Donaldson (President 1931/32), succeeded one another as Presidents of the IEE, and were influential in choosing their successors. Both had told Welbourn privately that they intended to nominate him as President, but in fact P.V. Hunter, Chief Engineer of Callenders Cables, became president in 1933/34. Hunter was something of a buccaneer, a man for whose engineering ability Welbourn had a high regard, but whose honesty he doubted. When a further possibility occurred that he might be elected for 1936/37, A.P. Young was preferred, since he represented the contracting branch of the industry, which felt itself to be neglected.

This was one of the great disappointments of his life; but perhaps the fact that the president has a great many social duties may have played its part. Welbourn was a non-smoker and virtually teetotal, and made no secret of his Christian moral principles; he spoke well and clearly, but no one would have called him an inspired after-dinner speaker. Many years later, when the writer became an Associate Member (now M) on Council, he gave him two pieces of good advice on speaking, the first of which was: 'Stand up, speak up and shut up'. This he himself always followed; but the second seemed to be beyond him: 'If you can think of three stories which are relevant and apposite to your topic, one for the beginning, one for the middle and one for the end, you can prose away for as long as you like in between, and people will still feel that you are human'. He took a great interest in the Students Sections of the IEE, but a talk which he gave to the Liverpool one in 1935 can only be described as sententious.

He was immensely proud of the fact that, as a member of Council in 1916, he had been the first person to propose that the Institution should apply for a Royal Charter. This was felt to be altogether too presumptuous by his fellow members; but when he was again on Council following the war, he once more raised the matter, and in 1921 the Institution was granted its Royal Charter.

In June 1913 he read his first paper since leaving King's College, 'Insulated and bare Copper and Aluminium Cables for the Transmission of Electrical Energy, with special Reference to Mining Work', to the Institution of Mining Engineers.[1] At a time when aluminium was scarcely being used for the purpose, this paper surveyed not merely the technical aspects of the matter, including jointing and the like, but also the economic, and more especially, the relative costs of aluminium and copper. In showing that 'paper-insulated lead-sheathed cables are cheaper than bitumen-insulated cables, whether the conductors be of copper or of aluminium', he takes a good hard swipe at BI's competitors. The paper was well received, and favourably commented upon in the engineering press; it made a major contribution to the development of the use of aluminium for transmission purposes. *The Times Engineering Supplement*, which appeared on Saturdays, reported it approvingly. In those days the editorials and comment columns of the engineering press carried weight.

His next major paper was awarded the Paris Prize of the IEE, for which he chose a work, Stills's *Electric Power Transmission*, in two leather-bound, gilt-initialled volumes, the second volume being reasonably demanding mathematically. The paper was entitled 'British Practice in the Construction of

---

[1] *Trans, Inst. Mining Engineers* XLV Part 5 (5 June 1913): 658–780.

High-Tension Overhead Transmission Lines'[2], and was given not merely to the IEE in London on 8 January 1914, but also to six of the local sections. Interestingly, P.V. Hunter, later Chief Engineer of Callenders, spoke in the discussion of the paper in Newcastle rather than in London; in those days the discussions at the various centres were all published in the Proceedings of the IEE.

The opening speaker in London concluded his remarks by saying that 'the paper is such an excellent summary of present-day practice and of the points that have to be considered in carrying out this sort of work that it will become the transmission-line engineer's *vade mecum*.' The paper emphasised the need for thorough planning, and for not starting construction until the planning has been completed in detail; and in particular, until all way-leaves have been obtained. It discussed the need for the IEE to make representations to the Board of Trade for parliamentary action to overcome the difficulties in obtaining way-leaves. It also discussed the need for more flexibility on the part of the Board of Trade with regard to its regulations. At every point it gave evidence of hard-won and extensive practical experience in the design and construction of power lines. The poles for the transmission lines which Welbourn considers are entirely wooden ones, and he firmly dismissed steel poles which effectively are only mimicking wooden ones. No mention was made of the lattice construction for masts which has since become universal for high voltage lines, and which, only ten years later, was to play such an important part in the development of the Grid.

While the paper was strictly addressed to the practical man in its attention to mechanical detail, it did not overlook the electrical design problems, and in particular those due to surge on the line. He made use of data provided by that year's President, Duddell (of oscilloscope fame) to support his advice on how to deal with them. Attached to Welbourn's bound copy of his paper is a memorandum, written to him by one of his staff twenty-one years later, drawing his attention to an American IEE paper. This shows that, using the recently developed cathode-ray oscilloscope, results had been obtained which were very different from those obtained with Duddell's more primitive electro-mechanical instrument with its much longer time-constants. Across the top of the memorandum is written in his own hand, 'Does this mean that all the advice which we and Merz and Maclellan and others have given for over twenty years is wrong?', to which the writer replies tersely, 'Yes'.

Welbourn's next two papers appear to have been based on work carried out by Dr F.J. Brislee, the works chemist, who, under the pretext of development, carried on a lot of research with him. The first of these papers was his Chairman's Address to the Manchester Local Section on 16 November 1915

---

[2] *Journal IEE* Vol 52 No. 226 (15 January 1914): pp.177–202, 217–239, 302–319, 434–44.

entitled 'The Production and Properties of Electrolytic Copper'.[3] In it he produces a lot of data on the properties of copper wire, and suggests that the British Standard for Copper Conductors should be revised. This appears to have aroused wide interest; doubts however were raised as to the modulus of elasticity which he gives for various types of overhead conductor, and which should be assumed in designing power lines; this affects the dip in them, and consequently the spacing of the conductors. As a result, he carried out more experimental work, and in a paper of only just over one page in length, published by the IEE in December 1917[4], he changed his recommendations for the value of the elastic modulus to be used in practice.

At the Institution of Civil Engineers Conference, 1921, Section VII, 'Electricity Works and Power Transmission', Welbourn gave the paper on 'Low Voltage Overhead Distribution'. This is essentially a discussion document with regard to standardisation by BESA (later BSI); and regulations by the Electricity Commissioners under the Ministry of Transport in accordance with the Electricity Supply Act 1919, some of which 'are widely disregarded'.

On 6 November 1922 he gave his Chairman's address to the Liverpool Sub-centre[5], without title, describing the progress which had been made in the use of electricity in North America compared with his previous visit in 1907. He asks why they have electrified to a far greater extent than we have done, and suggests that at least on the domestic front we needed to develop hire-purchase both for apparatus and for wiring, and also to give the public better service.

Following his visit to the USA in 1922, the IEE arranged a special meeting on 22 February 1923 at which Welbourn showed Kinematograph (*sic*) films showing the electrification of the Chicago, Milwaukee and St Paul railway, and discussed many of the matters of interest in connection with it. He ended by emphasising the value of such films in allowing young engineers, who might be thinking of working abroad, to visualise conditions there; and to realise that the stringent, safe, but also costly Board of Trade Regulations did not necessarily need to be followed!

His last paper was his Chairman's address to the Mersey and North Wales (Liverpool) Centre on 23 October 1933 entitled 'Load Building for the Grid'[6]. This was a very carefully based estimate of the increase in load which might be expected by 1940. He came to the conclusion that, as he later came to express it, the load would increase at a rate which represented doubling every ten years. It also attacks town councils which subsidise the rates through their gas works, and hinder the development of electricity.

---

[3] *IEE* 54 No. 251 (1 December 1915): pp. 54–62.

[4] *IEE* 58 No. 269 (December 1917): pp. 53–54.

[5] *IEE* 61 No. 313 (December 1922): pp.31–34.

[6] *IEE* 74 No. 445 (January 1934): pp.49–54.

The paper received appreciative notices in the engineering press, but was widely attacked as being ridiculously optimistic in a time of depression. *The Electrical Times* 'heartily commends his method of omitting the usual two or three pages of introductory and complimentary matter (sometimes apologetic and self-deprecatory) and coming straight to the point'. Six years after the paper appeared, when his estimates had already been exceeded, he could not resist rubbing in the fact to those who continued to doubt whether the electrical industry could continue to expand as rapidly as it had done in the past.

He was also a regular attender at meetings of the IEE, and in 1914 and again in 1915 made major contributions in the discussions on papers dealing with cables. He attended both from a sense of duty and also for pleasure. As a small boy the writer was taken to hear Sir Oliver Lodge at the IEE in London; today his name is largely forgotten, but he independently demonstrated electromagnetic radiation within a month or so of Herz doing so. As an undergraduate he accompanied his father to some not very exciting papers at the Liverpool Centre, when Welbourn would get to the meeting a quarter of an hour in advance, sit down, demand silence, and skim the paper thoroughly enough to be able to stand up and ask awkward and penetrating questions in the discussion.

In addition to papers to the Institutions, Welbourn also wrote a number of articles for the engineering press. His account book shows that in March 1907 he received £2. 17s. 6d. for 'copper position article'. In May 1912 he only gets £1. 0s. 0d. for 'tarif article' from *The Electrician*.

In a special number under the motto 'Look Forward', *The Electrical Review* for 17 November 1922 carries a long article by him entitled 'Some Considerations Concerning Cables'. The Editor clearly knew what he was doing in choosing him for the purpose. He starts by commenting on the economic depression and unemployment, and how the industry might provide work. He goes on to consider in particular the question of future working voltages both for cables and for overhead lines, and discusses the congestion under the roads of cities. In addition, 50 years before it became fashionable to do so, he writes: 'There is coming to our aid the general recognition of the wasteful methods by which we are using up our chief natural and irreplaceable asset – coal – and impatience with the pollution of our atmosphere, with the consequent destruction of our health and our buildings &c. In fact, conservation of coal is as necessary to our national well-being as pure air is to the health of our densely-populated country'.

On 20 November 1935, *Electrical Industries* published an article 'Developments in High-Voltage Cable Practice' which covers the use of oil-filled high voltage cables, and the alternatives being offered of gas-cushion and gas-filled cables for voltages up to 220 kV. This is largely an advertisement for the British cable making industry, with a discussion of the difficulties facing it due to the short transmission distances to be covered compared with those in many parts of the world.

Mr N.K. Bunn, who during the relevant years was his deputy in the Contracts Department, mentioned in particular in his obituary notice his years of service on the research committees on the heating of buried cables. The work was initiated in 1913 by the IEE, continued under the auspices of the Electrical Research Committee, and finally transferred to the Electrical Research Association on its formation in 1921. It was seriously hindered by the war, and the first report only appeared in 1921 with the second[7] in 1923. From the reports may be learned that Welbourn was a member of the Conductors Sectional Committee of the British Electrical and Allied Industries Research Association (May 1920) and also of the North East Coast Buried Cables Research Sub-Committee of the Institution of Electrical Engineers. This latter is otherwise comprised of representatives of Merz and Maclellan and the local power company for which they acted as engineers, whom in 1903 he had persuaded to buy 20,000 v. cables from BI. Interestingly enough, the other two great Chief Engineers, P.V. Hunter of Callenders, and P. Dunsheath of Glovers, took no part in the work of the committee, possibly because they had better internal research facilities of their own than did BI at that time.

He was also active in the Cable Makers Association Technical Committees, and in addition to being on the main one, is said by another member of it to have sat on over 60 technical committees; this was in the 1930s. He did a great deal of work on the committees of the British Standards Institution, and its precursor, the British Engineering Standards Association. He liked to tell the story of how, as a young man, he attended his first committee meeting, and was horrified by the way in which his seniors waffled for an afternoon without getting anywhere; so he went back to his office, drafted a specification, and distributed it at the next meeting. Unfortunately it was too perfect; the members of the committee tore it to shreds, and only many meetings later did a standard appear which was essentially the same as his draft.

He learned his lesson and when, at the first meeting of the next standards committee precisely the same thing happened as before, he again went home and drafted a standard. This time however he left plenty of undotted 'i's and uncrossed 't's, which the committee happily attacked, without ever bothering about any matters of substance. The committee's work was done far faster. He once caused consternation by suggesting that a standard format for standards was required.

After Welbourn's appointment as Chief Engineer at the end of 1927, a worried P. Good of the Electrical Section of BESA, and later Director of the BSI, wrote asking whether he could nominate someone to replace him on the

---

[7] 'Permissable Current Loading of British standard Impregnated Cables,' *Journal IEE* Vol. 61 Nos. 318 & 321 Vol./Issue (May and August 1923): 517–96 & 944–48.

Overhead Lines Standardization Committee, since he did not imagine that he will have time to attend to it.

The committee on which it gave him most pride to serve was that formed in World War Two by the CMA to issue orders on the use of raw materials in cable-making at a time when supplies were in short supply, or often non-existent. As the most senior member of the committee (he was 65 in 1940) he frequently found the other members wringing their hands, and asking how they were to build cables at all. He would remind them that in his younger days they had made cables successfully without many of the raw materials deemed essential by a younger generation, and drafted many orders to take account of the fact. He was greatly flattered that he was entirely trusted not to be doing so to the advantage of BI.

He was also very proud that the bicycle industry invited him fairly early in his career to act as arbitrator on the standardisation of threads for bicycles. Why he should have been chosen is far from clear, but possibly the industry had approached the BSI for someone with no preconceived ideas as to what was best in the mechanical engineering world, and that its Director had suggested his name.

Chapter 7

WORLD WAR ONE 1914–1918

Welbourn was almost 39 when war broke out on 4 August 1914. He was attested under Lord Derby's Recruiting Scheme on 29 May 1916, and transferred to the Reserve. He was never required to serve in the Armed Forces, since the BI was 'Under Government Control', as its letterhead stated, and he was regarded as being indispensable. A certificate issued to him on 19 May 1917 by the Recruiting Officer, Warrington, states that he was both Contracts Manager and also Chief of the Estimating Department. The only medical examination certificate which he kept (there may have been no others) is dated 10 July 1918 and puts him in Grade B. It may have been that he had had rheumatic fever as a boy, a common complaint in those days, and that this had left him with a weak heart.

He had been issued with a War Badge early on, and on 9 November 1915 he wrote to all his engineers suggesting to them (characteristically he did not tell them) that they should send to each of their men to whom they had issued a War Badge a copy of a circular issued by the Ministry of Munitions so that they may know how to answer recruiting officers and canvassers. The circular read: Extract from Lord Derby's speech at the Mansion House 19 October 1915. 'The War Office, the Admiralty and the Munitions Department have come to a thorough understanding and the man who can produce to a canvasser a War Badge issued by the Government has a sufficient answer to the request that he should serve his Country, because in his own Land he is doing all that the Country can call upon him to do.' He goes on to say that any employee who had a Badge, but nevertheless wished to join up, would be given as favourable consideration as possible. Only two days later Mr Dane Sinclair, the General Manager, sent out a circular to say that the company's business is being so materially affected by those who have already joined the forces, that anyone wishing to do so in the future must be given permission to do so. If given permission, he will be paid half his salary or wages in addition to his Service pay; if he joins without permission, he will get nothing.

In addition to his War Badge he was also issued with a khaki armband with a red crown embroidered on it. At some point Welbourn joined the Police

Burkewood Welbourn, October 1915.

Special Constabulary, which lead to him becoming a friend of the local police sergeant who lived on the Warrington Road in Rainhill, in a house which contained a cell. In some ways the war affected him less than most of his contemporaries, since he only lost one relative, one he had scarcely met, the husband of his wife's youngest sister. Three of his step-brothers served in the Canadian forces, and another in the Royal Navy, but all survived. No one who experienced the loss of 1,000,000 men out of population of 40,000,000 could be unaffected; one result for him personally was that he had the services of the same secretary, Nancy Webber, for 25 years.

His war-time activities, both within and outside the firm, continued mostly much as they had before the war. A letter shows him corresponding with Professor Marchant, Head of the Electrical Department of Liverpool University, with regard to his work on the heating of cables, and addressing him as 'Dear Marchant'. This meant that they were close friends, since in those days it was usual to address acquaintances as Mr so-and-so; if you got to know them very well indeed, you dropped the handle to the name; and only very rarely did you get on to Christian name terms. To the end of his life he addressed Mr Nisbett formally.

One exception to his normal work brought him into contact with an unusual circle of men: this was the Lancashire Anti-Submarine Committee, onto which he was nominated by the BI. It first met on 8 October 1917. This committee resulted from the feeling, early in 1917, that not enough use was being made of the country's scientific and engineering resources in combating U-boats. After Colonel Maclellan (of Merz & Maclellan) joined the Admiralty, where Merz was already Director of Experiments and Research, he talked with Mr (later Sir Holberry) Mensforth, General Manager of the British Westinghouse Co. of Trafford Park, (later to become Met. Vic., then AEI, and finally GEC). They organised a committee consisting of representatives of the Universities of Liverpool and Manchester, and eight local firms, all household names. It contained such notable personalities as Ernest Rutherford, a Nobel Prize winner, who was already working on sound detection, Professors Miles Walker and Marchant, E. Hopkinson, a younger brother of John, and a former Fellow of Emmanuel College, A.P.M. Fleming, together with 13 others, mainly engineers in industry. The committee, which was accepted and supported by the Admiralty in the most flexible manner, called upon people as diverse as F.C. Bartlett of the Cambridge University Psychological Laboratory to assist it. Welbourn recalled walking in the Fellows Garden of Trinity College in Cambridge discussing their problems with Bertram Hopkinson, Professor of Mechanical Sciences in the University, and son of his Professor at King's College, London.

The Admiralty wrote to the Committee on 1 January 1919 winding it up, and thanking it for its services. Reading its final report leaves a sense of astonishment at the amount of work, both experimental and field trials, which the committee

49

had managed to carry through in just over a year. The work was mainly in the fields of electrical devices for detecting submarines, of hydrophones, and of asdic.

The Committee held a final dinner on 7 February 1919 at which, judging from the signatures on the menu, all the committee managed to be present, as well as Captain W.W. Fisher RN who had been their official contact in the Admiralty. A good caricature of Welbourn on the program shows him with a hammer in one hand and a pot of pepper in the other saying: 'I sprinkles some pepper on the water, and when the Germun crew comes up for to sneeze, I 'its 'em on the 'ead with mi 'ammer'. The seven course dinner would have surprised him had a similar occasion been held in 1946 after World War Two. Welbourn left in his menu the notes for a speech: 'No experience of after dinner speaking. Sing of arms and the man. Navy night. Noble theme. Bairnsfather[1]. Army won the war while the Navy held the ring. Old Contemptibles. Territorials. New Army. All the Armies. All over the world. France, Italy, Salonika, Egypt, Gallipoli, Mesopotamia, India. Side shows combined with the hammerstrokes of British Armies. Foch's "Be proud". Not a martial nation, but we have every reason to be proud. Lancs part. Losses – Mousley[2] (*sic*). Col. Mclellan Major F . . .(?)'

The Admiralty had benefitted early in 1916 from the speed with which a contract for a telephone cable from Birmingham to Liverpool had been executed. The snowstorms of that year brought down all the overhead lines, and without the new cable the Admiralty would, for a long period, have lost contact with Liverpool, from which the war against the U-Boats was being directed. This was the first contract for which the superintendent was provided with a motor-car. During this snowstorm his wife bore the writer, Donald, on 11 February, while her husband was in London.

A small industry for making engineering taper broaches had long existed in Rainhill in the cottages on the north side of the Prescot Road on the Prescot side of the railway bridge. It had presumably started to serve the Prescot watch and clock industry, but by World War One it was making much larger ones and was exporting to France; Welbourn helped the proprietors with their business correspondence. The industry was still alive in World War Two.

From his early days Welbourn believed in equal rights – and duties – for women, but might have been dubious about the fitness of things when one of his engineers employed women to dig cable trenches for the Midland Electrical Company in 1917.

Welbourn was never an inventor-type, but in 1915 he was paid 10/- for the patents rights for a Pillar Shield. During 1916, after consulting Mr Nisbett, Mr

---

[1] *Punch* cartoonist. Tommy in shellhole, 'If you know a better 'ole, find it.'

[2] Presumably Moseley, the physicist.

Kerfoot and Welbourn, the Board introduced a staff pension scheme. After the War he became much involved with it, and for ten years was a trustee.

Welbourn's Cash Book throws interesting light on the large profits made by BI during the war, but it does not make clear what the company's pay policy was. It rather looks as though the company pursued a policy of freezing salaries after the beginning of 1915, because, while he had increases of £25 p.a. at the beginning of both 1914 and of 1915, he did not get another until 30 November 1918, (the war had ended on 11 November 1918), when part of his War Bonus was consolidated into his salary to increase it by £50 p.a. to £650 p.a. On the other hand, his basic income-tax was paid; this jumped in 1915 to 12½ % and 20% by 1918. In addition, he received a War Bonus which increased from £3. 16s. 8d. per month in 1917, when it was first paid, (his salary was £50 per month), to £8. 14s. 4d. per month (salary £54. 3s. 4d. in 1918.

In addition to this income, the Staff Bonus which had commenced in 1913, made payments to him of £31. 10s. 0d. for 1913, £55 for 1914, £86. 5s. 0d. for 1915, £120 for 1916, £180 for 1917, and £195 in 1918: apparently the BI had paid its shareholders 30% if it stuck to the rules of the scheme. Government control clearly did not run to dividend control.

His Cash Book also shows that during the war he sold a lot of his industrial and overseas investments to buy War Loan of various sorts, including War Savings Certificates in the names of his children.

Chapter 8

PEACE AND WAR 1918-1945

Between the wars, Welbourn travelled on business in 1922 to the USA and to Canada; in 1926 to Germany, Sweden and Holland; and in 1938 to the USA. He became Chief Engineer of the BI on 20 December 1927, and in 1935 received an Honorary M.Eng. from Liverpool University. He became a Director of BI in 1942, and retired on the amalgamation with Callenders in 1945.

By 1919 the cost of living was just about double what it had been in 1913, so that on a salary after tax of about £950 p.a. he was back to where he had been in 1912: but by mid-1919 he had a family of five, a daughter about to go to Oxford, and a son at Rugby School. Even with his declining private income, on which he had to pay tax himself, the situation must have been starting to look strained. His wife's private income had practically vanished, the management which succeeded her father having proved unable to cope with a rapidly changing world. The income from his father's and grandfather's estates had declined because the money had all been in property on 99-year leases. As a young man he had seen the danger of this, and advised the trustees to sell the property to sitting tenants whenever the chance occurred. Unfortunately they did not do so, and when the estates were finally wound up in the 1930s, he only received about £2,500.

However, in the middle of 1919 his war bonus was increased by £16. 17s. 0d. a month as compared with his salary of £56. 5s. 0d; his tax-free income for the year being £877. 4s. 0d. On top of this was a Staff Bonus of £270 tax paid. In 1920 his salary was increased to £80. 12s. 9d., but his War Bonus reduced to £8. 10s. 7d., providing a tax-free income of £1,006, together with '2/3rds Staff Bonus for 1920 of £258. 0s. 9d.'. In 1921 his salary is £84. 16s. 1d. with a War Bonus of £21. 9s. 4d., a tax-free income for the year of £1,272. 5s. 0d., and a Staff Bonus of £407. 1s. 1d.

During most of 1922 his salary remained constant, but his War Bonus dropped steadily from £16. 2s. 0d. in January to the end of April, then £13. 8s. 4d. for May and June, and £10. 14s. 6d. for the remainder of the year. The Staff Bonus was £407. 1s. 1d.

He received a kitting-out allowance for North America of £15, generous at a

The Family, 1919.

time when he paid 7 guineas for a suit from the best tailor in Liverpool. Following his visit to the USA in that year, Welbourn's value to the company was recognized, since Dane Sinclair, the General Manager, writes to him on 18 December 1922 saying that the directors have agreed to his salary being increased by £100 from 1 January 1923. 'You are aware that this is quite exceptional, as the rule was that in the ordinary course no increases were to be granted at present; but on the other hand the Board decided that there would be no further reduction of War Bonus at least until the middle of next year. With a view to preventing any complaints from other members of the staff, I think that it would be in the best interests of all that as little as possible was known of the fact that you had an increase. Therefore I am writing this letter privately. Yours faithfully,'. This should be read in the context of the fact that profits slumped badly in 1922, 1923 and 1924, although the dividend was maintained at 15%.

His salary and War Bonus remained constant during 1923 and 1924, while the Staff Bonus was £447. 1s. 1d. in both years. At the end of 1924, when he had just completed the building of his house The Croft in Rainhill, he had an overdraft at the bank of £1,062. 10s. 2d., compared with his tax-free income for the year of £1,246. 8s. 0d. From the beginning of 1925 the War Bonus was consolidated into salary, and his salary becomes £112. 3s. 4d. per month, or £1,344 p.a. The Staff Bonus was £403. 16s. 0d. From the beginning of 1926 his salary increased to £1,434 p.a., but in addition he was paid £46. 6s. 5d. for the expenses of his wife's visit to Germany with him, and the Staff Bonus was £525. His salary remained constant in 1927, when the Staff Bonus was £525 again. This appears to be the first occasion since 1913, when she had accompanied him on business to Ireland, that she did so again.

Following his Appointment as Chief Engineer at the end of December 1927, his tax-free salary for 1928 was £1,600 p.a., while the Staff Bonus was £600 – all free of income tax. In 1929 his income becomes more complicated, since at the end of April he received 'Rearrangement of Salaries Profit Sharing Bonus from January 1 to date £160'. In the following month his salary is £173. 6s. 8d. i.e. £2,080 p.a. tax free. In June and December he receives £162. 10s. 0d. 'Works Committee Remuneration'; and in June a dividend from the BI Guild Stores Ltd of 5/-. However the Staff Bonus for the year dropped to £179. 3s. 4d.

From January 1930 his salary was £2,150 p.a. together with £325 for the Works Committee and a Staff Bonus of £413. 7s. 10d., which was paid both on his salary and also on the remuneration for the Works Committee. In 1931 his salary increased to £2,250 and remained there in 1932 and 1933; no Staff Bonus was paid in these years, which represented the bottom of the depression. In 1934, however, the salary increased by £100 to £2,180 tax-free, with a Staff Bonus of £158. 0s. 6d. In January 1935 his salary increased to £2,625 tax-free, together with a Staff Bonus of £294. 10s. 6d., but he ceased to be paid for

Membership of the Works Committee. At this figure his salary remained fixed until he retired and became a director in 1942; unfortunately no further Cash Book survives covering his period as a director. He had, however, on the retirement of Mr Nisbett at the beginning of 1939, become a director of the Midlands Electricity Corporation, a fully-owned subsidiary of the BI, at a fee of £550 p.a. His youngest son believes that for his last three years he was earning about £4,000 p.a.

These figures should be compared with the wages of a skilled man which in 1939 was about £5 per week, including 25% piece work on a basic wage of £4. 4s. 0d. The cost of living figures over this period had changed from 100 in 1913 to 222 in 1919, increasing in 1920 to 257, and then falling rapidly to a minimum of 161 in 1934; in 1939 it was 182 and in 1942, 252 in round figures.

Thanks to the careful way in which he had invested in his early years, Welbourn was in fact able to afford far more than his salary would indicate; the most difficult point financially was probably about 1934 when he had two sons at Cambridge, one at Rugby, and his daughter was training for the mission field at the College of the Ascension in Selly Oak, something for which he insisted on paying. FHB (family hold back) was a well-known saying in the family when guests came to meals. This however did not stop him and his wife being able to afford two resident domestics, Mr Monks as gardener/handy-man, and casual dailies as well.

He felt that people should be paid properly for the jobs which they did; but his attitude to money was best illustrated during the winter holidays of 1932, when, after lunch on a Saturday, he went for a wet walk round 'The Stoops' in Rainhill with his son Donald, and discussed with him what he wanted to do. His son had no clear idea, but thought perhaps medicine. However, both Welbourn and his wife felt that their son needed too much sleep to cope with a GP's life. Engineering was discussed; Welbourn said that he and his wife had given all their children the best food that they could buy to give them healthy bodies, and the best education so that they might make the best of their abilities to serve their fellow men. He thought that his son had the abilities to take him to the top of the engineering profession, and that would bring the rewards of the world with it. That however was not the object. As Chief Engineer of BI he was largely responsible for 4,000 people in the Prescot works, and for the tradespeople of the town who depended on them. When, in due course, his daughter went into the mission field and earned nothing, he was entirely happy; and when his son Donald gave up industry for what initially was a far smaller income in the academic world, he was also happy.

Welbourn was always interested in people, and the Staff Guild, of which he was the first Chairman, was very much his baby. Speaking at its Silver Jubilee in 1944 he recalls how in May 1919 Mr Sinclair told him that the Chairman was much disturbed at the attitude of one of the staff in connection with a labour dispute which was in progress. The matter was urgent, and something had to be done to satisfy the Board as to the loyalty of the staff. After consideration, he proposed the forming of a Staff Guild with three objects: (a), (b) and (c). Unfortunately, no record appears to exist of what these were.

On the 27 October 1919 almost the whole of the staff met in the Picton Hall in Liverpool, with Welbourn in the Chair. At the end of a 'most exhilarating' meeting the Staff Guild was formed with him as its first Chairman, a post which he held for ten years, during which time the membership never fell below 90% of that possible. On his retirement he was presented with a handsome silver cigarette box – it caused some amusement among the staff that as a non-smoker he should ask for this – which held pride of place on his office desk and later in his drawing room. He was proud of the confidence which he had enjoyed among the staff. In those days people were unaware of the dangers of smoking, and many non-smokers carried cigarettes for their friends.

In addition to normal two-way traffic, discussions between the Guild and Management covered adjustments to the Pension Fund, the amalgamation of War Bonus and Salaries at the end of World War One, increased holidays for the staff, and generous support from the company for an annual social meeting at the Adelphi. These dinners in fact go back to at least 1911, for which a signed menu exists. His own holidays were only extended from two to three weeks after thirty years of service with the company.

The Guild attempted to negotiate special arrangements with the Prescot tradesmen, and when these failed, it established its own Guild Stores both at Prescot and at Helsby in 1921 and 1922 respectively; these were a form of co-op. The one at Prescot was just outside the works gate on the Warrington Road. It negotiated special terms with the Norwich Union and also with one of the car insurance companies, Leslie & Godwin.

In 1921 Welbourn wrote, for the benefit of the General Manager, a 'memorandum on the protection of the company against fraud on outside contracts' which in 1928 he copied to Mr N.K. Bunn, his successor as Contracts Manager, and again to Mr D.W. Aldridge in 1945, when the latter was responsible for all the manufacturing and contracting side of the BI. It starts by saying that the protection of the company against fraud with wages, petty cash etc. had always been difficult, and on various occasions a topic for discussion. Now that the Contract Department wages amount to about £3,000 per week, and since the amount looks like increasing in the coming year, the time seems appropriate to review the matter.

Quite clearly, someone had been impugning the honesty of his staff, and the memorandum, while clear, firm and lucid, scarcely conceals his anger. It starts by discussing the possibilities for fraud, and at the end of the first page he says firmly: 'In my opinion, the principal safeguard against fraud lies in the right selection of staff of high personal character'. For four foolscap pages he discusses the ways in which his Department tries to avoid any dishonesty going undetected, and then comes to 'Possible further safeguards'. 'The question, therefore, arises after consideration of the safeguards now in force and of all the circumstances of the case, whether you think it desirable and justifiable to incur the expense of employing a man to visit contracts to keep a check on wages and other possible leakages. Personally, I should welcome any move which would tend to relieve me of the whole of the standing responsibility, but before taking any decision to appoint a man, I would ask you to consider very seriously that it would strike at the foundation on which the Contract Department has been built, of putting every man on his honour and of then trusting him, within reasonable limits'. He then goes on to suggest how such a man might function, and what it would cost the company; and then to describe Callender's much looser controls. No more was heard of the matter, but he had been badly hurt by the insinuations against his staff.

In 1922 he made a long trip to the USA. A boyhood friend who farmed at Weston St Mary in Lincolnshire, Mr C.J. Atkinson, ten years older than himself, travelled with him for most of the trip. Each brought back a novelty, Welbourn the tuned vibration damper for power lines, Atkinson the white line for the roads, which as a County Councillor he introduced on the roads of Lincolnshire. The grounds for this journey were twofold. The Weir Commission on Railway Electrification had been set up by the Government, and a National Grid scheme for electrical distribution involving high voltage overhead lines was being discussed. Much experience in both these fields was available in the USA. On his return from the USA and Canada Welbourn wrote an immense and detailed report on what he had seen and learned. Possibly as a result of this trip, the BI obtained the first contract awarded for 66kv lines for the Grid in 1926.

Until the day of his death, Welbourn looked much younger than his years. Soon after his daughter had gone up to Oxford in 1920, he was one day in London and, with a little time to spare, decided to visit a customer who was complaining. The next morning Mr Nisbett asked him to come into his office and, chuckling, passed him a letter in which the Managing Director of the firm said that he was much obliged to the BI for sending to see him such an able young man, who had solved their problems efficiently for them, but that he felt that the BI really should have treated him with more courtesy, and sent someone more senior!

In 1921 Welbourn's mother-in-law had had to come to live with them, and the home became crowded. For £750 he bought the garden of a house just round the corner from where he was living, about an acre of land, and on it built The Croft, St James Road, Rainhill. The design was essentially taken from a book published by the Architectural Review, which showed a pair of semi-detached houses in Cranmer Road, Cambridge. The tender price was

£2,400, but the final bills came to over £3,000, and by the time it was finally finished, the builder, Joseph Lucas, who had built parts of the BI works in Prescot from the 1890s onward, was probably as fed up with Welbourn as Welbourn was with the builder! Quite apart from minor problems, a purlin was found to be blocking the attic stairs, and the hot water system developed airlocks due to not having been installed with proper drops in the pipes. The family moved in during October 1924. In that year he was sufficiently distinguished to be invited with his wife to a Royal Garden Party; the invitation caused something of a flutter in the village.

On the family front may be recorded the birth of his son Richard on 1 May 1919, the same day as the birthday of his mother-in-law, but more disturbing was the fact that his son Fred had developed 'glands', tuberculous infections in the neck which had to be operated on. As a result he was, for a year or two, shorter than his younger brother Donald, which resulted in problems when friends thought that Fred was the younger of the two. His daughter Edith was also causing problems. Having gone up to Oxford in 1920 she fell in love with another undergraduate, Gerald Hawker, who had already committed himself to becoming a priest in the Anglican church, but believed that he should remain celibate. Edith had a breakdown, and had to take a year off from Oxford. In due course they both became missionaries in different parts of India, both were invalided home, and in 1937 they married. Tom had already married in 1934.

Office accommodation after the end of World War One was so tight, that his office, as were a good many others, was built out of ammunition boxes left over from the war. Only when a new block was built in 1923 did he move into a spacious office, furnished in mahogany, with little to inform the visitor, save for the slide rule in the middle of the mahogany table which served as a desk, that he was in an engineer's, rather than a bank manager's, office.

At the time, the BI and almost every other cable company was experiencing terrible trouble with failures in high voltage cables which were not understood. One Saturday afternoon in the winter of 1925/26 he was digging the garden when the solution to the problem occurred to him. He stopped work, went to his desk, and wrote all week-end at a report for Mr Nisbett, which he handed over just as soon as it was typed. In the report he discussed the principle of what was later known as the Hochstaedter cable. Presumably in the course of a patent search, the BI then discovered that an American engineer, Hochstaedter, had in fact patented the same principle some years earlier, and that cables were being built to his patent both in the USA and also in Germany. Welbourn always believed that it was due to this report that he was appointed Chief Engineer on 20 December 1927. Mr Nisbett, who up to that time had held the post, had been appointed to the Board in 1923, as had Mr Sinclair, the General Manager. In the spring of 1926, Welbourn, together with his wife, made a visit to Germany for the World Power Conference in Berlin, but this was combined with a thorough investigation of what the leading German cable companies were doing in the field of high-tension (33/66 kV) cables, and the extent to which they were using Hochstaedter's patents under license. The results of this investigation, together with costings done at home, showed that the cables were more expensive than conventional ones, but that they were reliable, which conventional cables definitely were not.

In the autumn of 1926 he led a team of BI engineers to visit the Swedish firm of ASEA, the second largest manufacturer in the country. This was the result of an invitation from ASEA, and led on his return via Holland to a long and interesting report, which does not, however, make clear why ASEA had invited them in the first place. Nothing appears to have come from the visit except for a very limited exchange of technical information.

According to notes which he left, he started his job as Chief Engineer on 20 December 1927 with no staff, and only a vague verbal remit to provide technical inspiration for the company. His appointment led to at least 27 letters of congratulation. The letter from his old friend Neil Harris, Managing Director of Bullers of Tipton, the ceramic insulator manufacturers, may stand for many of them: 'It is always a joy to find a white man in a big position'. Colonel Tennant, the Works Manager, expressing the hope that further members of the staff may be appointed to the Board: '. . . congratulate you on your new appointment which I am sure you will occupy with credit until a still higher one comes along'.

Noel K. Bunn, Welbourn's deputy since 1913, was appointed Contracts Manager in his place. Born on Christmas Day 1885, he was almost exactly ten years Welbourn's junior, and up to this point in his career his salary had kept step with what Welbourn's had been at the same age. By the time that Bunn became Works Manager some ten years later, his salary was still appreciably below that which Welbourn was receiving when he was promoted. Did this represent Mr Nisbett's tightness on salaries, or did it represent Welbourn's reputation both within and without the company?

In 1928 preparation for commemorating the Rainhill railways trials of 1829 were started, and Welbourn became very interested in the history of the trials and of the building of the Liverpool–Manchester railway. George Stephenson's 'Rocket' had won the trials; but Rainhill was not only interesting for them. Stephenson had built across the railway in Rainhill the first skew-arch stone bridge to be built across a railway anywhere in the world, and it was still carrying the full weight of the Liverpool–Manchester road traffic before the building of the East Lancashire highway. When he first came to Rainhill, Welbourn had heard stories about how Stephenson had cut the first model for the bridge from a turnip, and then built wooden blocks from which the masons could work. Probably Stephenson had done more than this, and had done what mediaeval cathedral builders did: built a large model out of turnips. Sprayed with water to stop the model drying out, it could be inspected for two or three days. Welbourn got to know, and corresponded with, the leading historians of the early railways. He took part in the discussion of a paper by C.F. Dendy Marshall to the Newcomen Society at the Caxton Hall on 24 April 1929.[1]

One of the competitors in the trial, the 'Novelty', designed by Ericcson of 'Monitor' fame, burst a steam pipe during the trials, and was left by the side of the line. The engine had been recovered, and was in the Science Museum in London, without, however, one of its cylinders. One winter Sunday about 1929 Welbourn had such a bad cold that his wife would not allow him to read the lessons in church, so he went for a walk, which took him past the gas-works which were being pulled down. There he met, and chatted with, a very sad manager. As they walked round the works, Welbourn's eye was caught by a cylinder on a donkey engine, which proved to be the missing cylinder from the 'Novelty'! He organised its presentation to the London Midland and Scottish railway company; today (1994) the cylinder is exhibited in an old railway carriage at the back of the Rainhill village library, as part of a permanent exhibition relating to the Liverpool–Manchester railway. Alongside the cylinder is a report from the *Liverpool Post* of the meeting at which Mr B. Welbourn presided when the cylinder was handed over by the Gas Company to the LMS.

The BI had managed to avoid litigation over its products ever since its foundation, but soon after becoming Chief Engineer he had to spend an enormous proportion of his time over a period of about three years in connection with three different court cases. He found this work extremely interesting, and as a result he made a firm friend in F. Sellers QC, who later became a judge. He also got to know one of the juniors, William Geddes of Lincoln's Inn and the Northern Circuit, and suggested to him that he should write a book, which appeared in 1933, on 'The Liabilities of Directors of Limited Companies'; he was presented with a copy by the author. A letter Welbourn received when he was appointed a director of the BI suggests that about this time he might have been promised a seat on the Board.

The cases arose as a result of the 'Snail Case': Donoghue *v* Stevenson, which was finally settled on Appeal in 1932. A young man took his girl out for the day, and in a café she drank a bottle of ginger beer, which in those days came in a characteristic opaque roughened brown bottle. As she poured herself out the second glass, a decomposed snail appeared; she had hysterics, and became seriously ill. She sued the café, which pointed out that it could not check that the bottle was in order without pouring out the contents, and its defence was allowed. This created a new legal principle, allowing the vendor to associate the maker of the ginger beer as a defendant in the case. This led to a new field of litigation, and a rash of cases.

---

[1] Dendy Marshall, C.F., 'The Rainhill Locomotive Trials of 1829,' *Trans Newcomen Society* Vol. IX 1928–1929 p.92.

The first case which affected the BI was the so-called 'Bull-ring' case. An employee of the Brighton Tramways suspended himself from a copper bull-ring supplied by BI; it broke, and he was killed. His widow claimed against the Tramway company, which associated the BI as co-defendant. In what was generally regarded as a bad judgement, the judge accepted the BI's argument that it could not test every ring to destruction, and that sampling was adequate.

In the next case a man was killed in a transformer kiosk which had been built by the BI. The case was brought under the Factories Act, and the first point to be taken was whether a transformer kiosk was a factory within the meaning of the act; the judge found that it was. The kiosk had been made some 25 years or more previously, but fortunately the correspondence with regard to its design had been preserved, and BI was able to prove that the feature in the design which had led to the man's death had been specified by the electricity company which had bought it.

The writer forgets what the third case was; but this experience with the law caused Welbourn, when looking for amusement in *The Times*, which he read daily, together with the *Liverpool Post*, then a large format and weighty paper, to turn first to the fourth leader, but secondly to the law reports, where the *ratio decidendi* and the way in which judges distinguished cases often gave him ironic pleasure. One case that gave him particular satisfaction resulted from a woman being knocked down and killed by a cow on a zebra crossing. Under Common Law the man driving the cow was free of guilt, under Statute Law the woman had absolute right of way on the crossing.

One story that Welbourn liked to tell from this period, to illustrate the importance of experience and a good memory, was how, about nine months after BI had installed the first 66kV cable to be laid in the UK, it failed to earth. Electrical measurements indicated to within about a yard (or metre!) where the fault was, but the engineers on site could see no outward trace of it, as might have been expected, and had instructions not to cut out more of the cable than was necessary. Welbourn believed that 'the buck stops here', and as Chief Engineer went up to the site (was it near Newcastle, Merz and McClellan country?). He inspected the cable, rubbed it carefully with a lap, marked two lines on it, about 6" (15 cm.) apart, and told an astonished engineer to cut out that section of the cable. When it was cut out, he found what he had expected, and what his eye had spotted. While the cable was being laid, some disgruntled man had taken one of the 6" nails which were used in the cable-drums, had driven it into the cable, and removed it again. By sheer good luck it had not hit one of the conductors, and the cable was so well made that the insulation had taken all that time to fail. He was honest enough to admit that he knew what he had been looking for; he had seen exactly the same type of fault 30 years or so previously.

In 1929 Welbourn became a member of the Works Committee consisting of

Nisbett, Kerfoot, Bates and himself which ran the firm on a day-to-day basis. It is therefore not surprising that Sir Alexander Roger, who had been appointed Chairman of the BI in 1930, wrote on 17 June 31 to Welbourn asking him, next time that he was in London, to give his opinion on Waine in the Secretarial Office. On the 24 June Roger wrote again with regard to notes which he had handed to Welbourn, and asked for suggestions or alterations based on more detailed knowledge. His handwritten draft of his reply is dated 28 June, and Roger, on 1 July, is 'much obliged for your letter of 29 June which contains very useful matter indeed'.

In his letter Welbourn points out that Nisbett ('probably aged 65'), by now Managing Director, Kerfoot (58) the Company Secretary, and he himself (55) are all flat out, and need more time to think and to plan; assistance should be given to them in due course with a view to succession. In the works Colonel Bates is 65 and his deputy Colonel Tennant is 55. On a falling order book it is difficult to ask for increases of staff, but the finances of the firm need special care. The possibilities are to (a) appoint a Financial Director, or (b) find someone about 35 from the office of a Chartered Accountant, a Bank, or a Finance House to relieve Kerfoot of a lot of detailed work. The man should 'preferably be a public school man of wide outlook, and probably, by careful choice of the man, and without conferring titles, the matter concerning Mr Kerfoot's successor would settle itself'. He then goes on to discuss the effect on morale which Nisbett's and Sinclair's promotion to the Board had had, and suggests that there would be much to be said for having more working Directors – but he is embarrassed because this suggests that he is looking for seats on the Board for Kerfoot and himself.

This letter conceals the fact that Welbourn was becoming desperately worried for the future of the company, since he was the only manager who was appointing graduate staff. When he wrote 'public school' it was to save embarrassment; what he meant, and what he had said privately, was that he wanted Roger to approach one of the young Chartered Accountants who audited BI, W.H. MacFadzean of Chalmers, Wade, a graduate in economics of Glasgow University. MacFadzean was in fact appointed, and became Roger's successor as Chairman of BICC. Welbourn was very proud of his success in appointing such a man to someone else's department. MacFadzean, many years later, commented that he wiped his shoes twice before entering Welbourn's office!

Welbourn himself had begun collecting graduates into his department very early on. In some notes on the history of BI written in 1956, when he was 80, he mentions in particular that he was responsible for picking D.W. Aldridge, H.J. Stone, (both of whom became directors of BICC), P.R. Dunn, O.W. Minshull, G.H. Walton, O.J. Crompton, F.B. Kitchin, F. Mercer, N.K. Bunn and K.J. Kirkpatrick (now in Australia). They were known in the BI as 'Welbourn's boys'. He would certainly have mentioned his last appointment, had he known what was to come, since John Banks was to become both a Director of BICC and President of the IEE. Interestingly his successor Dr J.L. Miller is not mentioned.

F.J. Clements, who in due course became deputy to Mr D.W. Aldridge when the copper fire refinery was started in Prescot in the early 1930s to refine bismuth-free Rhone Antelope copper, wrote a brief history of the BI. In it he records how in August 1911 he, as a young graduate in metallurgy, was appointed to his staff by Colonel Bates 'as an experiment'. It does not appear to have been repeated. This appears to have been a unique event outside the Contracts Department, where Bunn continued the tradition which Welbourn had established there, and then in his department as Chief Engineer. The shortage in the succession in the works management meant that early in World War Two, Bunn had to become Works Manager.

It is possible that he had F.J. Baldwin in mind as his successor, but he died young and unexpectedly in 1937, and thereafter he considered P.R. Dunn. It seems probable that Vincent de Ferranti, who was frequently to be seen in the BI in those days (his father Sebastian de Ferranti had played a big part in the early days of the BI) persuaded Sir Alexander Roger to appoint Dr Miller from his own company. He was not a success. Dunn succeeded him.

Part of Welbourn's success in picking good men was his close friendship with Professor Marchant of Liverpool and also with Professor Cramp of Birmingham, but Stone was a Bristol graduate, and he took men with first class honours degrees wherever he could find them. The importance long term for the BI, and for its successor the BICC, can be seen from the fact that the BI organisation chart shows that in June 1943, the Management Group immediately under the Board comprised F. Waine (Commercial), D.W. Aldridge (Works) and W.H. McFadzean (Financial). The Home Sales Manager was Stone, and one of his three assistants Minshull. The Works Manager of Prescot was Bunn and of Helsby, Walton. The Contracts Department was being run by Crompton, and the head of the Estimating department was F.W. Gregory, a cousin whom he had encouraged to join the company around the turn of the century. The only one of these men not appointed by Welbourn was Waine.

In 1961, on his way to Welbourn's funeral, Bunn was invited to lunch with the BICC directors at Head Office. He wrote to Welbourn's daughter: 'During the lunch which I had with the Directors at Norfolk House, I was much interested – and gratified – to hear two of them (both from the Callender side) discussing your Father's achievements, and crediting him with having provided the company with more technically trained men than anyone else at the time, thereby having provided the skill that has made the company what it is. The result was that of the seven Directors present, five were BI men of your Father's finding and guiding'. Stone, who had been a director, was already dead, and McFadzean was overseas at the time. In fact, most of those present had been Divisional Directors. The only main board directors for whom Welbourn had been directly responsible were McFadzean, Aldridge, Stone and Banks.

Welbourn had a reputation for being very tight on salaries; many years later one of his technicians, D.C. Russell, who had served his time with W.H. Allen Sons & Co. Ltd. of Bedford, recalled how he had been recommended by them (as had D.W. Aldridge) to Welbourn, and told to get onto the bottom of the BI ladder however little he might be offered in salary. Between the wars, Allens trained more apprentices, both craft and graduate, than they could themselves employ, but took great trouble to place them when they had served their time. Russell had been earning about £6 per week on the test bed, including overtime, while looking round for a job. When asked by Welbourn how much he wanted, he replied £4, 'whereupon he almost lept from his chair with words to the effect "Good gracious, we only pay £3. 10s. 0d. to BSc, and you are not one of those."' He was offered and accepted £3 per week with 10/- out-allowance; the offer was doubtless accompanied by a direct but friendly gaze from the brown eyes partly hidden by very light-tinted blue spectacles.

Russell goes on to recall that 'Bunn's secret, and also that of your Father, was to let their staffs fix their own hours, and thus we were all on our honour not to let each other down. We worked not so much for the BI as for the interests of each other and our "own" bosses – said bosses certainly drove us hard, but we liked it that way'.

Professor E.W. Marchant had proposed on 7 October 1920 the formation of an Advisory Committee in Electrical Engineering for the Faculty of Engineering of Liverpool University. Welbourn was appointed as a founding member on 28 April 1921, together with Mr G.H. Nisbett from the BI, and also his friend Dr A.P.M. Fleming, who had served with him on the Anti-Submarine Committee. He was reappointed for five years on 27 April 1937, but the minute books of the committee indicate little about what was discussed. However, in 1935, the University conferred on him the Honorary Degree of M.Eng. He had hoped that his son Tom would become an electrical engineer, and follow him into BI, but Tom had no wish to live at home while studying at Liverpool – finances, which were relatively straitened in 1923, would have made it imperative – and had won a scholarship to Birmingham University, awarded by the Warwickshire Coal-owners Association to a boy from a limited number of Public Schools, to read Mining Engineering. This was done because the coal-owners were finding themselves faced across the table by trades-unionists who had been to university, by which they meant Ruskin House in Oxford.

Welbourn's career, and also the BI's, had a serious hiccup when Roger made one of his rare mistakes, and on 10 January 1935 appointed to the BI Board W. Travis, Managing Director of Connollys Cables, a subsidiary of BI,

My Father age 60

My Mother age 57

together with Mr T. Martin Harvey. In consequence the Works Committee was reconstituted to consist only of directors, these two, together with Mr Nisbett, who remained Managing Director. Welbourn's remuneration of £325 p.a. was consolidated into his salary. However, a Management Conference was instituted which had as its members the three directors on the Works Committee together with ten members of the staff, of whom Welbourn was one *ex-officio*, to 'consider, discuss and make recommendations to the Works Committee on all matters affecting the BI and its associated companies'.

As a result of Welbourn's visit to Canada in 1907, the BI had for many years enjoyed a very large share of the Canadian market for power cables. Some time in the early 1930s, probably after a visit by D.W. Aldridge in 1932, the BI had signed an agreement for the exchange of technical information with the Eugene F. Phillips Electrical Works Ltd. of Brockville, Ontario, and Montreal in the Province of Quebec. Probably this was intended as a first step toward buying out the company, which employed about 500 people in Brockville, and less than 100 in Montreal. The latter factory was only kept running for political reasons. In order to strengthen this agreement, Welbourn spent most of June and July 1938 in the USA and Canada, and was able to take his wife with him. At the end of July he produced a report on his discussions with Phillips Electrical, together with massive supporting documentation, largely written by the staff of that company. In the same folder are two other short reports, one on his visit on 2 July to the Hydro-Electric Power Commission of Ontario, to which C.H. Merz had given him an introduction. He obtained from it a confidential copy of a report on the Commission's experience with steel-covered aluminium, copper, and copperweld conductors, which had been suppressed at the request of the manufacturers!

The other report was on a visit on 21 June 1938 to the New York Edison Co. The writer, who looked after his affairs while he was away – no casual transatlantic telephone calls in those days! – recollects that Welbourn travelled by boat from Southampton to New York, since by then the Cunard Line had deserted Liverpool as a terminal. He initially visited his old friend del Mar, Chief Engineer of the Habishaw Cable Co., which in due course was taken over by BI. He also visited his friends from before World War One in Poughkeepsie, up the Hudson River, on his way to Montreal.

In 1939, on the retirement of Mr Nisbett, Travis and Martin-Harvey became joint Managing Directors. The new arrangements did not function well, and finally in 1942 Travis was asked to resign from the Board. To Welbourn the new arrangements were a great blow. In 1935 he was 59, mentally and physically fit and active, and had very much hoped that he might have been given the job of Managing Director. Many of his colleagues felt the same, and said so in letters of condolence after his death. Mr Nisbett had become unwilling to take any decisions, and he was feeling frustrated.

Britain's declaration of war on 3 September 1939 did not greatly affect Welbourn's job except for his membership of the CMA emergency committee on raw materials. In his private life all his children came safely through the war, and as in World War One, he lost no close relative, and only C.H. Merz among his close friends. On the other hand, the constant bombing of Liverpool proved very tiring. A stick of bombs was dropped across his home on the night of 8 September 1940; about a week later he wrote a graphic letter to the family, described what had happened, and characteristically analysed the lessons to be drawn from it. A bomb had landed on the front doorstep of the next house higher up the hill from The Croft, but the owners, sleeping on the sitting room floor, were uninjured. Their front door had vanished, and not a splinter of it was ever seen again. The garden of The Croft was surrounded by a red sandstone wall, a length of which, just opposite to where the bomb had burst, had been removed, but it had diverted the blast upward, so that little damage had been done to his home. He goes into detail as to the effect on windows of being open or shut, and of size of window on the usefulness of paper reinforcement.

When the crisis over Mr Travis came in 1942, Welbourn, who was already 66, was appointed to the Board of BI, and as a Consultant to the company, while three Executive Managers were appointed who were to attend Board Meetings. On the occasion of his retirement he gave two speeches, one to his personal staff, who presented him with a fountain pen, the other to the Directors and all the staff, who presented him with a canteen of cutlery to replace the one which it had given him as a wedding present forty-one years previously.

A photograph of his staff taken on this occasion shows a total of thirteen including Miss Nancy Webber, his secretary for 25 years. He records how the Chief Engineer's department had no staff when he took it over, and how it was then mainly concerned with matters with a heavy engineering bias, but with a foot in telephonic communication. 'Now it is definitely in the Radio Frequency cable picture'. The Department's Charter is 'to inspire all departments of the Company in technical matters'. F.J. Baldwin, before his death in 1937, had discovered that the Department was dealing with 202 matters.

To the Board and staff he emphasised his pride in becoming a director, and the importance to each member of the staff of feeling that he had got a field-marshal's baton in his rucksack. He reminisced about the past, and said that he negotiated the first orders to be placed in this country for 20, 30 and 60kV cables.

Welbourn kept 48 letters of congratulation, which included ones from all BI's competitors; they came too from his former staff and friends all over the world. One from J.A. Wilson says: 'I am very glad that at long last the promise made many years ago that members of the staff would be admitted to the Board has been fulfilled. (Of that proposal and its fate I have much inner knowledge,

My Parents with my daughter Ann Celia (b. 8 Jan 1944) at The Croft, Rainhill, 1944.

which left a nasty taste in my mouth!)'. Others also said bluntly that his promotion was long overdue.

Welbourn only left two papers from his time on the Board, one a most interesting and far sighted discussion paper dated 21 November 1942 on the probable position of the paper-insulated power cable business after the end of the present war. He takes a very brief backward look at the position at the end of World War One, but then goes firmly forward to look at the likely developments, and in particular the political ones such as Lease-lend, and the possibility of nationalisation of the power industry.

The other paper, unfortunately undated, deals with the question of the 'Artisan' house. This presumably was the 'pre-fab', factory built, which was produced in large numbers after the end of the war. Estimates are made of how many may be required, what and how much electrical equipment they will require, what BI can supply already, and whether BI should buy into various businesses so that it could supply the complete electrical equipment for the houses.

His work on the MEC was giving him great pleasure, and he made very firm friends among the directors and their wives. Social contact was made easier because his wife was having serious trouble with arthritis, and went regularly to the hot saline baths in Droitwich. He had looked forward to this work continuing for many years, but in 1945, when BI merged with Callenders to form BICC, and he retired from the Board, the electricity industry was also nationalised, and his MEC directorship came to an end.

The war years brought compensations to Welbourn and his wife in that Donald had married in 1941 and Dick in 1944, and their wives, as well as Tom's, were providing them with grandchildren. In the latter half of the war most of their children were tolerably safe. Tom, as a mining engineer, was in South Wales; Fred was working in the Student Christian Movement in London; Donald as a naval officer in the Admiralty. Only Dick, a surgeon in the RAMC, was in serious danger, having landed on D+14 in Normandy.

So ended forty-seven years in BI and rather more in the electrical industry. Many years later, when already eighty, he remarked that he supposed that he had been one of the more notable electrical engineers of his day (a very atypically immodest remark!), yet he had spent 90% of his life dealing with people, 9% with mechanical and civil engineering, and the remaining 1% with electrical engineering.

Chapter 9

RETIREMENT AND DEATH 1945–1961

Outside his work, Welbourn had few interests beside his family, his church and his garden, and he was unprepared for such sudden and complete retirement. He was invited to sit on the Finance Committee of the Liverpool diocese, where he was horrified to find a very amateur attitude to financial matters. He remained on it until he and his wife decided to leave Rainhill in 1951 – all their friends had gone – to go and live in West Kirby, not far from The Leas preparatory school on Meols Drive, Hoylake, to which they had sent their sons, and to which his wife was convinced that they would send theirs – but none of them did.

One interest, though, which enabled him to continue to make a contribution to the life of the neighbourhood, was Prescot Grammar School. He had become a governor in 1940, when Mr Nisbett resigned. The Headmaster quickly discovered that he had an ally who could think straight and come to the point. At the end of the war, with time on his hands, Welbourn busied himself with the new Education Act, and realised that it could be used to get a new chemistry laboratory for the school. In due course the Welbourn Laboratory was opened. He had also been successful, in connection with the school's 500th anniversary celebrations, in persuading the BI to provide scholarships to take boys up to King's College, Cambridge, (which owned much of the land in and around Prescot); and to Brazenose College, Oxford.

He decided, among other things, that the school needed a song, so wrote to P.H.B. Lyon, the Headmaster of Rugby, asking him whether he could write a song for it. Lyon, who had been one of the Georgian poets, replied that he was very sorry, but the bard had deserted him. He knew Lyon, who had become Headmaster in the middle of the writer's time there.

To the great regret of the headmaster of Prescot Grammar School, with whom he had worked for eighteen years, he had to retire from the Board of Governors in 1958, when he and his wife left West Kirby to live with their daughter, first in Greenwich and then in Caterham. One by-product of his interest in the Rainhill locomotive trials of 1829 was a prize which he presented to the school for the best essay on local history.

71

The Welbourns celebrated their golden wedding in West Kirby on a lovely day with all their children and their wives present; Fred had married soon after the end of the war. Some of their grandchildren were there too; but soon after that his wife's memory began to fail. On the first occasion when the result might have been serious, they had agreed to meet in a shop in Liverpool, and when she did not turn up, Welbourn hunted systematically through all her favourite shops until he found her sitting at a counter not knowing who she was or whence she came. After that she could never be allowed to go out alone, and Welbourn slowly became a nursemaid. They went to Droitwich for the baths, and they visited their family, but the load wore him down. Fortunately he was able to go on driving until he was well over eighty, giving up his much loved Rover for a Morris Minor. The writer tried to persuade him to write his autobiography, but unfortunately he got bogged down in trying to trace his ancestry with the aid of his half-sister Gertie. Had not the BICC decided in 1956 to write a history of the BI, he would have left very little in the way of records.

In West Kirby they were nobly supported both by Margaret Bennett, who had pushed the writer out in his pram as a baby, and Kate Canavan, another family retainer. Owing to age, both finally had to give up, the journey from Prescot being a long one, and Welbourn and his wife had to move down south to live with their daughter and her husband in their vicarage, first in Greenwich and then in Caterham. On one occasion, in an emergency, they both had to be moved into the Evelyn Nursing home in Cambridge because he was seriously ill, and his wife would not be separated from him.

They were very proud of their family, all of whom were married. At the time of his death, Edith was a most successful vicar's wife; her husband said that it would have been better if she could have been the priest and he the curate. Tom, the eldest son, had become a director of Powell Duffryn, and as a mining engineer was consulting all over the world for the International Bank. Fred, on the staff of Makerere College in Uganda, had written a notable book, *East African Rebels*, in which he discussed Mau-Mau as a heresy. As a result of this he was much in demand at Government House; the book opened up new perspectives on the coming of Christianity in the heathen world. The writer had become a Fellow of Selwyn College, Cambridge, had been on the Council of the IEE and had read a paper to it, to which some of Welbourn's former team ('Welbourn's boys', as they were known in BI) escorted him. Their youngest son Richard had, at the age of 39, been appointed in 1958 to a personal Chair in Surgical Science at the Queen's University of Belfast.

When Welbourn's end came it came quickly and unexpectedly. In the summer of 1961 one of Welbourn's 'boys', Minshull, had invited the author to visit the Erith factory which he was running, and afterwards sent him over to Caterham to see his Father. Welbourn's mind was as acute as ever, and the writer found

Four Generations of Welbourns at Glinton, near Peterborough 31 August 1947.
My grandmother, Clara Welbourn nee McClatchie, b. 23 Dec 1852, Father, b. 13 Dec 1875,
myself b. 11 Feb 1916 and Hugh Burkewood b. 21 May 1947.

Golden Wedding, July 1951.

L to R: Olga (née Dillwyn) and husband Tom, Mother, Gerald Hawker, Father, Donald, Edith (née Welbourn) wife of Gerald Rachel (née Haighton) wife of Dick, Esther (née Hendry) wife of Donald, Dick

himself hard pushed to answer all the searching questions as to what he had seen. He was delighted to hear that the BI had managed to halve the dielectric losses in its cables by applying modern control theory to keeping the tension in the paper constant as it was wrapped, and as a result achieving losses half those of Pirelli, one of its arch rivals. A few weeks later he was dead.

The reason for his unexpected death was probably twofold. Sir Alexander Roger, his long-time admired, but awed, chief, had died on 4 April 1961. Welbourn had wanted an Old Testament style parting, with all his family round his bed. For the first time for some years they were all in the country simultaneously, and it was unlikely that this would recur for another two years. His daughter alerted the family one scorching Sunday afternoon, when he had suddenly been taken ill, and his doctor said that he was dying. That evening all had managed to assemble; he saw each of them individually and gave them his blessing. He asked his medical son Richard whether he was dying, to which, as he would have wished, he was given the honest answer of 'yes'. The following Saturday, 1 July 1961, only a month before what would have been his diamond wedding, he died in his own bed, as he wished, with his wife and daughter by him.

Four days before his death, rambling, slightly delirious but not in pain, he started talking about a transformer works (was this ASEA?) and suddenly said, 'Yes, but let's get out into the shops'. Then his mind turned back to the BI. He kept repeating restlessly, 'Give me the BI to run'. Finally I said, 'But Father, you *are* running it, just look at Aldridge and Stone, Minshull, Dunn and Crompton'. He was still worried, and said, 'But are they big enough?', to which I replied, 'Of course they are, you trained them.' Then he was suddenly happy and peaceful again.

Often, when people reach the age of 85, few of their friends are alive to attend their funerals. Although fifteen years had passed since his retirement, the church was packed with his friends, mostly younger men whom he had helped in their careers. One or two of his oldest friends were there too, J.R. Beard, by now the senior partner in Merz & Maclellan, and N.K. Bunn from the BI. His ashes were placed in the churchyard of St Lawrence, Upper Caterham, one of his much-loved roses being planted on the spot.

The Times published a long obituary notice, prepared in a hurry by the writer, which was not entirely accurate, whereas that written by N.K. Bunn in the IEE Journal was. Sheaves of letters of condolence flowed in, the general tenor being one of admiration, respect and affection. Many looked back to the help that he had given the writers in their careers, and reflected their sense of gratitude for his leadership. Perhaps the last word should come from the obituary written by Bunn, his successor in the Contracts Department, and friend for more than 50 years: Burkewood Welbourn 'was a man of high ideals, which he lived up to with considerable success'.

75

Historical Background to letters written to his wife by Burkewood Welbourn when travelling on business for British Insulated Cables Ltd 1907–22

by

Francis West, F.R.Hist.S., F.A.H.A.
Emeritus Professor of History and Government, Deakin University, Australia

24 July 1995

Historical Background

Apart from their interest as a portrait of an Edwardian marriage and of the customs and usages of their period, Burkewood Welbourn's letters from abroad to his wife have historical interest because of the dates and places at which they were written. In Russia in the years following the 1905 revolutions; in Turkey soon after the Young Turk revolt of 1908; in the Balkans before, during and after the Balkan wars; in North America while Canada was developing before the First World War and the United States were booming just after it: the letters offer eye-witness testimony of an intelligent and observant professional engineer and businessman concerned with British exports of electrical engineering products.

For convenience the letters from Europe between 1908 and 1913 can be considered together, and those from North America, the earliest and the latest letters, can be similarly grouped.

Welbourn set off on the first of his Russian journeys on 28 February 1908. By Channel steamer from Dover to Ostend, he then spent fifty-two hours, two nights, by train across Belgium and Germany to the East Prussian border town of Wirballen – for there was no independent Poland between Germany and Russia – where it was necessary to change to Russian railways because of the difference of gauge. From Wirballen the line ran to the capital city of St Petersburg. He found the Russian train 'heaps more comfortable' than the Belgian and German ones, but he was less impressed with the city, where he stayed for only a few hours in a comfortable enough hotel, before an uncomfortable night-train journey to Moscow, the second largest city of Russia. There he was to negotiate, in conjunction with another British company, for the city cable contract for its new electric tramway system.

Almost from his arrival in Moscow on 3 March, he began to realise that it was doubtful whether he would get anything definite from the city government at all quickly. Three days later he heard that the *uprava*, the executive board of the city *duma* or council, was to meet in four days' time; after that he would know whether he and his senior colleague, Dane Sinclair, were to stay or leave.

Like many another British businessman, Welbourn soon began to be 'heartily sick of Moscow'. By the morning of 11 March 'we are still on tenterhooks and may leave any day or be here indefinitely'. Negotiations were proceeding with 'about as much speed as one would expect in a semi-oriental country'. By the evening of the same day things seemed to be progressing, and an answer from the *uprava* was expected on the morrow. When tomorrow came, however, he had to hope for an answer on the following day. By 14 March things had reached a critical pass, but four days later, at a round table conference with the *uprava*, affairs were most unsatisfactory, although they were promised a decision on 21 March. On 20 March he was hopeful but 'for downright torture these people take the cake'. The position was 'very trying' with so much at stake, and a national commercial fight in progress. On 22 March the promised reply of yesterday might come next Monday, and then possibly be only the jumping off point for further interminable negotiations and delays. By the following day 'we live in hope, and it is always "tomorrow".' When, on 24 March, the *uprava* finally promised the cable order to them, it could not be accepted until there was also a settlement with the associated company, Dick Kerr & Co. At that point the London office upset arrangements. By 30 March Welbourn's company could have had the order but it could not 'in honour' be accepted until Kerr's got theirs. The contract was finally secured, but not before the whole process had wearied and disgusted Welbourn.

His perception of Moscow, in a cold Spring, naturally enough was coloured by the slowness of the business dealings. The only relief was occasional visits to the Kremlin, to churches and to galleries, but these were only moderately interesting and seemed rather to be a way of killing time than a real pleasure. With the cold outside, and overheated, stuffy hotel rooms inside, with lack of much exercise to offset a heavy diet, Welbourn, like many British visitors, felt headachy and worried about his bowels. He missed fresh air and fresh fruit. What he did not perceive, indeed had little chance of knowing, was the complicated background of Russian municipal government which was concealed from his direct observation.

To any educated Britisher, the fact of revolution in Russia in 1905 was well enough known from newspaper reports of the more dramatic events. The less dramatic events were not so well reported; and it was these which had a closer bearing on business negotiations. Moscow had suffered considerable damage in December 1905, when the uprising had been violently suppressed, not simply by cavalry sabre-charging and infantry small-arms fire, but in some areas by artillery bombardment and fires. Some working-class districts had been reduced to rubble, but these were not parts of the city that Welbourn saw. He was aware of some of the consequences of the earlier troubles, for the Tsarist government kept up a surveillance which, to judge from his remark that he could not explain business to his wife by letter 'for obvious reasons connected with the P.O.', he was aware of. He was not aware of the circumstances within which the city *duma* and its *uprava* had to work.

In 1870, a few years after the liberation of the serfs by Tsar Alexander III, the imperial government had granted a City Statute as part of the 'Great Reforms'; St Petersburg and Moscow had respectively been granted an elected city council of 250 and 180 members. The city *duma* could, under this Statute, determine city services and the allocation of city revenues. It elected a mayor and a small executive board or *uprava*. The Statute also listed specific municipal responsibilities, which included public transport; and these could be independently exercised 'within the limits of the authority granted to it'. It listed also specific cases in which the central government might intervene. In March 1881, however, the Tsar was assassinated, and the imperial government then promulgated the Extraordinary Measures which provided for martial law under which central government officials and the army, especially the prefect or military governor appointed to the city, could control municipal government by decree, and by administrative action could, in effect, rule the city without *duma* or *uprava*. In 1892 a new City Statute reversed many of the provisions of the earlier one, restricting the franchise for electors to property owners whose payable property tax exceeded 3000 rubles: a 75% reduction of voters. The central government could veto the appointment of city officials or replace them with its own nominees; it considered all city officials to be imperial civil servants. The law still gave specific responsibilities to the city *duma* for local needs and well-being, but all decisions were open to review or rejection by the central government. The violent December 1905 revolution in Moscow ensured that the imperial government, despite Tsar Nicholas II's October Manifesto promising basic civil rights and a national assembly, did not relax its control even of minor matters – for example, cleaning the chimneys of Moscow. This was the administrative reality, not obvious to a visitor like Welbourn, behind the negotiations he had to conduct with the *uprava* of Moscow in early 1908.

There was a further complication which also could not have been obvious. Tsarist government policy, even when it did not reject modernisation, had no clear view of a policy for the cities; it had the peasantry and the countryside as its main focus. Yet Moscow, in the years after the 1905 revolution, was growing at a very fast rate, chiefly by the influx of peasants looking for work and for an escape from the hard conditions in the villages. R.W. Thurston (*Liberal City, Conservative State*, O.U.P., N.Y. 1987, p.20), concluded that Moscow's population growth was its most important single characteristic: 'not only did the city grow, but every year the rate of growth increased'. In 1907 the city, including the suburbs, had a million and a third people; by 1912 it was almost a million and two-thirds, a growth rate of over 4% per year. European cities like Berlin and Vienna had less growth; only New York had a faster rate of growth. With such population pressure the city rapidly spread, as property prices and rents rose in the inner areas and there was a search for affordable housing further and further into the surrounding countryside. Hence the pressing need to develop and expand urban transport. Hence the presence of Welbourn in Moscow on his cable company's behalf.

There was an obvious need for an efficient tramway network to move people from their dwellings to their place of work in or near the centre of the city, but Moscow's revenue came chiefly from property taxes, and even if the property owners who made up the city electorate were not as selfish as popular critics made out, the demands of the central government upon sources of revenue, and the competition of other demands such as public health – for Moscow had the deserved reputation of being one of the deadliest cities in Europe – and education, would have presented an urgent question of priorities for the municipal government. To raise the capital for a modern transport system meant, therefore, raising the money by borrowing, by bond issues on both the domestic and the international market; and every bond issue required the Tsar's approval which it might take several years to obtain. Moscow was (Thurston, *op.cit.* p.47ff) fairly successful in raising loans. From twenty-seven and a quarter million rubles in 1901, the city debt rose to 112 and a half million by 1912. This was the money which financed the tramways, and , once installed, they became the city's biggest money raiser. In 1901 horse-drawn trams were in operation, but their conversion to electric trams, although requiring large investment, and incurring an initial operating loss, by 1907 had begun to be profitable, and by 1912 were providing an income to the city of three and a quarter million rubles for the year.

At the time of Welbourn's visit, the city *duma* and the *uprava* were arguing over the issue of service to the inhabitants versus revenue to the city as the governing factor in tramway development. Should the city expand the hours of tram services and lower the fares, or extend lines to areas which did not promise an immediate return on the investment? At the time of Welbourn's visit the city's policy was beginning to shift towards the provision of services rather than quick profit, although the *duma* clung to the revenue as the largest part of the city's income. In 1913 M.A. Shtromberg published a book on the Moscow trams (cited by Thurston, *op.cit.*, p.144) which accused the city authorities of thinking first of profits and only secondly of service to the inhabitants, because they would not build lines into the less densely populated suburbs which would bring in less money. Such an argument plainly affected any decisions about contracts such as the one Welbourn was seeking.

Given the limitations upon the authority of the municipal government, and the delays and unpredictability of central government decisions on city affairs, together with the policy arguments in the *duma* about transportation policy, it is scarcely surprising that a British businessman should experience frustration at, to use Burkewood Welbourn's Russian phrase, this '*se chass*', this '*mañana* with knobs on' country.

His visit to St Petersburg in the summer of 1909 saw him more experienced in working for a Russian contract, but he had no great liking for the city, the capital and the largest city in Russia. He was there because of duty, and not because he wanted to be. Like Moscow, St Petersburg was undergoing rapid growth. Its population was over a million by 1890, and this more than doubled by 1914. Between 1908 and 1913, the growth of its industry meant that the value of its factory production increased by 60%. Such growth (documented by J.H. Bater, *St Petersburg: Industrialization and Change*, London 1976, p.213ff), caused the city to spread into the surrounding countryside with the consequent need for a public transport system, but compared with other cities, St Petersburg was laggard. From the early 1860s (Bater, *op.cit.*, p.271ff), horse trams appeared on the streets, but it was not until the mid-1870s that these had expanded to be in general use, run by a private company under franchise from the city authorities which took 3% of gross receipts of the company. In 1895 this amounted to only 86,000 rubles. In the 1890s the city *duma* did not renew the franchises, and bought one of the private companies running the horse trams as a step towards municipal control of the tramways. Litigation delayed complete acquisition. In 1902, however, plans were made to introduce electric trams, although none appeared before 1907, a later date than most other big cities, later even than Moscow.

St Petersburg, like Moscow, had city government by grant from the imperial government which exercised an even greater degree of control in its capital than in its second city. The Tsar and the central government were the major property holders in St Petersburg, and were exempt from property taxes. Not only could the *duma* be over-ruled but its revenue base was smaller than that of Moscow. To establish an electric tramway system, it was even more necessary to find the capital investment by raising loans through a bond issue. The Russian capital raised 9.5 million rubles on this market to extend the electric tramways, and by 1913 had purchased over 600 trams, but the original plan to extend the tracks had had to be revised downwards. By 1914 there was an extensive tram network, but the horse trams and the steam trams which had preceded electric still served outlying areas. One contemporary observer (H.W. Williams, *Russia of the Russians*, New York, 1915), noted that 'house-owners feared that the electric trams would mean an exodus to the suburbs and a lowering of rents'.

In 1909, when Welbourn came to St Petersburg, the electric trams had already proved a success. In 1908 they earned for the city 5 million rubles, the most significant single factor in the municipal revenue, and carried 83 million of the total of 148 million passengers on public transport. In the year of Welbourn's visit to secure a cable contract, the trams were carrying 162 million passengers (Bater, *op.cit.* p.277). But a separate fare was charged for each stage of a tram route, and the resulting multi-stage fare for most journeys to work still meant that tram travel was something of a luxury rather than cheap transport for workers; and upper class residents rarely used the trams. It was a common criticism, even more in St Petersburg than in Moscow, that the property franchise for electors meant that the city *duma* was dominated by a narrow circle of the richer, entrepreneurial citizens, and that the development of the electric tramways was designed to yield revenue rather than to provide services for the working population.

During his brief visit of less than three weeks, Welbourn could scarcely have been aware of the cross currents of municipal and national politics which lay behind public transport policy, but the decision to extend and electrify the trams had already been taken, and he experienced less of the frustration that had attended his earlier Moscow visit. The representative of the associated firm of Dick Kerr & Co., Malek, who had been with him in Moscow, now told him on 9 June that he had come out to St Petersburg three months too soon. Welbourn did not himself think so, but he recognised that there was a great deal of work to be done. How long it would take depended upon Malek and his business people.

Malek was actually in Moscow when Welbourn arrived in St Petersburg, to stay at the Hotel de France, about a quarter of a mile from the Tsar's Winter Palace (now The Hermitage museum). While he waited for his colleague, Welbourn filled in his time by walking round the city, and by taking tram journeys so that he could get a good idea of the scale of what was needed in the cable contract. There are no comments in his letters on the events of 1905. In January of that year a great march, led by Father Gapon, had attempted to reach the Winter Palace to present a petition to Tsar Nicholas II. The marchers were prevented from reaching their destination by cavalry and infantry attack, culminating in the violent repression which was internationally called 'Bloody Sunday', and which was well publicised in Western European newspapers. Since the suppression was by cavalry sabre and rifle fire, not by artillery as in Moscow, the city bore few physical scars. Welbourn saw and commented upon the equestrian statue of Tsar Alexander III which had been unveiled by the present Tsar Nicholas II just before his arrival, and he mentions another imminent visit of the Tsar on 11 June, for which no obvious decorations were visible; but he makes no political comment on well-known, relatively recent events. He was not unaware of politics, for he referred to Count Witte, whose residence he passed, as 'an able statesman who made the Treaty of Peace with Japan' after the Russo-Japanese war of 1905; and he referred to Stolypin, the Russian Premier whose house he also passed. He was necessarily aware of the strike by tramway workers on 15 June, noting that there was no associated disorder, but three days later that there was talk that the ringleaders of the strike might be deported from the city back to their villages for three years; they were costing the city £2,000 a day in lost revenue.

Despite another hint of political trouble in the background on 20 June, when he mentioned the news of the supposed attempt on the Tsar in the Gulf of Finland and the 'close scrutiny' which might account for the absence of a letter from his wife, Welbourn's concern was with his business. Before Malek's arrival from Moscow, on 9 June Welbourn spent four and a half hours acquainting himself with the various tram routes, and on the following day 'ventured' on a tram while looking over the routes. Two days later he caught the steam tram to the far end of a line into a suburb of wooden houses which were evidently summer residences, a line which carried a lot of passengers. Two days later still, he took an electric tram out to 'the Islands', and, two days after that, while waiting for a delayed meeting, took another long tram journey along the Schlusselberg road to join a river steamer on the Neva for an hour's trip, and then home by a very slow-going steam tram. By 18 June he was able to make an informed estimate of the work for which his company was tendering, and then to book his travel home via Berlin, where he and Malek planned to break the journey which would already have taken thirty-three hours from St Petersburg, before resuming across Germany, Belgium and northern France to the Channel, a journey which took equal time: sixty-six hours in all.

Having been successful in securing tramway cable contracts in both Moscow and St Petersburg, he was sent by his company to follow up negotiations which the General Manager, Mr Dane Sinclair, a 'telephone' man, had begun in 1909 in association with the National Telephone Company, in Constantinople, the capital of the Turkish or Ottoman Empire. In March 1912, Welbourn took the ferry from Dover to Calais and then the train to Brussels where he caught the train to Vienna and thence across Hungary, Serbia and Bulgaria to Constantinople, which he reached on 17 March after a leisurely, thirty-mile-an-hour journey across what he, correctly, called the Near East (the Middle East was then India; the Far East, China).

As Welbourn travelled across the Balkans in mid-March 1912, he was aware that they were 'the storm centre of Europe'. He knew that the king and queen of Serbia had been murdered seven years earlier. He knew that the present king was said not to be too secure on his throne but that the king of Bulgaria, which had proclaimed itself an independent kingdom two years ago and was reputed to be much more stable, was a strong governor. What he did not know was that on 13 March, the day before he left England, Serbia and Bulgaria, later joined by Greece and Montenegro (all of which had been under Turkish rule during the nineteenth century, and all of which had become independent as Turkey-in-Europe crumbled) had signed a treaty of alliance, and had agreed to a Balkan League to capture the remaining Turkish lands and divide them between themselves. Bulgaria indeed had hopes of capturing Constantinople. War did not, however, begin until early October 1912, although the shadow it cast before explained the passport checks and baggage examinations Welbourn mentions.

85

Constantinople itself had seen a revolt in 1908, when the Young Turks deposed the Sultan and replaced him with another who, they intended, should support the Army officers who intended, with a strongly nationalistic programme, to modernise an inefficient regime, long known as 'the Sick Man of Europe'. Indeed, the electric cable business was part of the modernisation of Turkey, and specifically a telephone network which would provide the communications needed to hold the empire together. The submarine cable across the Straits into Europe, which Welbourn mentioned on 23 and 24 March, was intended to help to shore up Turkey-in-Europe in the face of threats. One of those threats materialised in early April, while Welbourn was engaged in his business. The Turkish government, in the face of Italian demands in North Africa and in the Aegean sea, feared an attack, renewing that made on Tripolitania in 1911, and closed the Dardanelles to all shipping. On 6 April he reported the news that the Italians had blockaded the Turkish-held island of Rhodes, an action which delayed the re-opening of the Straits, the closure of which was causing an economic crisis in Russia which depended upon shipping being able to move through them into and out of the Black Sea. Despite wars and rumours of wars, however, Welbourn found that the Turkish officials with whom he had to deal were, like the Russians he had dealt with, unwilling to be hurried. He in fact briefly went back to England to discuss matters relating to Constantinople with the company, although he was sufficiently concerned about railway travel across the Balkans to contemplate an alternative route by train across France to Marseilles, and thence by ship to Turkey. In the event he returned to Constantinople by Channel ferry, by train from Paris through Salzburg to Vienna, but then took the northern route, to avoid Serbia and Bulgaria, across Roumania, which impressed him by its higher standard of housing and better clad people, to the Danube port of Constanza, from which he could take ship to the Turkish capital.

When he arrived in Constantinople on 3 May he reported that the Dardanelles would soon be cleared of mines and the Straits re-opened to all the banked-up shipping. He re-opened negotiations with the local contractor who would do the trenching and pipe-laying for the cables, and then examined the barges which would carry these drums of cable from ship to shore. While he was very busy with these details came reports on 9 May of the Turks capturing 110 Italians and six guns on one of the islands not far from the Dardanelles; and the Straits remained closed to shipping. Later in the day he had a final meeting with the local contractor, and struck what he thought was a good bargain. He would now be glad to be out of the place. He had indeed been hospitably entertained by the British expatriate community living just outside the city, but he had found the interminable interruptions and delays tiring, and the uncertain atmosphere of possible war somewhat nerve-racking. Travelling up the Golden Horn on 13 May, he had seen the collection of battleships which was the

Turkish navy: 'a disgraceful collection of out-of-date and largely useless warships'. He had also seen the much larger collection of shipping awaiting the re-opening of the Straits. He himself had to wait while a local lawyer completed the contract, but he was able to get away on 19 May, just as the Dardanelles were re-opened.

The first Balkan war broke out on 17 October 1912, when Serbia and Bulgaria, joined by Greece and Montenegro, launched their attack on Turkey. The Bulgarians fought the main Turkish army in Thrace, winning the big battle of Lulé Burgas, and later capturing Adrianople, although they were unable to take Constantinople. The Greeks took the port of Salonika, four hours before Bulgarian forces arrived, and the Greek fleet occupied the Aegean islands. The Serbs took Macedonia. On 3 December the Turks concluded an armistice, and a peace conference opened in London two weeks later. While it was sitting a *coup d'état* overthrew the government in Constantinople, the army commander-in-chief, Nazim Pasha, being murdered; and the war resumed. The Bulgarian capture of Adrianople, the Greek of Janina, and the Montenegrin of Scutari, however, forced a peace settlement on the Turks by the Treaty of London, signed on 30 May 1913. Under its terms, Turkey ceded all her dominions in Europe west of the line Enos-Midia, and the island of Crete. The Balkan states, however, quarrelled over the division of the former Turkish lands; in particular, Serbia took almost the whole of Macedonia, part of which had been promised to Bulgaria under her treaty of alliance with Serbia. On 29 June 1913, Bulgaria therefore attacked her former allies, Serbia and Greece, without, so historians such as A.J.P. Taylor (*The Struggle for Mastery in Europe*, Oxford 1954, p.497) and E. Lipson (*Europe in the 19th and 20th Centuries*, London 1949, p.279) have said, warning.

On 7 June 1913, Welbourn was on his way back to Bulgaria and Turkey. He again crossed the Channel to Calais, and then took the train via Paris, Munich and Vienna to Sofia, capital of Bulgaria. After Vienna, the Balkan troubles upset railway arrangements, delaying his arrival in Sofia by a whole day. He began to understand what was meant by the words 'a nation under arms', for he passed troop trains and bivouacs at most stations, and all tunnels and bridges had armed guards. A Bulgarian fellow-traveller repeated what was commonly said in Britain before Welbourn left: 'it is all a game of bluff'. Nevertheless he also learned that the Serbian and Bulgarian armies were encamped on opposite sides of the frontier, although he was unlikely to see all the tents owing to darkness. A good many people, he wrote, seemed to think that it might be best to settle now and perhaps for all time the mastery of the Balkans, but if anything should happen, his wife was not to worry about him; there were two railways out of Sofia to ports on the Black Sea, and on one of them one could also get to Bucharest in Roumania, and so to Constanza and by steamer to Constantinople, the route he had used in the previous year. He had taken care to get a passport from Sir Edward Grey, the British Foreign Secretary, for 'Travelling in Europe'.

He reached Sofia on 10 June, staying at the Grand Hotel Bulgaria, opposite the royal palace. He saw no warlike signs on his arrival, but the train had been searched by the military near the frontier, and he was told that it was useless to post a letter from Nish, in Serbia, because it would not get through the censor. He proposed to see if the Bulgarian censor would frank it. Incoming letters were probably also being censored, he told his wife, so it was necessary to write in generalities. He noted that inflated war prices were being charged in the hotel, where both the British and the German military *attachés* were staying, dining together in the garden, while the Belgian minister or consul was to be seen lunching with a Turkish cavalry general who had been captured at Adrianople. The regime in the city was severe: all theatres and cinemas closed, all cafés shut early. He saw General Ivanoff, the Bulgarian hero of Adrianople, an unaffected elderly man with an iron-grey goatee beard and moustache, quietly dining with one or two other officers, without any of the applauding or staring which would have happened in London or America. Sofia nevertheless impressed him. The electric tramway work had been well done, the open wire work on the telephone lines looked quite good, and the telephone directory showed 1200 subscribers already.

Welbourn expected to stay three days in Sofia, meanwhile inspecting the very interesting hydro-electric works in the mountains which provided the city with power and lighting, and the State coal-mine at Peruik. While he awaited a colleague from Newcastle, he played some hard tennis, and watched military aircraft circling low overhead. And he heard the rumours which circulated in the disturbed political atmosphere. He heard the news of the murder in Constantinople of Mahmoud Sherkel Pasha, a fine-looking man who had been pointed out to him when he was there, an event he said he had been expecting by way of revenge for the death of Nazim Pasha. He heard that the Tsar had written to King Ferdinand of Bulgaria and to the Serbs, an intervention designed to effect a settlement of the dispute between the two countries. And he experienced a severe earthquake which shook the hotel on 14 June. His business work, not very arduous, was occurring at an unsuitable time, for people's minds were occupied with military and political matters of great importance.

Since the ordinary rail services were upset by military traffic, he left Sofia by car on 19 June for Stara-Zagora and Bourgas, from the latter place catching a ship to Constanza, and from there a steamer to Constantinople. The anticipated war broke out when Bulgaria attacked Serbia and Greece on 29 June, certainly without a declaration of war but, historians notwithstanding, without surprise, given Welbourn's eye-witness testimony to the preparations on both sides. On 20 June, from Bourgas, he reported the news that Bulgaria had given a 48 hour ultimatum to Serbia and Greece, although he could not vouch for its truth.

Such circumstances made business very unsatisfactory, and it also delayed his departure. Not until 24 June was he able to reach Constanza, because of shipping delays in Bourgas and then in Constanza, and only on 25 June did he arrive in Constantinople, four days before war started. The Turks, with the Bulgarians defeated by the Serbs and the Greeks, were able to re-take Adrianople, and the Roumanians who had been neutral in the first Balkan war, now joined in the attack on Bulgaria in order to take Dobrudja. The second Balkan war ended by the Treaty of Bucharest in August, Serbia and Greece being the big gainers, and Roumania and Turkey minor ones. But Welbourn had concluded his business in Constantinople by 7 July, and left via Odessa to avoid the fighting. His telephone cable business in Constantinople was fairly quickly concluded, since Turkey's involvement in the second Balkan war was peripheral, and in any case there was a British cruiser, H.M.S. *Black Prince,* for the protection of Britishers, anchored off Constantinople.

By contrast with his visits to pre-First World War Europe, Welbourn's North American trips were unexciting, if professionally more interesting. He went to Canada in the summer of 1907 to examine the state of an existing market for his firm's cables. He spent more than half his time in Old Canada, the provinces of Quebec and Ontario which had been settled respectively by the French in the 17th and 18th centuries, and by the British at the same period, with an influx of United Empire Loyalists after the American War of Independence. These were the two provinces which, together with the two eastern seaboard provinces of New Brunswick and Nova Scotia, were created the Dominion of Canada by the British North America Act in 1867. Like the United States, Canada was a federal system of government, with a division of powers between the provincial (or State) and the federal governments. When he left the eastern provinces, Welbourn travelled west by rail to Manitoba, with its provincial capital at Winnipeg, which joined the Canadian federation in 1870. Beyond Manitoba lay the prairie provinces of Saskatchewan and Alberta, opened up by the building of the railroad, and only becoming provinces of the Dominion of Canada two years before Welbourn's visit. His destination, however, was the western, Pacific seaboard province of British Columbia which had joined the federation in 1871; but only after the promise by the federal government to build a transcontinental railway.

The Canadian Pacific railway on which Welbourn travelled west was built, with considerable government loans and concessions to the railway company, between 1881 and 1885; and another trans-continental line and a Grand Trunk line were still being completed while he was there. The growth of western towns and cities was stimulated by the railway, and business by their demand for electric power, in large part generated by hydro-electric plants in the Rocky Mountains, with the consequent demand for high-voltage cable. This was the background to Welbourn's visit.

During this trip, it became clear to him that the business would have to be developed with an American partner, rather than in competition with American companies, and he recommended that a marketing agreement should be made with the General Electric Company of Schenectady. This successful arrangement was behind him when he paid his second visit to North America in the summer of 1922. Most of his time then was spent in the United States, with only a brief visit to Toronto, capital of Ontario, just over the border. The post-war years which, as remarks in his letters show, were in Europe ones of a sluggish recovery from the war and from war-debts and reparations, in the United States were boom years in a creditor country. Welbourn went there to examine American expertise and skills which might contribute to his company's tendering for the proposed British railway electrification scheme and for the overhead cables necessary for the proposed National Grid, in the mid 1920s.

Welbourn was plainly impressed by the scale and efficiency of American enterprise which had been stimulated by the war effort, and which was encouraged by the Republican Administration of President Warren Gamaliel Harding. Harding had defeated Cox, the nominee of the party of President Woodrow Wilson, the Democrat who had struggled to keep the United States involved with the League of Nations and world affairs, after an anti-League presidential campaign. With the rejection of the League by the United States Senate, the election of Harding in 1920 had seen an American withdrawal from international politics and concentration on home development; and that of course by private business enterprise. Welbourn noted that American electrical engineers were still working out solutions, and were willing to admit it and to learn from British and other experience. What impressed him was their energy and the general air of optimism. What he did not mention was some of the attendant shady dealing. There was a whiff of scandal about Harding's presidency, in particular the Tea Pot Dome affair, concerning land leases for oil exploration in California and Wyoming, which led to the resignation of the Attorney General in Harding's administration, and some subsequent criminal prosecutions.

In his letters from North America, Welbourn reflects the circumstances of doing business in a free enterprise society under a federal system of government with limited powers of intervention, an interesting contrast with his experiences in eastern Europe, doing business under despotic governments which had the power, the capacity and the need to intervene in the affairs of all their subjects and the foreigners they dealt with.

Francis West

90

Letters written to his wife by Burkewood Welbourn AKC, MIEE, aged 31, travelling on behalf of the British Insulated and Helsby Cables Ltd ('the BI') to Canada and the USA in 1907.

(Editor's note: In 1907 the BI had become worried about its Canadian Market, and sent Welbourn to investigate the situation. On his return to Prescot he recommended, in a brief but pithy report, that the BI should come to a marketing agreement with the General Electric Company of Schenectady and that it should send over an engineer as its resident manager. He found that a letter, written at his instigation by the GEC, had already arrived, and to it he drafted a reply which was sent by BI. He also put forward the names of two possible men for the job of manager, of which one was accepted. The result was that the BI captured the 11,000 v cable business in Canada for many years.)

R.M.S. *Umbria* in Mid Atlantic
July 20th 1907

My very dear Wife,

It is a long time since I had such a lump in my throat as when I had to say goodbye to you this afternoon. I was glad you had to go off quickly – I couldn't have stood it long and it would have been harder for you.

I have had time to examine my surroundings now. There are only 38 first-class passengers, according to the printed list, and so I have my cabin all to myself and ought to be comfortable.

The cabin steward and I have had a talk about various arrangements. He will try to fix up a bath for me at 7.30 a.m. Also, it is not usual to dress for dinner so I am relieved on that score. I found my port hole open and the cabin much fresher.

I have sampled the afternoon tea – it was acceptable but not very refreshing with milk only. I have arranged with the second steward that I shall occupy seat No. 2 at the Purser's table.

I have exchanged remarks with two or three men – one of them is the clean shaven man with a boy of about 9 or 10 years. He is a very decent sort and has been here only 3 weeks – chiefly in N. Wales in connection with some proposed

91

cement works near Llandudno.

The brown little boy (with the brown clad mamma) seems a spoilt little rascal and his nurse has just carted him off in her arms – protesting.

There is only one name in the passenger list that I recognize – Mr Beals C. Wright. I believe he is one of the American tennis champions who has been over here playing for the English Championship and been defeated.

I thought it so very kind and thoughtful of Mrs Nash[1] to come down to be with you after I had gone and I appreciate the attention to you very much.

Please give my best love and kisses to the children and very much to yourself from your loving husband

Burke

Please keep all foreign stamps and post-marks for the children's collection.

It would have been so nice to have had you with me	S.S. *Umbria* Sunday July 21st: 1907 5.15 p.m. English Time 5.42 p.m.

My dearest,

The sea is giving the ship more motion now and, therefore, I am setting out to write today's budget lest I should be 'unwell' later. I feel somewhat uncomfortable already. The sea looks very smooth and there is scarcely a ripple to be seen.

We got into Queenstown about 7.15 this morning but did not go into the inner harbour as it was smooth enough to stay outside and let the tender, with additional passengers, come out to us. The inner harbour was not very clear because of the morning haze. The snapshot of it cannot be at all a good one. In the bay, there were large numbers of sea gulls, chiefly white, but I noticed a few grey ones also. They were scrambling for food thrown to them and prefer meat to bread.

Boats came out conveying women with Irish linen, shawls, bog oak, blackthorns but did not do a thriving business.

We left at 9.40 and, by noon, had covered 45 miles by the log. The boat seems to be travelling well and we are now crossing this Devil's Hole – the deepest part of the Atlantic. There was no Service, this morning. There is a rule that the Captain must remain on deck until land disappears.

I got a snapshot of the Fastnet lighthouse. The S. coast of Ireland is very

---

[1] Mr R.P. Nash was manager of the electrical power generating plant in the BI in Prescot, and was responsible for its distribution in Prescot and the surrounding villages.

uninteresting. We passed, fairly close, the *Canadian* – a Leyland boat bound for Boston, U.S.A.

We are now out of sight of land but there is still communication by Marconigram, via Crookhaven, at prices which are prohibitive for ordinary purposes and ordinary purses. The minimum charge is 6/- for 12 words, including address and signature, plus the ordinary land charges for telegrams. I hope it will not be so monotonous all the week. A few porpoises and Mother Carey's chickens have been most welcome as a diversion. Some people thought they saw a whale but there was considerable doubt about it. The people are getting more sociable. On deck, my chair is between a lady – name unknown – and a man. The latter is a decent sort and is one of Geo. Smith & Son of London. We buy copper from them, at Prescot. The lady is single and opened the conversation. She is English and has travelled to and from several times. She makes herself pleasant.

At my table at dinner, last night, two out of six men were in evening dress so I suppose I must follow suit tonight (if I am well enough). It is not very encouraging for me to hear someone 'going it' in the next cabin – just started! You remember that on the Irish boat?

We get salt-water baths in the morning and I am having one. The sea temperature off Queenstown, this morning, was 64°F. I expect we shall be running into the Gulf Stream before long. I have had a short talk with the ship's doctor, this afternoon, but am not much attracted to him. I hope to find out the engineers tomorrow. Although so fine, it is distinctly chilly on board without active exercise.

It is now 6.17 p.m. (E.T.) and I picture Tommy just going to bed and the Churchgoers assembling. I am going on deck now for fresh air.

> July 22nd: 1907
> 11.0 p.m. (English)
> 9.30 p.m. (Ship's Time)

The day has been very uneventful and I have kept more or less comfortable by taking all my meals on deck except breakfast. This was a modest meal – a cup of tea and some dry biscuits – in my berth. I got up early and shaved after taking my salt-water bath.

I have not extended my acquaintances very much. I have had a good talk with an elderly lady with white hair – a fellow sufferer and a companion in meals. One man from Florida has been staying with the William Osborns (the cutlery people) in Sheffield. They seem to have given him a good time motoring in Derbyshire.

The day's run to noon today was 446 miles (nautical). This is a good performance and we are expecting to reach New York on Saturday evening but not to land until Sunday morning.

We have had clouds and no sun all day. I am told that the sea was rough last night. I slept well and knew nothing of it. I had about two hours sleep again this afternoon. It really is *very* slow on this boat with so few saloon passengers. The doctor says there are, in addition, 190 2nd class and 600 in the steerage – chiefly emigrants. On the whole, it seems creditable to remain up. A few have disappeared today altogether with mal-de-mer.

One feature of the day is the publication of the newspaper – *The Cunard Daily Bulletin* – at 2½d or 5 cents. In it, there are published the messages received by the Marconi apparatus. I was interested to see that the King's Prize at Bisley has gone to an Australian.

There is precious little news to send and day by day it will get less, I expect, until we reach New York. My thoughts are very frequently with you and our two children. I did not expect Edith would feel the parting, on Saturday, so much as she evidently did.

July 23rd: 1907
10.0 p.m. (Sea Time)

This has been a most uneventful day. When I looked out first, this morning, the sea was almost without a ripple. About noon, the rain started and lasted about 3 hours. Then it got fine until about 7.30 when the rain poured down. Breakfast was the only meal taken below today. The others I had brought out to me on deck, where my companion is an elderly lady travelling alone. The children have been the one bright spot today. They have been lively and playful. This afternoon, after a 2-hours' sleep, I played deck quoits with them. This morning I had about 10 minutes at the piano and there is some talk of getting up a concert for Friday night. The run to noon today was 467 miles and the doctor says we are 50 miles further on than on the corresponding voyage, last time, and that he expects we shall get in on Saturday night.

I have discovered a very nice elderly man from Adelaide who knows the Hon. Tom Playford – 'Honest Tom'.[2] It proved quite an interesting topic tonight.

July 24th 1907 8.35 p.m.

I shall write very little tonight. I have come to bed early after the most

---

[2] The Playford family were distant Welbourn relatives.

uncomfortable day we have had so far. The ship is pitching and I want to hurry up to get to sleep for fear lest I should be ill. I have spent the whole day – 12 hours – on deck.

July 25th 1907
10 p.m. (Sea Time)
1.25 a.m. (English)

We are now at the end of another day. You will see I quote English Time – I have kept my watch unaltered so that I can picture what you are all doing at once when I look at it. I hope you will not imagine this is a pleasure-trip for me. It's hard work fighting against mal-de-mer day after day. Tonight I feel rather better but still I have had all my meals on deck. Some people on board are *very* ill. The whole day has been fine although getting more cloudy as the day went on. Now the rain has started and there is lightning – a fine sight at sea. We have seen a little phosphorescence tonight also. Tonight there has been a good phonograph playing in the saloon. One of the pieces was Melba's singing of 'Home Sweet Home'. My unmarried deck neighbour seems to have developed a flirtation with the ship's doctor. They have been together most of the afternoon and evening.

I have done very little reading – so far. I finished off 'Sir Charles Dowers' and now have read a few pages of *The Woman with the Fair*.

People all round seem to be getting more friendly and chatty. It helps things along. One great bond of interest at noon each day is the run for the last 24 hours. Today it was 453 miles. Previously, it has been 440, 467, 446. We are more than 2/3rds of the way from Liverpool but we do not expect to be able to land until early on Sunday morning.

The vessel has rolled a good deal today at times but I am thankful to say that dreadful pitching has ceased. I hope I shall have forgotten this week's experiences before I have to set out on the return journey. I should not like to have to face it again for a week or two.

Perhaps you think I am harping too much on this sea-sickness topic – but it is very real to me. The rest has certainly done me good and I have lost the very sallow look which I had when I came on board.

This evening, the 2nd class passengers had a concert on behalf of the Liverpool Seamen's Orphanage but I did not go to it. Later – on deck – there was impromptu singing and dancing by some girls who are supposed to belong to a theatrical party. It was very inferior and we soon got tired of it all. There is some talk of our having our own concert in the Saloon tomorrow night but I don't know if we shall. Our numbers are so few.

You will be very busy now in making all preparations for going to Rhyl where I shall address this letter. I hope Lucy will be able to go with you on Monday.

July 26th 1907
5.30 p.m. Sea Time
9.40 English Time

Tonight we are to have a concert and I am to sing 'King Arthur' although I don't really feel up to it. We had a very rough night – tropical rain and lightning for hours. The ship rolled a lot and hardly anyone seems to have had a good sleep last night. I am still so-so but Mr Smith, who has been alright so far has not appeared today and is pretty bad, I hear.

Our run to noon was 456 miles leaving 640 miles to N.Y. There seems to me no chance whatever of getting ashore tomorrow night.

I expect I shall be in N.Y. or neighbourhood until about July 30th and to get up to Montreal about August 2nd or 3rd and to be there at the Windsor Hotel for fully a week. It seems to be the business headquarters of Canada. I will arrange there for letters to be forwarded.

I am sending a separate note to Edith and Tommy which should arrive when this does. Please get E. to send me one of her own notes. I am very sorry I am not to be with you on "wedding night" this year. I have been wondering whether you would like me to get you a skin in Canada for lining a coat or perhaps a fur muff and boa to match? Please let me have your views. Of course, I do not know what they cost but they should be cheaper than in England. I must go now – I must go on deck again for fresh air.

R.M.S. Umbria in Mid Atlantic
July 26th 1907

My dear little Edith and Tommy,

Tomorrow night, sometime, we expect to reach New York and to go on shore on Sunday morning early. Before we get there, a ship comes to meet us with a doctor on it. He wants to know if anyone is or has been ill and, if no-one has an infectious complaint, he will give us 'pratique' and say we may go ashore.

We have very few people on this part of the ship but among them is a bright little boy named Douglas – four years old – and even more energetic than Tommy. He is the little boy that mother saw on the ship last Saturday in Liverpool. Another boy, Willard Wentz, an American, is very bright and plays all sorts of games such as deck quoits and shuffle-board and he does them well.

There is another boy – George, 12 years old – a Nicaraguan – who has been at school for three years at Freshfield near Southport. He says I ought to send Tommy there when he is old enough. He sleeps in the next cabin to me and he has been very bad all the week with sea-sickness. He is so looking forward to getting to New York tomorrow and to meeting his father, mother, 3 sisters and two brothers who live there.

Then a little girl with very fair golden hair comes to see us, pretty often, and plays great games with Douglas.

Tonight there is to be a Concert at which I am to sing 'King Arthur' but I do not feel very well and so I do not expect to get on very successfully. We have had a beautiful morning – much warmer than before. I think we got into the Gulf Stream. The water suddenly got 10 deg. hotter from 58 to 68 Fahr.

The picture on this paper is that of this ship. When I come home again, I expect and hope to be in a bigger one still.

I hope you will send me a nice letter soon and get Tommy to add his mark. I expect you are breaking up today for the holidays and saying goodbye to your governess.

My best love and kisses to you both
from Father

I mean to send you some p.p.cs. Pl. keep them and put them in an album.

July 27th 1907
12.10 noon (Sea Time)
4.55 p.m. (English Time)

Our concert went off well last night but before a necessarily small audience. The result was £7 odd for the Seaman's Orphanage. I sang, as an encore 'Funiculi, Funicula'. I got one of the very few encores.

We passed the Nantucket lightship at 8.30 a.m. today – 223 miles from N.Y. – and 190 miles from Sandy Hook. It is clear, therefore, that we cannot land tonight but shall do so tomorrow (Sunday) about 8 a.m.

Today is very lovely with strong West Wind fairly cool. It seems certain that the frightful heat wave has left N.Y. but of this I expect to know a good deal more in a few hours.

I don't know how it is done but we can post letters before landing and for 1d. as against 2½d. on shore.

Now goodbye – I am much looking forward to receiving a good long letter from you in Montreal about Thursday next.

My best love to you and the children and kisses too from
Your loving husband
Burke

This hotel does not really stand
in splendid isolation like it
does here (Illustration on notepaper)

Hotel Belmont
Forty-second St and
Park Avenue
New York
July 28th 1907

My dearest

I have been here, in this sky-scraper, for about an hour and a half and am glad to be off that rolling ocean for a time. As I write, I still seem to feel the ship's motion. I am thankful also to be able to have a quiet day in which to rest and think. We got into New York Harbour about 8.00 p.m. last night but too late for going ashore and so we anchored in mid-stream. I am sorry not to have been able to photograph the famous Sandy Hook but it was too dusky. This morning, again, it was too early to get the Statue of Liberty in the Harbour.

It is a very fine approach to N.Y. at night. On our right (starboard) was N.Y.'s pleasure resort – Coney Island – one mass of illumination. The buildings are outlined with electric lights. On the port side were North Beach and South Beach, similarly illuminated but not on such a vast scale. I hear that a big fire broke out at Coney Island at 2 a.m. Some of our passengers saw it from the ship. People got very friendly towards the end. One young boy of 21 from London was a general favourite and seems to have a shower of invitations to visit people here. He had a violent flirtation with a young girl from Kentucky who has been studying singing in London and sings very sweetly. I warned him, this morning, not to play fast and loose with her. She's too good for it and he only needs years and a guiding hand to turn out a good man. At present, he is young, too impulsive and too generous.

I had very kind messages awaiting me, at the ship, on arrival, from Miss Way.[3] They are staying at the sea at Westerly, Rhode Island, 3¾ hours from here. I have been trying for ¾ hour to get her on the long distance telephone but we get no answer. So I have written to say I expect to reach there about Tuesday evening and to stay one night; it is somewhat out of my way for Montreal but it can be done. It is not the shortest way.

I had practically no trouble with the Customs people on getting ashore. Instead of entrusting myself to an exorbitant N.Y. cabby – the shortest ride is one dollar or 4s. 2d. – I sent my luggage by an express company at a cost of 80 cents, say 3s. 4d., and took the Elevated Railroad at 5 cents myself. I saw more of N.Y. that way. I noticed two fine 'homes for the blind'. Apart from the height of the buildings, width of streets and tramways everywhere, I really do not see much different here from a big English city. This is, of course, a first

---

[3] Born 3 February 1822, died 26 January 1924. His account book shows that he lent her 7/6 in 1897. Had she been visiting his Uncle Fisher, who had been in the USA as a young man?

glance opinion. There is not half the excitement of being in a country where you do not understand the language.

To revert to the ship for a moment – the tips cost 4¼ dollars. The people come and ask for them in the most unblushing way. I have, only once, in England, seen it done so openly. One Irish lady – a Miss Ferris – who came on board at Queenstown, last Sunday, was left very ill through sea-sickness and the orders were that she was to go to hospital. A nephew was there to meet them and they refused any other offer of help.

I am going off, now, to find out if my luggage has come and I will continue this later. My room here costs 2½ dollars a day and is a quiet inside one on the third floor. The whole place, so far, reminds me somewhat of the Midland Hotel, Manchester.

Please keep all picture post cards and any other mementos which I may send.

Later – 8.00 p.m.

After a light lunch about 2.00 p.m. – cost $1 – which, at home, would have been about 1s. 9d. or 2/-, I set off for a stroll. I was introduced to Green Corn at lunch. It is young maize not stripped but cooked on the parent stem. It is best covered with butter and then eaten *au naturel* i.e. with the fingers. I went down a part of Fifth Avenue – *the* fashionable residential street of New York and then into Central Park. About C.P., I enclose a note for Edith. It is curious to see the notice outside some churches here 'Closed for the Summer'. I saw the Fifth Avenue Baptist Church which has lately secured the popular Rev. C. F. Aked from Pembroke Baptist Church Liverpool and which is run by 'Standard Oil' John D. Rockefeller. It is among the closed ones. After leaving Central Park, I went to the Presbyterian Church in Vth Avenue and heard an excellent sermon on God having a plan and a purpose for every one, in life. I enjoyed the service and hearty singing lead by a – presumably paid – tenor of good training and most excellent voice method. I have heard of this American system before. There is no choir. It was all so restful after the bustle and heat, outside.

I failed utterly to be impressed by Fifth Avenue. The buildings are unimportant, architecturally, and are typical solid John Bull in type. There is an endless stream of motor buses, motor cars, cabs, private conveyances, going along it as, indeed, there seem to be in all the streets round this very central hotel. The whole place is alive on Sunday and I wonder what it can be like on a week-day. The unbroken noise, outside, of the tram cars is appalling as I am now writing. It makes me glad of an inside room. It is really quiet there.

After church, I strolled along to the Greek Restaurant, close by this, and had afternoon tea *à l'Anglais* – apparently to the surprise and disgust of the foreign

99

waiter. It was most acceptable to have two large cups of weak tea. The heat here is of the very thirst-provoking kind and it is difficult to keep resisting the iced water which is constantly offered. Before my tea came, it was served to me as a matter of course and free-of-charge. It is natural that it should be hot here. It is, I am told, on a level with Madrid in point of latitude. It should be cooler in Canada – about 400 miles further north. I believe there is not so much moisture in the Canadian air and so the heat is not felt in the same way, as here.

I want you to realize the difference in time between here and Liverpool. It is exactly 4 hours 48 minutes but it is taken as 5 hours. It is much more convenient for everybody. We are 5 hours *later* than you e.g. at noon here, it is 5 p.m. with you. I often reckon-up the corresponding English time so that I may picture what you are doing at home. At this moment you are, I expect and hope, fast asleep. No doubt you have had, and unfortunately so, a busy week in preparing for Rhyl and when I am getting up tomorrow morning you will be about arriving there. It seems rather topsy-turvey, doesn't it? Last night, on the *Umbria*, I was shewing your, and the children's, photos to one of the married ladies. She was so very kind and nice about it and I had another very big lump in my throat. It brought you all so close to me again. Now I have set my back to this Canadian work (and I can see it is going to be a hard and trying time) I want you to help me all you can. I know you will. I quite forgot to say that I want you to deal with all my letters, that you possibly can, while I am away and only to send on to me the really necessary ones that need my personal attention. I should, however, like you to keep all letters for me to see, later.

I am now going to write my letter to baba to send with this.

My best love and kisses to you all

Your loving husband Burke

Hotel Belmont
Forty-second St and
Park Avenue
New York
July 28th 1907

My dear Baba

It is now half-past eight, at night, here and half past one tomorrow morning at Rainhill. Please ask Mother to explain this apparent conundrum to you. It is hot here – much hotter than it was when I left Rainhill and I have been sitting in my bedroom without my coat and waistcoat trying to get cool.

I am getting tired now. We had to get up about six o'clock this morning, and have breakfast at seven so as to be quite ready when the steamer got alongside the Cunard Co's wharf at New York. I came most of the way from the ship to this big hotel by an Elevated Railway i.e. one which runs above the streets.

Underneath, on the street surface, are tramcars and below ground is a Subway with trains in it. All these various conveyances are worked by electricity.

This afternoon, after dinner, I walked to the Central Park which is a big space of 840 acres in the centre of Manhattan Island and contains a Zoo, but very much smaller than the one you saw in London with Coz. Elsie.[4] I did not see quite all of it as it was so hot and – whisper softly – very smelly on such a hot day. There were some things which you would so much have liked to see and I am going to tell you a little about them. First of all there was a real American Bison Cow with such a very pretty little baby calf having its tea. Then I saw some fallow deer – like those in Lord Derby's park at Knowsley. We must take you there, one day, to see them. After this, I saw some beautiful birds – cockatoos, parrots, Java sparrows (like ours only with feathers which make them look like canaries), some English birds such as thrushes and starlings (looking very miserable) and some very pretty ring doves.

The lions and tigers were mostly fast asleep and seemed stifled, in their cages, with the heat. Their coats were in beautiful condition. There were some beautiful baby leopards. I saw two elephants eating hay. One was ever so much bigger than the other and about the same size as the one you rode on. I saw a great big brown bear in a den cut out of the solid rock, a wolf, a fox and some big birds something like swans, which were fast asleep standing up each with its head tucked under one wing. I saw several rabbits in a wired off enclosure. They could run out on the grass but had a big house to go into if they wished. I expect they do wish, very much, when it rains or snows.

I saw such a lot of people in the Park and at the Zoo. There were lots of girls and boys and the younger ones mostly looked very pale-faced town children – not like you and Tommy. They cannot get out into good country air as you two can.

Best love to you and Tommy
from Father

Hotel Belmont
Forty-second St and
Park Avenue New York
July 29th 1907
9.35 p.m.

My dearest,

I am coming to the end of a very long 'wedding day' anniversary. I could not sleep after 4.15 a.m. and have been working practically ever since 5 a.m. and shall not finish until about 10.30 tonight. I have to be up and breakfast about 7 a.m. tomorrow to go off to look at some copper smelting works in

---

[4] Elsie Gregory was the daughter of his favourite Aunt Emily. She exhibited regularly at the RA.

Carteret, New Jersey. In the afternoon, I leave for Mrs Gray's for the night and expect to be in Boston on Wednesday afternoon and perhaps in Albany, the same night, about six hours away, and to be in Montreal at the Windsor Hotel on Aug. 2nd.

About two days after you get this you will, I expect, be hearing from Prescot asking whether you are willing to join me in Montreal and go on to Japan. I have expressed my willingness to go, if they wish it, and conditional on your being willing to go with me. I am telling you at once so that you may arrange with Mary and Nurse Booth to take care of the children at Rainhill with Lizzie. Madge has now left school and is available for looking after your mother. I should expect to be back in England about Dec.1st and certainly before Christmas. *A quick decision is necessary as Prescot is to cable me in Montreal on August 9th giving their and your decisions.* If you are willing to go, you had better write or wire to the works, on hearing from them, asking Mr Kerfoot[5] or Mr Brooker to come and see you at Rhyl at once and talk things over. They have your Rhyl address. I have given them full particulars about booking your passage out etc. so as to relieve you of all that trouble. You would, of course, ask to be consulted about your actual berth in the ship. The travelling would be first-class throughout. I have asked them to consult Mr Sinclair[6] about the kind of clothing required at sea and in Japan and to have you properly advised. You had better ask for a copy of my letter to Prescot. You would need to leave Liverpool about September 1st – to meet me in Montreal about September 9th.

The advantage to the company is very obvious. If I am at Vancouver, I am only 12½ days from Yokohama and am more than half way from England. They were intending to send someone out shortly – at least Mr Sinclair has spoken of it several times lately to me.

Now about money matters – Prescot would buy your tickets and hand them to you – free, for the time being. You have ample funds to get your clothing, leave Mary with housekeeping and funds for a month or more, bring £25 with you for oddments and you can arrange with Mr Kerfoot to pay say £25 a month to Mary and the balance into my current a/c at St Helen's to meet my mother's fortnightly payments. You can also arrange with Mr Varley to pay my grandmother's 30/- on the first of each month. Mary, of course, need not spend all the money if she does not need it but can save it up. It occurs to me you might be able to get Nurse Booth, perhaps, for the children for part of the time. She and Lizzie could easily manage without a second maid.

On the passage out, you would give the following tips:-

---

[5] Mr Kerfoot was Secretary of the BI.

[6] Mr Sinclair was General Manager of the BI. Welbourn accompanied him to Moscow in 1908.

102

Table steward		5/-
Cabin stewardess	)	5/-
If you are sea-sick and needed extra attention then	)	7/6
Boot cleaner		1/-
Bath attendant		1/6
Deck steward	)	2/-
If you have many meals on deck then	)	4/-

I want you to decide whatever you think is best about coming if you are asked to do so from Prescot. If the offer comes, it will be an exceptional chance of seeing an interesting and outlying part of the world as well as seeing something of Canada especially Winnipeg, the Rockies, British Columbia and Vancouver.

You should get Baedeker's *Japan* – if they publish one and bring it out. Also there will be letters to bring from Prescot. The two green trunks marked EW and BW will do admirably. You should get Lowe to put the Welbourn in full on each and to add Rainhill, England. One trunk would go into your cabin and the other into the hold of the ship. Let the works arrange all this for you. Choose the lower berth in the cabin if you can. It is not advisable to bring any superfluous jewellery. Also bring very little actual new clothes, wear them once or there will probably be trouble with the Canadian Customs people.

Ask Mr & Mrs Hyde to get for us all the introductions – social and business – they can from their Japanese connections in London. Also get any others that may be forthcoming. Mr Sinclair can provide some, as he lived there some years, in the seventies.

You need warm clothes for the sea travelling, borrow another rug and bring me my big black coat please.

Love to you all – in great haste for the last post

Your loving husband

Burke

Weekapang
Westerley, R.I.
31/7/07

Dearest,

I got up here last night – it is 7 miles from the Westerley Station – and I was met by Miss Way in a motor car. It is beautiful here, right on the sea. The water is only about 50 yards from this Bungalow which is named 'Port of Rest'.

Mrs Gray is here and her eldest daughter's boy, Richard Pitkin aged 2. Her son's wife and boy Robert Gray are in a cottage close to. He is 11 days older than Tommy and as heavy or even heavier.

I only have time for this note. I leave here this afternoon and go to Boston to get the sleeper to Albany. I am so looking forward to hearing from you when I get to Montreal on Friday.

Best love to you all

Your loving husband

Burke

en route Westerley – Boston
31/7/07

Dearest,

I got up to Mrs Gray's about 9.30 last night – went to bed 11.30 – got up soon after 7.0 a.m. and had a good long day in the sun. This morning we talked and walked and held a great baby reception. Also of odd neighbours. They dropped in to the Piazza of the wooden house quite freely. Mrs Gray went out to lunch with friends in Westerley but returned before I left at 5.40 p.m. She sent her love to you and seemed very pleased to have seen me, heard of you and seen the children's photographs. She repeated her very kind invitation for us to visit them in their Hartford home in the winter season.

In the afternoon, we had about an hour's sail on the Creek near the house. They have their own boat but used a friend's today – the Lumsons.

At 5.40 p.m., Miss Way and I left by motor for Westerley and I caught an earlier train for Boston than I had intended – by good luck. I intend to leave there for Albany tonight by the sleeping car.

I am writing this in the Parlor Car – a great institution in the fast trains here. You pay for an armchair – reserved for you for the whole journey.

I want now to continue my notes on New York. First about the Belmont Hotel. There are some very admirable features. There are 4 or 6 lifts in regular use. When a letter comes, it is sent to your room. If you are not there, a slip is left telling you where to get it. Similarly with a parcel.

In the upstairs corridors, there are wall plugs to which the men attach a pipe and nozzle and go along cleaning the carpets by vacuum process. This is a great advance in cleanliness and time-saving over English methods.

My bedroom was small but leading out of it were two cupboards. A *large* one for clothes and a smaller one containing a large wash basin with hot and cold water, plenty of towels, a fresh piece of soap in a paper cover, dentifrice etc. In this small room were 8 electric lights which could be on all together, if desired. The bed clothes were very light in weight – because of the heat. You will have noticed the height from the pictures on the hotel letter paper. It is very conveniently situated opposite the Grand Central Rly Terminus. Also, from the hotel there is a direct entrance to the Electric Subway trains. This is an 'elegant' feature of the City. It contains four train roads. Two for local service, with frequent stopping places, and two for express trains which run from one end of New York to the other and only stop at a few definite points.

I was not the least bit sorry to leave N.Y. last night – its just the noisiest place I have ever been in.

The sky-scrapers are a great feature – in one I went up to the 23rd storey. I don't think it went much higher. In these high buildings, the lift arrangements are admirable and they travel quickly. In this building, the local service did the first 14 floors. The express skipped 14 and began at 15 upwards. I saw the famous streets – Broadway, Wall Street and Fifth Avenue also Madison Square but had not time to see the Thaw – notorious Roof Garden there. I did see the Tombs prison where he is now.

Outside New York in the country, by far the largest number of the houses, of all sizes, are of wood. I was not prepared for this. We are just entering Providence where the Waterons family live but, of course, I cannot stay to see them although Miss Way says they want me to do so.

We have just stopped and opposite the Station on one side on elevated ground is a magnificent building, the recently finished Capitol where the Rhode Island State legislature meets and where the Courts of Justice sit. The dome of it reminds me of that of St Paul's Cathedral.

The railways, generally, remind me of those in Germany. The engines have cow-catchers and ring a bell as they go through the stations and suburbs. There are no platforms, in our sense, and people walk about the lines and climb up from steps or move into the trains. I have for you the menu of the train dinner, last night on the N.Y.; N.H. and Hartford Railway. Just left Providence – 7.22 p.m. and expect to reach Boston about 8.30 and dine there.

The luggage arrangements are immensely superior to ours. You hand over your trunks to the Railway Co and get a Baggage Check for it. You do not need to see it into the train. You just claim it at the other end on arrival by surrendering the Check. If you come out, have everything in trunks – no small parcels – they are a great nuisance as these trains and steamers are arranged. The only thing to have in the compartment is a suit case containing one or two nights' and days' requirements on the train. This my new suit case will do and, also, I have with me my Gladstone bag. Also remember on the train each 1st class passenger is allowed 150 lbs only of free baggage, i.e. 10 stones 10 lbs but it does not seem to include the hand baggage in the compartment.

Aug. 2nd 1907

Since I wrote the above, I have had a busy and tiring time. On Wednesday evening, I got up to Boston about 8.30 p.m., dined there, and strolled round the town and saw some of the decorations and illuminations in the streets in connection with Old Home Week Pageant. I left by the Sleeper and reached Albany about 6.30 a.m. I went and had a bath, breakfasted, wrote letters and then went to look at the Cable and some other parts of the gigantic engineering works of the General Electric Co. at Schenectady. They now employ 15,000 men and, until recently, had 17,000. Just fancy dismissing 2,000 men at once! More than we employ at Prescot altogether. I got back to Albany by the electric *tram*, which goes along the open road at about 40 miles an hour in parts, about 5.0 p.m. and spent the evening in dining, reading, writing more letters and went over to get the Sleeper for here, before 10 p.m. Of course, I had to miss the beautiful scenery of Lake Champlain and the Adirondacks Mountains by coming at night. I got here at 7.15 a.m. and, again, I bathed, breakfasted and met, by appt., Ernest Kaye from our Prescot works who is out for Bates[7] and Peard about annealing furnaces. He has gone away tonight and I am rather glad. I got somewhat tired of him after 12 hours or so of his society. He is a very intelligent foreman.

I have done some business today but not as much as I should have liked as my trunk did not turn up until late and so I was minus my letters of introduction until about 6.0 p.m. I was so disappointed on reaching here this morning not to find a single letter from you or anybody. This has disappeared as I have since received three separate lots including your most acceptable budget. It was a capital idea of yours to utilize your diary. I much admired your promptness in writing to Mr Varley[8] about the best interest on the deposit a/c. Your M.U.[9] tea seems to have been a tremendous success and I am glad of it. It was sure to be so when you took in hand the organization of it.

It is very sweet of both children to think of me so continually. Will you please thank baba for her chocolate and say I much enjoyed having it and eating it. It is very thoughtful and neighbourly for so many friends to keep looking you up. I will send a p.p.c. or a note to Mr & Mrs Collingwood – also to Lyon House.[10] I have done so to Clinton, the Thomas's[11], Aunt Emily[12], and Mr Hackworth.[13] I am just on the verge of starting work properly – probably be *in media res* on Monday next and then I do not expect to write much except to you and the Works. So far, I have had a useful time from the business point of view.

So far as I know, we escaped the fearful thunderstorm of July 21st. On two

---

[7] Colonel Bates was Works Manager at Prescot. The Bates-Peard annealing furnace for copper rod was licensed world-wide.

[8] Manager of Parrs Bank, later part of the Midland Bank.

[9] Mothers' Union.

[10] Where he was in digs when he married.

[11] Joyce Thomas had been his best man at his wedding.

[12] His much beloved widowed aunt, Mrs Henry Gregory.

[13] His guardian.

nights at sea we had very vivid sheet lightning and it was very fine to see it in three entirely different parts of the sky. There was heavy lightning here for a short time this morning. I saw one very vivid flash of forked lightning. Did I tell you, we saw some baby whales – about 30 feet long – just before getting to N.Y.? I did not actually see them but I clearly saw the water they spouted up into the air.

The time here is as N.Y., i.e. 5 hours later than you.

Have I told you how *frightfully* expensive everything, except railway travelling, is over here? As far as I can see, it is 2 to 2½ times more costly than with us. Money seems to melt. I fear the Works will open their eyes when they see my expenses sheet later on !

I am sorry Harry[14] has been unkind to your mother. You do not give me any clue. Had she written or spoken to him or Hilda or had your father repeated to him some remarks of your mother?

Mrs Thomas' letter is most kind and is the real Mrs T. that I like and know is always there below the surface. She told me, quite lately, that her bark is worse than her bite. I also had a note from Joyce about the entrée dishes and saying he has to undergo an operation which will necessitate a week's bed. He does not say what it is but I suppose its those varicose veins again.

I should leave J and A's[15] a/c unpaid for the present.

I suppose now that you are all quite settled at Rhyl. After this, I think I shall address letters to Rainhill.

It is getting late now and I must soon go to bed. Goodnight, my darling.

Best love to you and the sweet children from

Your loving husband

Burke

Room No. 437
The Windsor Hotel
Montreal
Sat August 3rd 1907

Is there any news about Owen Clarke and Valparaiso yet?

My dearest,

I had the best night's sleep of the week, last night. This morning I used Donaldson's[16] introduction to R. M. Wilson and was most kindly received. I

---

[14] Harry Appleyard was the eldest brother of Welbourn's wife. He was married to Hilda.

[15] Johnson and Appleyards Ltd of Sheffield was largely owned by his father-in-law.

[16] J.M. Donaldson was a close business and personal friend, and the editor's godfather. He had worked in Canada for some years.

am hopeful this will lead to considerable opportunities of doing business and I have an appointment with him for more definite business at 9.30 a.m. Monday.

After leaving him, I went to Henry Morgan & Co., the leading sporting goods people here, and talked 'Imperial Green Dot' Golf Balls on Helsby's[17] behalf. There is nothing definite yet. Their skilled golfer has two for trial and also, this weekend, four will be used by members of 'the' Royal Golf Club of Montreal including the ex-champion of Canada and by the Secretary. I should much like to establish this for the Helsby people and for my own credit.

This afternoon, I took the Hotel Coach ride round Mount Royal – $1 – from the top of this public park, one gets a fine bird's eye view of Montreal, the St Lawrence River, the Lachine Rapids, and (in the U.S.A.) the distant Adirondack Mountains. There is an Indian reservation[18] on the opposite side of the river and I have arranged with a tourist Yankee, here, to visit it tomorrow afternoon and to return by steamer through the Rapids. They are not dangerous and it should be a novel experience. As I expected, lots of people are away on summer holidays but it has not affected me much, so far. On Monday morning, I expect to start a busy week and not to leave here until about Aug. 10th. I should like to get up to Quebec for next Sunday, if possible. It is said to be a very fine city. Frankly, I am very disappointed in Montreal as a town. It is made hideous by all the electric wires for light, power, tramways, telegraphs being run overhead mostly on unsightly wooden poles of all shapes and anything but straight or vertical. The tramway tracks and road surfaces are in a disgraceful state – quite unworthy of such an important and wealthy place. Such a condition of things would not be tolerated in England even in a small town. Some few of the buildings and banks are fine structures. This hotel with 800 rooms is, probably, the largest. Opposite is the R.C. cathedral – a ½ size model of St. Peter's, Rome. The Can. Pac. Rly Terminus – the Windsor Station – is very fine and massive looking in the castellated style. Other important buildings are the McGill University, the Hospital, the Grey Nuns Convent, The Bank of Montreal.

I am very glad to hear, tonight, that the English mail is due in tomorrow. I am expecting a considerable further budget from you, then. My first letters to you should now be arriving at the other end. Tomorrow I hope to see Donaldson's friend, Father Wood, and to attend his morning service.

Today, I have been buying a few Canadian things – souvenirs – two brooches for you, one each for the children and one for Lizzie but I think I shall

---

[17] The BI's Helsby factory made golf balls, and also tyres for motor cars, besides rubber insulated cables.

[18] Kahnawake, where his granddaughter Dr A.C. Macaulay F.C.F.P. was to organise the building of its hospital, of which she became medical director, in the 1980s.

not entrust them to the post. I intend the children's to be their birthday presents from me.

If we go to Japan, Miss Way can furnish us with two intros – one, curiously enough, to a Rev. Welbourn, an American missionary.

There was one feature of the ride today which I enjoyed very much i.e. the view of the Park Ranger's House and more particularly the garden. The latter was chiefly beds made up in patterns and reminded me so much of the similar ones which we saw together in the Tuileries Gardens.

By the way, if you come out please bring a large tin each of black and brown boot polishes and some Seloyts. Boots cost 5 1/2c (five pence) a time for cleaning. We could save quite a lot by doing our own.

Sunday August 4th 1907

Today has not been especially eventful. This morning, as usual, I could not sleep after 6 a.m. so I got up at 7.10 and dressed leisurely. After a light Sunday morning breakfast, just after 8.0 a.m., I went for a walk, took a few snapshots (in a bad light) and found out Father Wood's church – St John the Evangelist in Ontario St. I had a letter of introduction to him from Donaldson. He seems a dear old boy. He has asked me to go up to supper tonight at 8.30. The 11.0 a.m. service, at his church, is Choral Communion with sermon on the 1st Sunday of the month. As you know, I do not care for this service. The music is too diverting. He sent his young organist to take me to the R.C. church, this afternoon, to hear the music. At the Cathedral, the 3.15 p.m. service seemed to be 'off', for some unexplained reason, so we went on to the Church of St James opposite the Bank of Montreal and the Maisonneuve Statue. There is a magnificent organ there, lots of singing, priests and boys and light candles and incense. The priests etc processed round the church with two candles and a figure of Christ on the Cross at the head and a figure of the Virgin Mary at the rear of the long procession. As the sermon was starting (in French) we left.

At 2.45 this afternoon torrential rain fell for about ½ hour. The weather is quite cool and very overcast. I am told that July is the hottest month here and I am glad not to have to face much heat. I am afraid, however, that some of my clothing will be unsuitable for September and that I may have to buy my winter vests and pants here – I wanted new ones in any case. I find there is a Jaeger depot here, fortunately. One of my pairs of boots has started hurting me in walking. The lining seems to have worn through right at the big toe and I fear there is no remedy. The boots are in excellent condition. It will be a great pity if I have to discard them. I fear they would be too small for Russell. This clothing question is important. If you are coming out, you will need a plain warm coat –

say ¾ length – for the various sea journeys (4 in all) and a good warm plain tailor made costume for that and the train. You want to have as few washing things as is practicable. Washing is $1 (4s/2d.) for 12 articles ie 4¼d. each nearly. I have already told you about the boot-cleaning. The tipping nuisance here is rampant, also. The waiter expects not less than 10 cents per person, at each meal. I have been looking into things roughly and find I shall be rushed to get away for England by the middle of September – if you are not coming out. If you do not come, I can leave out Winnipeg until then and that will make things more comfortable for me, at this end.

I have been missing you so much today. I feel sure that my sleeplessness would all go if only you were here.

The Yankee tourist left Montreal, this morning, instead of keeping his engagement with me so I have not shot the (Lachine) rapids nor seen the Indian Reservation.

I am surprised to find that the shops inside the Rotunda of this hotel are open and doing business today.

I am disappointed, too, that the English mail, due at 10.30 this morning, has not come in. No-one seems to know why.

Goodbye, now, and best love to you and the children.

Your loving husband

Burke

> The Windsor Hotel
> Montreal
> August 5th 1907 10.20 p.m.

My dearest,

Very many thanks for your expected letter which reached me here today and bringing the home news down to July 27th. I have come to the conclusion that it is best for you that you are not on this Canadian trip with me, at this stage of the proceedings, as I am having to work really hard. Today, I got up at 7 a.m. and am only finishing now and am tired out so I shall write no more of this tonight.

> August 6th – 6.15 p.m.

I am frightfully busy and have no time to send you a decent letter. I am, at this moment, expecting two men in to dinner with me and must close.

My best love to you and the children.

Your loving husband

Burke

My dearest,

I am so sorry I have had to write you such skimpy notes in the past two days. There are limits to the capacity for one pair of hands and my excuse is that I have been at full stretch – from 7 a.m. to 11 p.m.

There is such a lot to be done here and I am trying to do it well. I expect to get out of here on Friday night or Saturday for Quebec or I may go there earlier and return here before going to Ottawa and Toronto etc. A good deal depends on my cable from the works which I expect to get on the 9th or 10th.

One thing is now certain and that is that I must go out to British Columbia, while in Canada, and it will fit in well with the Japanese trip if I am to go there.

I have another tough day before me today. What makes it hard work is that I have to meet some of the keenest brains here not one a day but several and the 'stretch' is severe. I have to turn from one subject to another like a barrister from one to another. I expect to complete this later on.

Later

I go to Quebec tomorrow night and probably return here about Monday or Tuesday. Only just time to send my love and kisses to you all.

In great haste
Burke

The Windsor Hotel
Montreal
August 8th 1907

Dearest

I have had to send you the scrubbiest notes for this last few days and this must be the same. I am just giving a few minutes after breakfast to this. I have had no letter from you since Monday and it is now Thursday.

I am working awfully hard for the firm. On a week day, never less than 7 a.m. to 11 p.m. Yesterday 7 a.m. to 1.30 a.m. this morning. I have been up since 6.30 a.m. again, packing and writing prior to going to Quebec by boat tonight, leaving at 7.0 p.m. with Mr Hanson, my very good financial friend here. He is a trump! I dined with him, last night, at the second best club in Montreal and afterwards he came here with me and introduced me to still other important people in this electrical firmament. I expect to be back here on Monday afternoon and to stay another 2 or 3 days.

I am so looking forward to getting a cablegram in 2 days' time saying you are to come out and that we are to go to Japan together. I feel sure that the

Japanese trip would be very different to this and that I should have much more free time to give to you – apart from the long spells – with no work to do – on the ships.

I am keeping wonderfully fit and well and do not feel the loss of sleep. In fact, I am rather enjoying the 'lust of battle' and feel I am making a good impression here for my Co.

Must stop now.

Best love to you and the dear kiddies from

Your loving husband

Burke

S.S. *St Irene* 10.30 p.m.

We are now en route for Quebec where I intend to post this tomorrow morning. It is a lovely night and the boat is very steady and well appointed. Of course, we see little of the scenery but it is not very interesting, I am told.

BW

Chateau Frontenac
Quebec
August 10th 1907
10.30 p.m.

My dear Wife,

I want to thank you very much indeed, for your long letter of July 30-31st which reached me today and which I had to read in patches. I have had such a week for work. I got here from Montreal yesterday morning about 9.0 and got to bed at 3.30 a.m. this morning. I have been up again since 7.45 a.m. and intend to do no more work until Monday. I have quite made up my mind, now, how the B.I. should tackle most of the Canadian trade and that is why I was up so late last night – writing a 10-page letter giving my views. I hope my recommendation to send out a man *at once* to be in Canada about Sept. 1st to meet me in Montreal, will be acted on. From Sept. 2nd to 14th there is an electrical exhibition here and, at the same time, meetings of three engineering associations at which some 2000 delegates are expected. By that time, I shall know some members of them and could introduce our representative in an unique way and send him off.

I received the cablegram from Prescot, last night, telling me not to go to Japan so now I can plan out my itinerary. I expect to be back in Montreal <u>about</u> Sept. 4th. Before then, I want to go to Toronto, Ottawa, Winnipeg, Rocky Mountains and possibly Vancouver so you can see I am in for a busy month. I leave here tomorrow night by the Richelieu and Ontario Navigation Co's boat which goes down to Montreal via the St Lawrence. The river is over a mile wide as far inland as Montreal. It is a wonderful national asset to the country. In addition, there are numerous and large waterfalls which are being harnessed for electrical developments. The country is immensely rich in timber and minerals. Mr William Hanson has gone back to Montreal tonight. This afternoon (Sat.), his niece and Mr Reid went with me to visit the Montmorency Falls, a few miles from here. They are 285 feet high and I got about 5 photographs. I have only done 17 in all yet but hope to get more, later on. The films are 6d. a dozen cheaper here than in England. This is a most beautifully situated place. It is one of the finest sights I have seen anywhere. The whole place teems with historic interest. Tomorrow, I expect to go on the Heights of Abraham and see where Wolfe fell.

I expect to leave Montreal at 1.30 p.m. on Wednesday next for Toronto and probably shall be at Niagara Falls on Saturday or Sunday or both. I think you had better address me, next, at the Queen Alexandra C.P.R. Hotel, Winnipeg. I expect to be there about Aug. 23rd to 27th and can arrange for forwarding of letters. There may be some delay in receiving letters owing to the uncertainty of my movements after that. For delivery after Aug. 27th you had probably better send to me at the Windsor Hotel, Montreal, where I may expect an accumulation of news on reaching there again.

Closing rapidly for last post 11.00 p.m.

Best love to you all

Burke

Yes – have that corn out.

Chateau Frontenac
Quebec, Canada
August 10th 1907

My dearest,

My sudden scare to finish my accompanying letter was of no use. The last post is 8.0 p.m. not 11.0 p.m. It is now somewhat doubtful if you will get this in time to let a letter catch me at Winnipeg. W. is 2 days by train from Montreal. Anyway, you had better write there and I can arrange for forwarding of letter. I expect to go up to Rossland in the Rockies and, if I go to Vancouver, I shall have to retrace my steps to a good extent to get on to the main line again. When I get back to Montreal again, I expect to map out my itinerary, take my tickets and so on.

I am glad to say that I have found out in time that furs here are about twice the price of the same thing in London. People here buy, or get friends to buy for them, in England! So that little idea is 'off'.

I am glad you are so comfy at Rhyl. I am wondering what you are doing about staying on after the 12th or whether you are going to Ingleton? I have seen nothing of Mr Cook – journalist – but I know a party has been out here.

We have had nothing like so much hot weather as I expected but today has been glorious and hot. We have had quite a lot (here they say 'quite a little') of rain – torrential rain – and lightning, especially in Montreal.

I really *must* go to bed now so goodnight, my dearest, and God keep you and the babes safe and well until my return.

Best love from
Your loving husband
Burke

Chateau Frontenac
Quebec
August 11th 1907

Dear Edith,

This is where I have been since Friday morning early when I got here from Montreal by the river H. Lawrence steamer *St Irene*.

I want to tell you about the expedition which I made yesterday afternoon to Montmorency Falls. We left here by an electric railway which can run at 43 miles an hour and we got there in about ½ hour. The first thing to look at was the Waterfall which is 285 feet high and perhaps 150 feet wide. I have some photos of it (I hope). Then we saw the outside of Kent House which is now used for refreshments. It is the house where the Duke of Kent lived, a long time ago. He was father of our late Queen, Victoria. What you will be most interested to hear about is the animals which are kept there by Holt, Renfrew & Co. – the world-famous furriers. Most of them were given, I believe, by the Dominian Government and are in splendid order. There were wolves, foxes, white and brown bears, beavers, marmots, pheasants, owls, deer, swans and so on but no lions or tigers. It seems to be an exhibit of Canadian animals only. There was also a bison but no little calf as at New York. We got home about 7.0 p.m. very tired. It had been very hot. This morning (Sunday) I have been for a walk over the Quebec Golf Links which are on the Heights of Abraham. I saw where the English and French troops met in battle; and the place where Gen. Wolfe died is marked by a not-imposing monument. I snap-shotted it and got, in all, about 9 this morning.

This is a very beautiful place in which to spend a few days and, very much, I wish mother was here to enjoy it with me. I expect to see it, again, on my way home, next month. It has been broiling hot this morning but now (1.0 p.m.) it is cloudy and cooler. I am quite ready for lunch after my walk.

I am leaving here tonight by boat for Montreal again and, perhaps next

Saturday or Sunday expect to see the famous Niagara Falls and then shortly go West to the Rocky Mountains. It takes 4 days and nights in the train to go from Vancouver to Montreal and there are 21,000 miles of railways in Canada.

Give mother and Tommy big hugs and kisses for me and ask mother to give them to you from me.

Love to all

Father

I wonder if you leave Rhyl tomorrow?

Chateau Frontenac
Quebec
August 11th 1907

Dearest,

Just a line before leaving for Montreal in a few minutes. Will you please send my blue suit in a strong parcel 'to await arrival' at the Windsor Hotel, Montreal? If you are not at home, will you ask Mrs Nash to get it? It is in the attic chest of drawers. I have written to Edith. This morning was awfully hot and this afternoon is cloudy and quite pleasantly breezy and cool. I intend to finish and post this in Montreal tomorrow.

Montreal August 13th 1907

I fully intended to finish and post this last night but a most unusual and acceptable occurrence prevented my doing so. I finished dinner soon after 8.30 p.m. and went to my room and got sleepy over the evening paper and the big heat here in a few minutes. I turned the light out and lay down on my bed to rest awhile. The next I knew was that it was 5 a.m. I undressed quickly, got into bed and slept until 7.55 a.m. – nearly 11 hours in all. I can tell you it did me a lot of good. Today has been again a very full one as I am clearing up and going on to Ottawa tomorrow en route for Toronto, Niagara and Winnipeg and the Rockies.

The weather has been 'hot' here at last and one seems to exist in a sort of Turkish bath when walking out of doors. I had two hot baths yesterday and expect I should have had a third if I had not gone to sleep.

Many thanks for your long letter enclosing the one from Becan. I am sorry about Mrs T. I had just posted a note to her when your letter came. I am tired now and intend to go to bed. It's late.

I think you had better send my big black coat to await me at the Windsor

Hotel, Montreal by Sept. 10th at latest. I shall need it on the voyage home, I expect.

Best love to you and the children.

Your loving husband

Burke

The Windsor Hotel
Montreal
August 14th 1907
7.45 a.m.

Dearest,

This is our engagement day! Many happy returns to it. I am busy packing etc. prior to leaving.

Burke.

The Russell House
Ottawa, Canada
August 14th 1907

Dearest

It is now 8.35 p.m. here – at about this hour, 8 years ago, history was being made for you and me. I remember it so well; and I have no regrets. It was a great day, for good, in both our lives. I did wish you could be with me, last Sunday, in Quebec. It is such a lovely place and you would have thoroughly enjoyed it. Fortunately, for me, I am frightfully busy and working like a nigger. Added to this, I have at last succumbed to diarrhoea and have had to resort freely to brandy to keep myself going – in addition to dieting. I have just managed to pull through and, tonight, I feel almost well again. We had a sudden change in the weather – went very hot and all day long I felt like being in a Turkish bath and had 2 or 3 warm baths a day to keep clean. I have been very fortunate at Montreal and here in getting a bedroom with attached bathroom. It is a great convenience. It contains a lavatory and washbasin with h and c water also.

I got here – it was such a rush to get off from Montreal – about 1.30 p.m. today. This afternoon, I have interviewed, at the Government offices, the Deputy Ministers of 'Public Works' and 'Trade and Commerce' – also the General Supt. of Telegraphs in the Govt. service. I have had little time to 'see' Ottawa except the Govt. Bldgs and Offices. They are *very* fine. Tomorrow, I shall be busy and intend to go on the sleeper tomorrow night to Toronto and, from there, see Niagara. I am in a difficulty about giving you an address – except the Windsor Hotel, Montreal. I think all letters had better go there. I am glad you have been so comfortable in Rhyl. I felt sure No. 27 would be O.K. and I hope No. 24 will be ditto. I wish I could send you over some of the occasional bursts of heat from here. I have not lost many things yet. I left my razor strop at home and had to get another. I left my toothbrush on the ship and, this morning, I left my macintosh in the train but recovered it. I left my umbrella at Mrs Gray's. That's the sum total.

I have taken several snap-shots lately. I have not yet had time to get my photo taken and saw no place I cared for in Montreal. Here there are two or three decent looking photographers and I may get it done tomorrow.

I, too, am getting brown but not so black as at Aberystwyth – 8 years ago.

I expect to be in Toronto until August 19 or 20th – then go by the Lakes to Fort William – thence by train to Winnipeg and there be until about Aug. 27th. From there I expect to go to Kootenay and Rossland in the Rocky Mountains. I do not know yet whether I shall get to Vancouver or not. I think I ought to go but I want to be back in Montreal for the Electrical meetings by September 5th or so.

Have I told you how kind Mr William Hanson has been to me? I had a letter of introduction to him from London. He is a very well-to-do, if not wealthy, man. He dined me at his Club, introduced me to all kinds of influential and useful people, took me to Quebec and has now given me various letters of introduction to carry me on. His niece said he had been making very nice remarks about me and gave me to understand I should be further entertained in Montreal in September.

The time is slipping away now and in a month from now I hope to be on the eve of leaving for home. I shall be very glad to get back.

Best love to you and the children. I will try to write for their birthday.

Your loving husband

Burke

The Russell House
Ottawa, Canada
August 15th 1907

Dearest,

I have had my photograph taken today by Pittaway of Sparks St., here. I have just seen the three negatives – two of them look quite hopeful – and on Friday morning, I am to have the proofs in Toronto. I hope to have a finished one to send to you early next week. I have paid $6.00 (25/-) for this dozen and I hope you will be quite happy now I have carried out your request. I propose to keep 4 – one each for you, the children and myself. The rest are for Joyce, Mrs Thomas, your mother, my mother, aunt Emily, aunt Loui[19] and two to be

---

[19] Mrs Richard Trist.

My Father, Ottawa 1907.

decided later – but please don't promise them to anyone. When I get home, I think I shall, definitely, go in for Freemasonry. Apart from the good fellowship, it will, I believe, be of considerable benefit to me in mixing among engineers. Most engineers smoke and drink and, so often, I feel unsocial and at a loss. Freemasonry would be a useful link of another kind and more binding. I think I told you Mr Marsh had said he would get me elected into his Lodge?[20]

Fortunately, out here, drinking is not universal and I have only seen about four people the worse for drink in Canada. Also, there is a general air of prosperity that we do not see at home and, so far, I have not seen any signs of slum life. I am told, too, that there is far less immorality here and that it is largely due to the Roman Catholic element, which preponderates in the old French districts of Canada – especially Quebec and Montreal. Also, the French-Canadians working class are said to be real plodders and much the most reliable.

I have got about 6 snapshots today in this orderly town. It is the Government Headquarters for all Canada and the parliament sittings are held here. Also, the Dominion Govt offices are here and the buildings, containing them, are very attractive.

I have not been outside the town, at all.

Tonight, I go on to Toronto by the sleeper. Please give my love and kisses to the babes and with many for yourself.

Your loving husband

Burke

I have not seen Mr Cook nor heard the date of Joyce's wedding. Have you?

King Edward Hotel
Toronto, Canada
August 16th 1907

Dearest

Through moving about, I am having such long gaps between your letters. It is days since I had a letter from you. I have tried to write to you every day and have only once failed and then through falling asleep – about which I told you.

I have travelled all night and reached here about 8.15 a.m. I was in bed from 10.40 p.m. to 8.40 a.m. The grits come in freely but there is almost room for two in the sleeping berths on the trains. One can get a fair amount of sleep. The train was about an hour late in arriving. This hotel is a fine one downstairs. My room has not yet been allocated to me but I know I am to have one with a bath attached.

---

[20] He never became a Mason.

The weather seems cool today. Yesterday was lovely in Ottawa. Brilliant sunshine tempered with wind. I left my letter to Dr Courtenay from Joyce but he was out. Mr E. S. Eddy (another letter to him) is dead. I have one for use here (socially) from Miss Arnett to Mr Bolton. I suppose you are sending a final note of good wishes to Joyce for his wedding day? I have written him from here. Poor Mrs Thomas is evidently very upset – she writes me that Joyce is a spoilt child and is acting as such!

I will write in a day or two for the children's birthday.

Must close now.

Best love and hugs for you all from your loving husband

Burke

I wrote home and to Aunt Emily yesterday.

King Edward Hotel
Toronto, Canada
August 18th 1907 Sunday

Dearest

I cannot make out what has happened. I have had no letter from you for six days now although I left very careful instructions in Montreal about the forwarding of letters. My only consolation is that I have none from Prescot either and conclude everything has gone astray.

I was to receive, yesterday, from Ottawa, the proofs of my photographs but they have not come and there is no further mail here until 9.20 tonight.

It is curious to note the changes in this country. Quebec is decidedly R.C. and French. Montreal is about 2/3rds R.C. and French. Here, the Protestant element is predominant and one sees no French names and language.

Yesterday, I had one of the big experiences of my life and it would have been perfect if you could have shared it. Being Saturday and an off business day – for the afternoon – I made a bolt for Niagara Falls. I caught the 2.00 p.m. boat across Lake Ontario. It was crowded with excursionists and I talked with an American on board. The boat called at Niagara-on-the-Lake – a very small village on the Canadian side of the Niagara River just at the mouth of the river. It has a fort – Fort Missisanga. On the opposite bank – the U.S. – there is Fort Niagara. From here to Queenston, the river is moderately interesting. I got off here and took the International Electric Rly to Table Rock by the Falls on the Canadian side. The Rly climbs round and round the hill on which stands Brocks Monument and then winds along at the top of the steep bank of the Niagara Gorge. At several places, one gets a glimpse of the river and the Rapids. The Canadian side is undoubtedly the best one to go to for the Falls – especially in the afternoon, when the sun is at ones back and shewing up the

Falls to the best advantage.

First of all, we came opposite to Niagara town on the American side and saw two fine railway bridges across the Gorge – those belonging to the Grand Trunk Rly and the Michigan Rly. Just past the second is the American Falls, a wide expanse of water about 165 feet high, 1,000 feet wide and nearly straight, when seen end-on. About a quarter-of-a-mile further on are the Canadian Falls – the Horseshoe Falls – so named because of the shape. They are indescribable in beauty and <u>strength</u>. The water falls about 185 feet with such force that it rebounds from the bottom in geysers very frequently (It is about 1,000 *yards* in width at this fall) higher than the Falls itself. Also there is much spray but, fortunately, the wind was in the right direction and I did not get much of it on me.

On the Canadian side is a beautifully kept National Park with well cut lawns etc. On the American side is a regular trippers and manufacturing town.

I have about 14 photographs in all of the afternoons outing.

To come home, I walked across the foot bridge over the Gorge and came back (by the Lower Route of the same Cos Gorge electric railway) close down to the water, all the way, and got a splendid view of the Rapids and particularly the Whirlpool Rapids where Captain Webb lost his life in a foolish attempt to swim them. The boiling, churning and swirling of the waters in this Gorge are indescribable. We got back to the boat at Lewiston at 7.40 p.m. and reached here at 10.45 p.m. – half-an-hour late. We met a Toronto journalist who was kind enough to take me in hand and shew me the points quickly. He was a decent little man and was taking his two young boys – about 7 and 10 – to see the Falls. I promised to send him a few snapshots to commemorate the days outing. I did not buy any illustrated book at Niagara for you. I looked at one, fairly expensive, but it gave such a feeble idea of the reality that I decided not to buy but to rely on my own snapshots for you. Up to date, I have about 48 snapshots and expect to get as many more of this wonderful – wonderful – country which God has blessed with very many natural gifts. The chain of fresh water lakes, emptying into the St Lawrence form an unique outlet for the merchandise of the country. Then there is water power available for the asking in millions of horsepower. Timber also – in Quebec province alone, there is one belt of 100000 sq miles of good spruce awaiting capital and men to develop it, get it to the St Lawrence and export it to England etc.

What is wanted here is money and good class men. There is no doubt this is a very magnificent country of opportunities for enterprising men. There is a great lack of poverty – in the English sense. There is a general air of well-being. Of course, there are drawbacks. The cost of living in Montreal is stiff. A very small flat costs 70 a year. A good servant 40. Clothes about 1/3rd more than at home. Food – probably 1/3rd more. Electric light 7½d. per unit against our 4*d*. Water is charged at 7% on the rent – say 10 – a year against our 2 (about). I have been rubbing it into these Canadians, and the Americans too, that they have to pay the piper for living behind Tariff walls. Toronto is cheaper than Montreal. For instance, Miss Hanson told me that they come here to do their outfitting and it pays to come these hundreds of miles. Also, they get their furs from London, whenever possible.

I will continue this later.

This morning I went to St James Cathedral (Protestant), heard excellent singing, the boys voices being very good, and a very good and practical sermon. After lunch, I laid down for 1½ hours and think I slept for a portion of the time. Then I had tea and went for a good two hours walk round the city, with the aid of *Baedekers Guide* and the map therein, which is good and clear. I saw the fine Parliament Buildings, in red granite and sandstone, its well kept grounds and the Queens Park behind it. Still further, on the opposite side of the Park, is another fine University building but not large. From here, I went East into the chief residential district. There are some good houses. I enquired about one well built new house in a sidestreet. It was not as large as our Toll Bar house but just about the same ground to it. I was told the rent would be about 65 a year and the selling price about 1000.

I had rather a rush to get home, have a hasty dinner and get to the Metropolitan Methodist Church at 7.0 p.m. I enclose their programme – the singing is quite good but it is rather too much like an entertainment. At both services to which I have been today there have been splendid congregations.

I forgot to tell you how beautiful it was on the water, last night, with the moon shining brightly.

Today, I have taken another 11 snap shots. I hope to get a number more in Winnipeg but, especially, in the Rockies around Rossland B.C.

It is so funny, over here, because of the heat, to see people using fans vigorously in the places of worship. In the Presbyterian Church, in New York, each pew had in it about 6 of the palm leaf type.

As you can see, this hotel is a large one and it is decorated more finely than any that I have been into, on this side. It has large and small paintings, good furniture and fittings and the room, shewn above, has large painted frescoes in similar style to those in the Liverpool Kardomah.[21] All the hotels, at which I have stayed, have been good but this beats all, in most ways. The Chateau Frontenac at Quebec was very good, too, and well appointed. The Windsor Hotel at Montreal is the hugest. I believe the Place Viger there at the C.P.R. terminus is excellent but I did not go inside it.

The large hotels in Canada have the advantage of being modern. In most of them, one can either have a room and pay separately for meals (this is called European plan) or else a fixed charge per day (American plan). Here I pay $4.00 per day for bedroom with bath attached and for three meals. It is really

---

[21] A well-known coffee shop and restaurant in Liverpool.

cheaper than the same thing would be in London. I like it better because there is not the trouble of paying at each meal or of signing a check.

Toronto is the best-paved and kept town that I have been into yet. I suppose it is because of the comparative absence of the French and R.C. element. There is said to be a good deal of corruption in Montreal municipal officers and the town is certainly very indifferently cared for.

I must stop now to write to the children for their birthday. Please let Edith send me a note of her own.

Best love and hugs for you all from
Your loving husband
Burke

I have said little about the business side of this trip. I reckon, when I come home, there will be no-one on our side of the Atlantic, who knows more of the Canadian Cable situation than I do.

King Edward Hotel
Toronto, Canada
August 18th 1907 Sunday

Dear Edith and Tommy,

I am writing to you tonight because it will be your[22] birthdays on the 30th and I expect it will take just about all the days from now until then for this letter to reach you. It will have to go ever so many miles in the train in order to reach a big boat. This big boat will be a steamship and it will carry this letter right across the Atlantic Ocean to England. Then it will again have to go into a train to get to Rainhill. I do not know which way it will go from here to get to the big ship but I expect it will go to Montreal. It may go to New York, instead. Some letters do go that way.

I hope you will both have a very happy birthday and have a nice fine day so that you can have some of your friends in for tea and games. I am bringing for each of you a little silver brooch with a Canadian emblem on it.

I have taken such a lot of photographs and I do hope they will turn out nicely so that you may enjoy seeing them when you grow up. I should, very much, like to bring mother and you, both, out here, one day to see this wonderful country.

I want you to ask mother to tell you all about the wonderful waterfalls which I saw at Niagara yesterday. One day, this week, I have to start on a long, long journey to Winnipeg and then on into the Rocky Mountains at Rossland in British Columbia. I expect I shall get so tired of railway travelling in this warm – sometimes very hot – weather.

---

[22] They were born on 30 August 1902 and 30 August 1905 respectively.

Now, goodnight, and once more, I hope you will have a very happy birthday. I expect you will both be very brown for it, after your months holiday at Rhyl.

My best love and hugs and kisses for you both,

Father

King Edward Hotel
Toronto, Canada
August 19th 1907 8.30 p.m.

Dearest

Its 8.30 p.m. and still no letter from you. Whatever does it mean? Are you all ill?

There is a party of journalists here, tonight, guests of the Can. Pac. Rly. Co. (C.P.R. for short). I asked one of them if Mr Cook was of the party. He said no but he was in another party, out West, guests of the Canadian government. So I may find him at Winnipeg or in that quarter of the globe.

The hotel is very animated tonight with the journalists and underwriters who are here as well as a big tourist element. The regular orchestra (about 4 players) keeps letting off music, of the tum-tummy order, at intervals. One night, they were really good and gave selections from Carmen and Faust. We have had another beautiful day but not an appallingly hot one. This morning, I went to Hamilton – 39 miles away – to see the Canadian Westinghouse Co. and had the least cordial reception of any place since my arrival. I have had a busy and important day and have sent home two cablegrams to the works. I expect to leave on Wednesday or Thursday en route for Winnipeg.

I learn that there is another mail in at 9.20 tonight. I do hope there will be something from you. I have not had the photo proofs either. I sent you a considerable budget early today and tonight I have no news to send you.

There are important developments out here but, so far as I know, they will not interfere with my return home by the September 20th boat from Montreal. There is not a good boat until that date, I think, but I am not sure yet.

Your loving husband.

Burke

Kisses <u>etc</u> to you all

<u>Later</u> Mail in and still nothing. Over a week now since I heard from you.

King Edward Hotel
Toronto, Canada
Tuesday August 20th 07, 11.0 p.m.

Dearest

Still no news and it is now over eight days since I had a line from you. What does it all mean? I suppose it is due to postal vagaries. I have done my utmost in the way of giving clear instructions about forwarding from Montreal.

Today, I have been busy up to the last few minutes and now I am tired and want to go to bed in readiness for a long day tomorrow. I have two or three people to see early in the day and then I go to Niagara, again, by the 11.00 a.m. boat, primarily to look at Power Houses, at the Falls, for my general engineering knowledge and benefit. Incidentally, I am getting very useful information on a variety of subjects.

I expect to go from here to Winnipeg on Thursday by the Lake route i.e. Owen Sound via Sault-St Marie (the Soo) to Fort William and thence by Rail. I shall probably arrive in W. on Sunday morning.

Although I wrote to Russell,[23] I have had no reply. Perhaps he is too busy with harvesting and is working all the hours there are.

Best love to you and the children and I *do* hope I shall soon hear from you.

Your loving husband.

Burke

King Edward Hotel
Toronto, Canada
August 21st 1907 9.30 p.m.

Dearest

Still nothing from you.

I have just returned from a second visit to Niagara – a visit which has added considerably to my professional knowledge. We have nothing, in England, like this latest water-driven electric plant of the Electrical Development Co. of Ontario. Their power is being transmitted by bare overhead wires to Toronto for the purpose of driving the trams and supply of power and lighting. The wires have to go 80 miles round the end of Lake Ontario. It seems almost uncanny. The Falls, themselves, do not seem less wonderful. In the Gorge, at the narrowest places, the water heaps up in the middle thus, (sketch) instead of running flat.

Last night, I spent about two hours in looking over the Terminal station in Toronto where this power is received and sent out to the Lighting and Tramway companies.

I have practically decided, for various reasons, to cut out the Lake route and to face the railway journey to Winnipeg – arriving there about 6.0 a.m. on Aug. 24th.

I think I shall cable to Prescot, if there is still no news from you when I reach Winnipeg.

Goodnight, now, and best love to you all

from your loving husband Burke

---

[23] Russell Welbourn, his half-brother, had emigrated to Canada.

Dearest

I am still without any English letters although I only left Toronto at 1.45 p.m. today and wrote, again, some days ago to the Windsor Hotel, Montreal. Will you ask Mr Nash to let them know at Prescot in case they have sent any letters to me that needed an urgent reply. I have had no letters at all since Aug. 12th from England.

I have cut out the Lake route – to save time and also to avoid the rough weather on them. I expect to reach Winnipeg, now, on Sat. morning at 9.25. The travelling is fairly comfortable today but slow. This is Grand Trunk Rly and the distance is 227 miles – time 1.45 to 9.40 p.m.! We join the Trans-Canada at North Bay C.P.R. and go, without changing, from tonight until Sat. morning.[24] The country, today, has been very barren, from the farming standpoint, but the woods and lakes have been very fine, indeed, in places. Now the beautifully golden-yellow harvest moon has risen and I hope we shall soon be able to see the country, again, for miles. This is very sparsely populated country and the railway has only a single track.

Mr Bolton, very kindly, came down to the station to see me off today and, incidentally, took payment for the Canada bracelet which I am bringing for you. He is leaving for England again on Sept. 21st. Did I explain that he is the man to whom Miss Arnett gave me a letter of introduction? At Toronto, there is to be a big exhibition from Aug. 26th to Sept. 9th. It is an annual affair and brings crowds to the City. I fear I shall be very weary of travelling before I am a week older. Probably, by then, I shall have done Winnipeg and be at Rossland, in the Rockies. There are various English people, in this train, but they seem a most unsociable lot. A Canadian-Scotchman is the only man I have talked with and that at dinner. He is a good sort – clear headed and knows the country well. I wish you could be here, with me, now the worst of the business rush is over. You could, and would, enjoy it very much, I am sure. Everything is so novel. Travelling is pretty expensive out here. In the towns, I think the ordinary householder must find things fairly expensive. So far as I can see, we could not live in the same style and with the same comfort without an expenditure of quite 2½ times what it is now. I am always telling these people what a price they have to pay, personally, for living behind a Tariff wall.

In 5 days time, it will be the children's birthday. I wrote to them from Toronto. Within that time, too, I expect there will be a Mrs Joyce but I am without definite news of the date of the wedding. I wrote to Joyce on the supposition that it would be on the 26th. We are due at N. Bay in an hour or so

---

[24] Welbourn had always used a 'cut-throat' razor, but bought a Gillette Safety Razor for this train journey. He cut himself the first time that he used it.

and then change trains quickly and go to bed. I hope to find a post box there.

Best love to you and the children with kisses and hugs from
Your loving husband
Burke

en route Toronto-Winnipeg
August 23rd 1907

Dearest

I posted a letter to you at North Bay last night when I changed trains. I have not had a very restful night and feel tired and wishful for a nap.

The lakes we passed yesterday were some of the Muskoka Lakes. Away from the line are some of the favourite holiday haunts of Canada.

The first place we stopped at after rising, this morning, was Missinate – there seemed to be about 3 wooden houses including the station. Since, we have stopped at White River to change engines. At times, we get very pretty peeps at Lakes, streams etc but with purely wooded country is rather uninteresting on the whole. So much of the timber has been cut, dead trees left standing and the young trees look much like large bracken.

In another hour or so, I expect we shall reach Heron Bay and then skirt Lake Superior for 200 miles to Port Arthur. That stretch is said to be very fine. It is difficult to realize that all this green country will be a mass of brilliant red, in a few weeks time, and that it will be hidden under feet of snow and ice from early December until April.

After passing Port Arthur, we put our watches back another hour so that 12.00 noon will be 6.00 p.m. with you. We are due to reach Winnipeg at 6.00 a.m. tomorrow. The travelling by day is more comfortable than by night. This is really a very fine car for day travelling – plenty of room and not many people. The meals are very fair, too, and the waiters are respectful. We still have black men to make up the beds and keep the carriages clean.

In the undergrowth in the woods I see a lot of one kind of very light purple flowers – I think it must be phlox.

On Monday next, you are due home at Rainhill. I do hope I shall find you much better for the change and rest. You needed it more than the children. I expect they will have enjoyed it all, thoroughly. I fear you have had indifferent weather. I have seen odd paragraphs in the papers about it.

The day has been a disappointing one. We have had three lightning storms and a good deal of rain and mist. It quite spoiled the 200 mile ride along Lake Superior. I think it would have been very beautiful. The Lake seems to have some large islands in it.

We stopped at a few places – the most important was Fort William where passengers by the Lake steamers join the train. During the storm at 1.00 p.m.

and for an hour afterwards, it was quite cold. The lightning flashes were very vivid and quite violet in colour.

At Port Arthur, we saw a 7,000,000 bushel grain elevator and store – the largest in the world and belonging to the Canadian Northern Rly. That and Fort William are becoming quite important places with that Rly in addition to the C.P.R. and the Grand Trunk. I am told that there is much unexploited mineral wealth on the Canadian side of the Lake. On the U.S. side there are the famous copper mines – the best in the world. We changed an hour backward at Fort William. At Brandon and Laggan, there are also changes of one hour – making the difference between London and Vancouver times, eight hours. I am glad it is getting on towards bedtime. I have to get up about 5.45 tomorrow morning in order to leave the train at Winnipeg at 6.00 a.m.

I have not yet found out anything about Mrs Chamberlains[25] brother – John C. Bell – but don't tell her so yet. I may be able to get something before I leave.

Goodnight – I intend to post this at Winnipeg in the morning.

Best love to you and the children and many kisses and hugs from

Your loving husband

Burke

Delighted to find your letters on reaching here (nearly 3 hours late) this morning. Writing later. BW. 24/8/07

The Canadian Pacific Railway Co.
Royal Alexandra Hotel   Sunday August 25th 1907
Winnipeg, Man.

Dearest

After reaching here at 9 a.m. yesterday, getting my room (252) with attached bath, shaving, bathing etc, I proceeded to look round and used a few of my letters of introduction. The one from Joyce to Mr Alan Ewart, solicitor, was most useful. He is a nice little man and going to be married to an American lady on Oct. 23rd. He is curiously deformed in one hand, foot and side but he seems very cheery and goes everywhere and seems to know everybody. He asked me to lunch at his bachelor hall, i.e. the house in Portage Avenue where he lives with two other bachelors. We had it alone as the other men were away. They have a nice comfy place and an admirable servant – a Chinaman – whom they call Peter. He cooks and waits so nicely and they regard him as a treasure. Probably, he is going with Mr Ewart when he marries. There was a railway magnate, Mr Ogilvie, on the *Umbria* who has Chinese men-servants at his

---

[25] Neighbours.

house in Cuba. He spoke most highly of them and their honesty.

After lunch, Mr Ewart took me to the Club here – the Manitoba Club – in Portage Avenue and made me a temporary member, for my stay, and introduced me to another railway magnate, Mr White, 2nd Vice-President of the Canadian Pacific Railway – the one I am travelling on and the only Canadian railway which yet runs from the Atlantic to the Pacific. The Grand Trunk are pushing on with their trans-continental line also but it must be some years before they can get through.

I had to leave him about 2.15 p.m. to keep another appointment with Mr Philipps, the manager of the Tram and Lighting undertaking here. After leaving him, I went out to the Country Club, on Mr Ewart's invitation; it is about 9 miles by tram. He drove out with his young sister – a girl of 17 or 18 – who is visiting here with friends. Her home is in Ottawa. Afterwards, he came to dinner with me, about 7.30, and then we went up to the Club for a short time so that I could see some English newspapers. I had only seen one – the overseas *Daily Mail* – since leaving. I regret that I did not arrange for the *Times Weekly* edition to be sent to me regularly, while away. I got to bed about eleven and have had quite a good night. On Friday night, too, I slept really well, although it was in the train.

Today, I intend to go easily and get some exercise. I have not discovered the church yet but intend to go to one service today.

The air is fresh and bracing here with brilliant sunshine – very much like a hot English spring day with cool nights and mornings. I intended to describe, briefly, the Country Club. It is composed, mostly, of members of the Manitoba Club and is only used in the summer. The club house is right on the bank of the Assiniboine River at St Charles – S.W. of Winnipeg – about 8 miles. It has a large verandah, protected by fine wire netting to keep off the flies. Some members were playing golf – others were playing polo on ponies. I got a number of snapshots. The grounds are quite interesting and wooded. The rest of the country round here is *very* flat – like that around Glinton.[26]

Winnipeg itself is a pleasant surprise. It has two very wide main thoroughfares – Main Street and Portage Avenue. At a guess, I should say each one is about 70 yards wide. There are some very fine substantial stone and brick buildings evidently put up as permanencies. Winnipeg has certainly come to stay as so many of the railways converge on it. It is also the most important place on the edge of the farming part of Canada. The population is about 100,000 and has (I hear) more than doubled in the last six years. The street railways system seems very good and well done. The trams, themselves, have no superior in Canada. The power for the trams and lighting is transmitted by overhead wires, for 65

---

[26] His mother lived in Glinton, near Peterborough, on the edge of the Fens. Her second husband, also named Welbourn, was a distant cousin of her first.

miles, from the Lac du Bonnet where there are developed water-falls.

I tried to find Mr George C. Bell – Mrs Chamberlain's nephew – but I find he has been promoted to be manager at Banff, one of the most lovely spots in Canada, and through which I expect to go by rail but not to stop at. His mother is with him, there. I have written him, now, enclosing his aunt's letter and saying how pleased I shall be to take a reply to his aunt if he will entrust one to me. I have also asked for information about his uncle, John C. Bell, and I have written to Mr Bolton in Toronto asking him to try to glean some news of him, also. I was unable to find a Mr Strickland in Toronto, who was a lumber man, but I did not try very much. I was too occupied, in other ways, and really forgot it until too late. I am trying to make up for it, now.

I am so sorry at the lack of harmony over Joyce's marriage. Mrs Thomas has, as she says or hints, lost control of her common-sense for once in her life and I fear she (and others) will regret it. I think it is pretty certain that Miss Arnett has let it be understood that she will not be bossed and means to paddle her own canoe – *hinc illae lachrymae*! I am glad you are writing to Mrs Thomas and trying to help in keeping her cheered up. I have sent her a few notes, too, and intend to write to her at Marlow, today. I heard from Joyce on my arrival here and now know that August 28th is the date.

Your letters, received yesterday, only bring my news down to August 10th – a fortnight old – I hear there is another English mail tomorrow morning and I hope that will bring more letters. I intend to leave here on the evening of August 27th en route for Rossland and Vancouver and may be back here about September 6th. I propose to make a break here to get letters and a rest (two days travelling from Vancouver) and then to go to Montreal – another two days straight going.

This is a very fine C.P.R. hotel – opened July 1906 – and intended, I should say, to meet the requirements of Winnipeg when its population reaches three times its present number. There is some elaborate wood carving on the ceiling in the dining room. Last evening, a small orchestra (about 5) played and, tonight, I understand they have about 30 players and a free really good orchestral concert. I was surprised last night, at 10.30, when God Save the King was played, that no hats were removed and no one stood up.

It *was* kind of Mr and Mrs Collingwood to look after you so hospitably. I have sent them two p.p.cs and must send more. I don't think you will be able to complain of lack of correspondence after the start. You have had a very regular stream from me since the commencement to arrive.

I am still without any news from Russell although I have written him twice and invited him to visit me here, today. I am glad to hear that Madge[27] is going

---

[27] Madge Appleyard, a younger sister of his wife. Her elder sister had been at this finishing school.

to Chateauroux. I hope it will do her good and cure her of some of her selfishness.

Please thank Edith and Tommy for their letters. Edith's is quite a creditable production.

I have heard nothing about Owen Clarke and Valparaiso. Is there any news?

It is now time to look round and find a church for morning service so I must finish now and begin another letter, later.

My best love and longings for you and the children and hugs from

Your loving husband

Burke

The Canadian Pacific Railway Co.
Royal Alexandra Hotel   Sunday August 25th 1907
Winnipeg, Man.   8.0 p.m.

Dearest

I have had a most pleasant and welcome surprise, this evening – the arrival of your two letters and p.p.c. of Rhyl bringing your news down to August 14th. I cannot remember whether I gave you this address but rather think I did and so I may get a further budget from you by the direct English mail which is due here tomorrow morning. After writing you, this morning, I went to church. The music was a considerable feature of the service. It was taken at a great pace and I had another experience. I could not see the choir until they walked out, at the end of the service, singing a Recessional hymn. Then I discovered that the soprano voices were those of girls – girls dressed in black cassocks, surplices and college caps (mortar boards). The costume is most taking! I got in about 1.00 p.m. and, since then, I have not been out again. This afternoon, I had a nap and a read and then got your letters about 6.00 p.m. I had dinner about 6.30 p.m. and since 6.00 p.m. the orchestra has been playing and it is surprisingly good – in fact, very good. Just now, there is a ½ hour interval. The second half of the programme looks more solid and I am expecting to enjoy it very much. The hotel is pretty full tonight. The orchestra seems a great attraction.

I have written to Mrs Thomas and my mother today, also to Mr Ruthven-Murray and sent p.p.cs to Mr & Mrs Collingwood, Edith, aunt Emily, Mr Riseley and Stirling. I think I shall send one to the Dodds soon. I intended to do so, before, as a little surprise.

It has been overclouded all the afternoon and is quite cool tonight. I am glad your first two weeks at Rhyl were as pleasant in the weather. I hope very much you have had it the same right up to this evening – the last evening. I have scarcely read anything since I left home except skim through the papers. I don't want to, somehow. Sometimes, I wish I could get hold of a fascinating love

131

story just to rest my brain and divert my thoughts. I have not read *It's never too late to mend*, which has so fascinated you. I propose to finish this tomorrow. By the way, as you say nothing about it, I suppose your money arrangements are turning out alright?

August 26th 11.35 p.m.

Many thanks for 2 p.p.cs and for the letter tonight. I have no time to write a proper letter. It has poured with rain all day.

Love B.W.

The Canadian Pacific Railway Co.
Royal Alexandra Hotel   August 27th 1907 9.30 p.m.
Winnipeg, Man.

Dearest,

Many thanks for your further letter bringing your news down to the 16th. I am frightfully busy again. I only got to bed at 2.30 a.m. and was up at 7.0 a.m. again. I have been going hard all day and have to finish packing and catch the night train at 10.15 p.m. going East for Rossland B.C. I expect to be travelling solidly for 2 days. I am uncertain when I get there. I expect to be in Vancouver by September 2 or 3 via Revelstoke and shall have seen more of the Rockies than the average tourist. Better address letters to Windsor Hotel, Montreal to arrive up to September 19th.

I am sorry this must be such a scrubby note but I really have no time for more. Tomorrow, in the train, I shall have, I expect, plenty of leisure.

Best love to you all and kisses from

Your loving husband

Burke

en route West from Winnipeg
August 28th 1907

My dearest

Rather than keep you without a letter, I sent you a brief note from Winnipeg last night just before going to the train. Now, after breakfast, I am writing this in the hope that I may be able to get it into the post at Regina. You have my detailed news down to Sunday night – Aug. 25th. Since then it has been business-business and hard going too! On Monday, I lunched with a Mr W. Burney at the Club and he dined with us at the hotel in the evening. Afterwards,

132

we went to his digs and played bridge and had music until after 11.00 p.m. Then I had to make it up by working until 2.30 a.m. writing and packing.

Yesterday, again, I had a hard grind and only just caught the train, with about ¼ hour to spare, at 10.15 p.m. I did not have a very good night --- it was so cold. After a good breakfast, and this air does make one hungry, I am writing this to you and a short one to Prescot. I have conversed with three fellow-passengers so far. There are more in the train than in the Trans-Canada. I find I am due at Rossland at 11.20 p.m. tomorrow night. The country is not at all interesting. I have not seen much wheat yet and that has been quite green. I was hoping *very much* to see mile after mile of waving golden fields but the harvest is so late that it seems certain I shall miss it.

I don't know when this will reach you as we are now nearly 3 days journey from Montreal. I expect you are quite settled again at home by now and Joyce married. I hope the excitement will not be too much for Mrs Thomas. We have lost another hour and are 7 hours behind you. At Vancouver, it will be 8 hours. I expect to be back in Montreal on September 9th or 10th – about the time you get this.

Pl. thank Edith and Tommy for their letters – I hope they will enjoy their birthday. I am glad Rhyl has done you all so much good. Have you heard yet from Chateauroux about a French help?

Here's Regina.

Love

Burke

Canadian Pacific Railway Company
August 29th 1907
S.S. *Kuskanook* on
Kootenay Lake

My dearest,

This is part of the journey in B.C. which can only be done by water. I have been in the train since 10.00 p.m. Tuesday night until 3.00 p.m. today (Thursday). We left it at Kootenay Landing (lost an hour by the change to Pacific time) and are now en route for Nelson B.C. from whence I get a train to Rossland and am due there at 11.20 p.m. tonight. I do not know how long I shall be there but hope to leave there at 6.40 p.m. tomorrow by rail and go up most of the way to Arrowhead (due North) by lake steamer and thence to Vancouver via Revelstoke by rail. I left the main line at Dunmore Junction, near Medicine Hat, last night about 9.30 p.m. and went straight to bed and had a fair night. When I first waked up we were still in flattish country and stopped at a small wayside station. Sometime after – about 7.30 a.m. – I waked again and found we were stopped opposite the Summit Hotel in the Crows Nest Pass.

I got up quickly and while washing we passed three sister peaks called the Three Sisters. They were very fine sharp pointed mountains of bare rock and sprinkled with snow. I think the height is about 9,000 feet.

Today has really been very disappointing as the weather has been wet, cloudy and misty and the sun has not broken through once. It has spoiled, very much, my first peep of the Rockies and my impressions are indifferent. I understand there is much more magnificent scenery on the main line from Revelstoke to Banff which I pass on my way back to the East. This morning we went over a loop line for 3 miles and only actually advanced 200 feet forward! This was to escape the mountains. One really fine thing we saw, for about 20 mins, was the Goat River valley down which the railway runs. At the end, the river crosses in a Gorge under the railway. The water dashes through an opening in the rock perhaps 12 feet wide. The walls of the Gorge look straight and about 150 feet high. We saw a lot of lumber work going on in various places, also coal and silver mining, and ovens for converting coal into coke for use by the smelters in the Rossland district. The forests along the railway are much spoilt, as pictures, by the devastation caused by sparks from the engines causing fires. It is quite disappointing and one sees forests, for miles and miles, with numbers of dead or half-burnt trees in them. It was much the same in the Muskoka Lake district between Toronto and North Bay. Today, we passed one considerable lake – Mojie Lake. This is one of considerable size – not wide but long. It is perhaps a mile wide with high wooded mountains on each side. This particular trip is 51 miles and I believe the Lake goes further still.

There is on the boat (and was on the train also) a lady returning to her husband at Nelson after a years absence in England. She has her little girl of 4 years with her. She interested me very much, because she is so like our Edith at the same age. The same large wondering eyes, same coloured hair, same length and dressed in the same way and even similarly dressed and, more odd still, sucks her first finger! She is very shy and wont make friends. The only thing she would take an interest in was Edith's and Tommy's photographs.

I may, possibly, get a letter from you in Vancouver but, more likely, I shall get nothing until I reach Winnipeg, again, about September 7th. It is now 12.15 a.m. (midnight) with you and I hope you are all fast asleep. It has been much too dull for snapshots so I have bought some good p.p.cs. I sent 10 spools to Letall from Winnipeg to have developed and printed for you.

Best love to you all and kisses round from

Your loving husband

Burke

Hotel Allan
Rossland, B.C.
Aug 30th 1907 5.55 p.m.

Dearest,

Although it is now August 31st with you, I hope the children have had a happy birthday and have enjoyed themselves. I suppose you will have let them have in a few of their young friends.

I am having a somewhat wasted day. The man I came specifically to see is away although he telegraphed to me in Winnipeg to see him here today. He does not return until 11.20 p.m. tonight and there is no train out of here until 6.40 p.m. tomorrow. There are only 2 trains per day from here on the C.P.R. This is the end of the railway in this part of the world.

I posted a letter to you in Nelson (I left it with the booking clerk at the Railway Stn to do it for me) written on the S.S. *Kuskanooka* on Lake Kootenay. I had a silly journey here from Nelson. We left at 7.15 p.m. and were due here at 11.20 p.m. Instead of that we had a long, long wait at Castlegar Junction and reached here, tired out, at 1.00 a.m. I slept well and did not rise very early. I met quite an entertaining Yankee who came on here but he leaves tonight for Revelstoke and then goes to Mexico. He has to leave his wife twice a year for two months, each time.

Today, I have been to the Le Roi Mine No. 2 and seen Mr Couldrey, the manager. He is a Liverpool man, went to the University and knows Frank Bradford. He took me all round but not down the mine. I have a piece of the ore which contains Copper and Gold. Tonight, Mr M. Kibbin, the Can. General Electric Co's representative, is coming for me and to put me up as a member of the Club. He has given me various local information.

This town has a somewhat dead appearance. A few years ago, it had a great boom and there were about 8000 people, 42 licensed drinking saloons, 12 gambling dens etc. Now there are about 5000 people, 12 l.d.s., not much gambling and many empty shops and houses and the town has shaken down to be a fairly respectable mining town. It is in a lovely situation surrounded by hills. Again, I have had bad luck – the weather is very wet and I have had to fall back on p.p.cs. to bring home. I am sending a general view of the town to Edith by this post. Please keep it.

It is a great nuisance, being kept here 24 hours longer than necessary. It interferes with my other plans and makes Sunday travelling a necessity, now, I fear. I don't know when this will reach you. This place is fully 4 days from Montreal.

I hope to find a few letters from you when I reach Vancouver.

Best love and kisses to you and the children from

Your loving husband Burke

This is the most primitive hotel I have struck in Canada!

Dearest,

My recent letters will, I fear, reach you at irregular intervals. My last one written on the afternoon of Aug. 30th would not leave Rossland until yesterday. This will probably be posted in Revelstoke where I get the main line train for Vancouver. Yesterday was just as *perfectly* beautiful at Rossland as Friday was wet and disagreeable. The main street of the town – Columbia Avenue – is 3,400 feet above sea level. The train climbs up 1,500 feet in 7 miles from Trail and winds round and round the mountain sides. The atmosphere is wonderfully clear. One mountain was 36 miles away and only looked, to me, about 10. Other high ones which looked about 30 miles were really about 300 miles away in the State of Idaho. We had a brilliantly hot sun and cloudless sky all day long and, today, we have just the same. If you could have been with me, these interludes are what we should so thoroughly have enjoyed together. As it is, one feels one's spirits rise in this exhilarating atmosphere. Yesterday morning, I found myself whistling 'Che Faro'. I had a long busy day, yesterday, and was with Mr L. A. Campbell almost all day and he saw me off at 6.40 p.m. He is a good sort and a capable engineer. We talked all the morning in his office. After an hour's interval for lunch, he brought out his light carriage and fine pair of horses and took me round to see some of the electrical installations at the mines. It was most interesting to me to see all this and to discuss all sorts of engineering questions with such a clear-headed energetic man.

I think I told you there are only two trains a day into and out of Rossland and only one of them is of any use for reaching Vancouver. I got on to the boat at 9.30 p.m. and wrote business letters until 11.30 p.m. and then turned in. I had a cabin all to myself and was much more comfortable and had more room than on the *Umbria*. I had the window wide open all night and was fully awakened before 6 a.m. by the bright sun pouring in. I got up at 7.00 a.m. and dressed and shaved leisurely and breakfasted shortly after 8.00 a.m., also leisurely. I had about five minutes on deck before breakfast as the boat had stopped at a wayside landing. There was a group of 21 men mostly sitting and smoking. One man was shaving. There was one wooden house of fair size, three small canvas tents and two long wood huts built of poles and with mud (or something of that sort) filling the crevices. These latter were, I fancy, huts for animals, fodder, tools and so on. Did I tell you I saw an Indian canoe, the other day, before reaching Kootenay Landing? It was cut out of a solid tree and there were 3 Indians in it. I was not at close range and could not see it very minutely.

This lake is very beautiful. It seems about ¼ to ½ mile broad and it takes about 10 hours to go from Robson to Arrowhead i.e. from the South end to the

North end. Although the sun is so hot, the breeze comes off this fresh water in a cold chilly way that one does not feel, at sea, from salt water. The water is a peculiar colour. It is a sort of sapphire pale green and milky. It is not a bit clear and the surface is like glass.

I do not know what time we left Robson except that it would be in the early hours of this morning. It is now 10.00 a.m. or 6 p.m. English Time and I imagine Rainhill Church Bell just beginning to ring for evening service. There is no service for me today or next Sunday so far as I can see. I expect to be travelling again next Sunday and to arrive in Montreal at 6.30 p.m. on Monday September 9th (11.30 p.m. English Time). We may be hours late. It is really very wonderful how the trans-continental service is done, so well as it is, over a single line, 3,000 miles long, with passing places only.

I have been expecting a cablegram from Prescot for two days and it has not reached me. I expect, therefore, I shall have to cable from Vancouver. It affects the question of the date of my leaving for home and I advise you to ask Mr Nash to enquire from Mr Kerfoot and so keep you posted in developments. So far as I know, there is nothing to prevent my leaving for home on September 20th, as planned. I cannot book my berth until I hear from Prescot. Of course, I have had no letters from you or anyone else since leaving Winnipeg on August 27th.

We have just cast off from a fairly important landing place. Evidently a line (branch of C.P.R.) runs to it. This Lake is entirely enclosed by high mountains but I got one peep just now of a more distant mountain with a good lot of snow on it. I do not seem to have any more news now so goodbye for the present. Lots of love and kisses to you and the children from your loving husband

Burke

When you get to know from me or Prescot what boat I leave on, find out from Prescot what line it is and write to them in Liverpool enclosing 6*d*. stamp and they will wire you when they know the time of expected arrival of the boat in Liverpool – so that you may meet me if the hour is a reasonable one. They get Marconigrams advising them of the progress of their ships. B.W.

Vancouver Hotel
Vancouver, B.C. Canada
Monday September 2nd 1907 8.10 a.m.

My dearest,

I regret to say I did a stupid thing yesterday at Revelstoke. After posting my letter to you there in the hope that it would help to reach you more quickly, I found a notice above the box – not a very conspicuous one – saying that the box was to be used for West-bound letters only. Then I discovered another box at the other end of the station building for East-bound letters. It has put me on my guard for the future. Probably that letter will come here and reach you at the same time as this one.

Both Saturday and yesterday were just glorious days and the sun was broiling hot especially yesterday afternoon at Revelstoke where I had to wait 1¾ hours for the train. The heat is a dry heat not moist as in Montreal and it is quite bearable even in the glare of the sun. I had a stroke of luck here catching the last Trans-Canada of the season and so I got here at 7.00 a.m., only ½ hour late, instead of 11.00 a.m. as expected.

I have not yet got a room – the hotel is packed. I understand that a boat leaves for the East (West from here) this afternoon and then there should be plenty of vacant rooms.

The weather here is wretchedly wet. I hope it will clear up so that I can get out and see something of the big trees in Stanley Park. I have just breakfasted in this comfortable hotel – a nice change after the Allan at Rossland – and was looking forward to a day's rest and holiday. Today is Labour Day – whatever that means – and so a public holiday. Losing 24 hours each at Rossland and here, of course, knocks on the head my chance of seeing some of the finest scenery in the world at Banff and also of seeing Mr Bell, there (Mrs. Chamberlain's nephew).

I got a good number of snapshots yesterday and there should be some good ones because of the bright sun and clear atmosphere. I wish you would get Mr Nash to enquire from Mr Letall whether the 10 spools I sent him from Winnipeg for development, have arrived and if there are some good negatives among them.

At first glance, this looks a substantial sort of town. I understand it was virgin forest here until about 22 years ago. The travelling is made quite endurable by meeting other business men – some of them like me in having to leave wife and family for regular trips. Business conditions *have* changed hugely since the days of our grandfathers. For instance, letters posted in England on Friday August 23rd were delivered in Toronto on Friday August 30th. That seems to me to be very wonderful.

I am disappointed not to find any letters here from you today but, perhaps, some will come on the next train.

You have now been back from Rhyl for a week and I wonder whether you have found any help yet, for the children, likely to be of a permanent character? Later Must close to catch post,

Best love
Burke

(Editor's note: letters for the next ten days have not survived.)

My dear Wife,

I have cabled to Prescot today saying I am sailing on September 20th and I hope you will have this information tomorrow direct from the Works or via Mr Nash.

I was glad to have four splendid letters from you, all together, by this morning's post and also one from Glinton. Russell wants to go lumbering next winter and so I have sent him a letter of introduction to a man in the lumber trade at Vancouver whom I travelled with, last week, in the train, from Vancouver to Winnipeg – Mr J. F. Clark, a thoroughly good sort and *very* well informed. In my opinion, B.C. is the best province in Canada for opportunities and it has the climate most similar to our English one and is not frost-bound in the winter.

I agree to your taking Mrs Knowles'[28] class on September 22nd and, if this is not too late, I suggest 'Patience' as a suitable subject and as one in which you have had considerable training for the past two months – like myself. You don't know how glad I shall be to get back to you and the bairns.

It is not possible for me, at present, to write you such long letters as you are sending me. The convention meetings are now over and I am feeling somewhat more rested. I intend to leave here about September 17th for Quebec to have a little fresh air before sailing. It is very quiet there but is much more bracing than Montreal. You need not be afraid of accidents here in travelling by rail. The average pace is about 30 miles per hour, only, and the accident of which you read was quite an exceptional one.

Please thank Edith for her painting (which is excellent, if un-aided) and chocolate and both her and Tommy for their various remarks which show I am not forgotten. I am glad to hear you have Alice Hay to help and I hope she will be a success. It is good to know, also, that the German lady[29] is considering us favourably. All your arrangements seem to be admirable. There is just one thing – I agree to this lady coming on condition that you personally, benefit by taking more rest and not wearing yourself out as you have done this year. If you do not benefit, then this outside work must be dropped for a few years. I am quite clear that you cannot go on as you have done since Tommy came.

Tomorrow, if fine, I am to go out to one of the Golf Clubs with Mr Oliver and see some crack players. On Sunday, I expect to go to Father Wood's Church in the morning and, in the afternoon, I am going to Mrs J. P. Cooke's for afternoon tea at 4.30.

---

[28] Wife of their doctor.

[29] Fräulein B.E. Roth who was at the same finishing school as Madge Appleyard.

I have written Albert Cook on a business matter which may be of use to him and have thanked him for remembering the children's birthday. I want to write to Glinton now and go to bed fairly early.

Best love, missus mine, and kisses for you and the wee ones from
Your loving husband
Burke

I suppose you have written to Mrs Gray for us both?

The Windsor Hotel
Montreal
Sept 15th 1907

Dearest,

This afternoon, I took tea with Mr Donaldson's friends Mrs and Miss Cooke. They received me very kindly and I stayed about an hour and a half. The two sons of the house are out West. Mrs Cooke used to live at Crosby and has two sisters in Liverpool.

Today, the heat has been very trying. I went to church this morning but was not attracted by anything except an able sermon by a clergyman schoolmaster. This afternoon, I spent two hours on my bed and had some sleep. The sun was hidden but the heat was considerable in the absence of breeze. It is now nearly nine o'clock and I propose to go to bed very soon. I propose to continue this tomorrow.

Sept 17th

I sent you a note yesterday and doubt very much whether this will reach you before I do. I am getting more rested now and the weather, today, is not so trying – in fact there is quite a pleasant breeze. I have such a lot to do, tomorrow, before I leave at 2.00 p.m. for Quebec. I have a man coming here to see me tonight and I want to dine before his arrival.

Best love to you all
Burke

Canadian Pacific Railway
Atlantic Service
R.M.S. *Empress of Britain*
Sept 20th 1907 (Friday)
Quebec 6.10 p.m.

Dearest

I propose to jot down a few notes, daily, to complete my log of my trip, for your benefit. I wrote you last on the 17th and had a very busy time in Montreal until I left at 2.00 p.m. on the 18th. I went round saying goodbye to various people and giving away cable samples. A large box of samples came from Prescot on the 16th and I had *such* a job to get hold of them. I only got possession from the Customs and the Shipping Agents on the morning of the 18th, after a struggle. Just before leaving Montreal, Mr Jas. Sutherland gave me lunch at the Canada Club, took me to the Windsor Hotel to collect my baggage and then took me to the C.P.R. station at Place Viger and saw me off to Quebec. I forgot to say that Donaldson's friend, R. H. Balfour, lunched with me on Monday and his friend, R. M. Wilson, on Tuesday.

I had a Mr John Macfarlane of Westmount as my travelling companion from Montreal to Quebec. He would be about 55 years old and made himself very agreeable. I saw him, also, in the evening at the Chateau Frontenac although he could not get a room there. I did not get one for some time but finally succeeded by urging my claims on the C.P.R. as a traveller by their boat to England. I was fairly busy all day yesterday. In the morning, I saw Mr Edw. A. Evans and andMr L. G. Denis again. In the afternoon, I had afternoon tea at Kent House, where the Duke of Kent used to live in Quebec. It is now a curios shop and most delicious teas with cakes are served. After that, I used Mr Sutherland's letter of introduction to Mr Norman Fletcher who took me through the showrooms of Holt Renfrew & Co – the celebrated furriers. You may remember my writing to Edith about their live animals at Montmorency when I was at Quebec before, last month. They have some lovely things such as sable muffs at $1050.00 (£210), sea otter skins, unmounted, at $600 etc. They have a lot of bear and other skins like the one which Joyce sent home to his mother. There was one of a red fox at $12.00 (about 50/-) which I should have liked to get.

This morning I was busy packing until about 10.15 and then went to see Mr Denis again. Donaldson's friend, D. S. Barton, came to lunch at 12.45 p.m. and then brought me to the boat. Instead of sailing at 3.0 p.m., as advertised, we are not leaving until 10.00 p.m. owing to the over-seas mail, bringing people from the corresponding boat at Vancouver from China and Japan, being late. It is disappointing as it probably means that I shall not get home until Saturday, September 28th, instead of on Friday evening. It also makes the time go slowly – just waiting about on board. I was very drowsy and lay down at 4.00 p.m. and slept or dozed until nearly 6.00. It is now 6.30 and the bugle is going for dressing for dinner.

This is a much smarter ship than the *Umbria*. I am writing in the Music Room. It is panelled in satin wood and upholstered in figured greenish blue velvet. There is a large smoke room in light oak and brown leather and a small library. I am advised by Mr Morris to get out Bradley's book on Canada.

I have a large cabin on the top deck and, so far, have it to myself. Probably I shall have it all the way but cannot say definitely until we leave Rimouski. I have arranged for my morning tub at 7.15 a.m. and am first on the list. I have not yet got my seat at table allocated. I have laid in Seidlitz powders and Chloretone (3 grs. dose) for sea-sickness and hope to pull through with their aid. I must go and wash now.

Sept. 21st

We were delayed by fog until about 9.00 a.m. today and, in the night, we had much blowing of the vessel's foghorn. This was not conducive to sleep. The fog cleared about 9.00 and the sun has come out. We stopped at Rimouski for the mail-pilot boats to come out and now we are under way, finally, for old England and home. I have had time to take stock of a few fellow-passengers. I have seat 118 at table – the Chief Officer's. On my left is an elderly Londoner – W. Herbert Anderson – a very good sort and gentleman of considerable experience in world-wide travel. On my right is a young man – Mr Lyon of Toronto. He is bound for London to complete his medical studies at the London Hospital. He has been there before. After dinner, last night, Mr Anderson and I walked the deck until 9.00 p.m. and I turned in about 9.30 and got up at 7.15 a.m. for a warm sea-bath. It is nice to be gaining time and putting one's watch forward, once more.

Reverting to Quebec – the C.P.R. has bought up property surrounding the Chateau Frontenac, on the land side, and is pulling it down in order to extend the Hotel. The new portion is to be in Louis XIV style. The porter is to wear costume of the period. There is to be a regular portcullis and, after a certain hour at night, a pass-word is to be used for gaining admittance. This will be very much in keeping with the quaint French character of Quebec and people will be able to see for themselves without going to France. It is expected to 'tickle to death' (as they say here) the American tourists.

We have, on board, Lord Loreburn – the Lord Chancellor of England – Mr John O'Connor M.P. with him and Mr Hamar Greenwood M.P., a Canadian born, whom I heard speak at the Canadian Club lunch at Vancouver. You will remember my telling you about it.

At breakfast, each passenger was presented with a nicely-got-up Saloon Passenger List which I am bringing with me. I have come to the conclusion that this vessel is 'chalks ahead' of the *Umbria* for comfort especially since I have found that I have my cabin to myself. No one has joined at Rimouski for it. The passengers do not yet seem a very sociable lot but, perhaps, they have scarcely had time to shake down together. I hope some enterprising person will get up a concert for one evening.

Probably we shall see icebergs tomorrow or Monday in the Newfoundland region.

We have just had morning service in The Saloon. It was so nicely conducted by Canon Brooke and was short and cheerful, with no sermon. We had four hymns: 'Glory to Thee who safe has kept', 'Hark! my soul, it is the Lord', 'All people that on earth do dwell' and 'Fight the good fight with all thy might'. They went well and heartily and there was a large congregation drawn from all parts of the ship.

Although the fog is not dense, we are still in it and the fog horn sounds at intervals and did so all night. We had (for me) a most curious experience yesterday afternoon. We could see, straight ahead, what looked like a cloud resting on the water. Of course, it was a bank of fog. It looked very beautiful with the brilliant sun shining on it. I took a photograph of it and am anxious to see how it turns out.

We are still in the placid water of the Gulf of St Lawrence and I do not expect to be 'on the roll' and clear of the Straits of Belle Isle, Newfoundland, until tomorrow. It is almost as steady on the ship as in one's own house. There is a little vibration in this, the Music Room, from the engines but it is difficult to realize that we are going at the rate of something like 18 knots an hour.

I am reading a most charming book which Mr Morris recommended to me – A. G. Bradley's *Canada in the 20th Century*. It would be a good book to have in our house.

I have just been making my preliminary preparations for combating the rolling motion tomorrow and hope to escape the mal-de-mer. Probably, though, I shall not feel well enough, on the succeeding days, to write very much.

Letters written to his wife by B. Welbourn AKC, MIEE, aged 32/33, Contracts Manager of British Insulated and Helsby Cables Ltd, ('the BI') when travelling on business for it in Russia in 1908 and 1909.

(Editor's note: Welbourn went to Moscow with the BI's General Manager, Mr Dane Sinclair, both to obtain a contract for tramways in conjunction with the firm of Dick Kerr of Preston, and also to start negotiations to build a cable factory in Russia. Sinclair was a telephone man by background. The tramway contract was successfully landed: whereas the negotiations with regard to making cables in Russia started in a promising manner, but later foundered.)

Hotel Victoria	London Feb. 28th 1908
Northumberland Avenue	8.50 p.m.

My dearest,

This is the first free moment which I have had in which to write to you. Mr Taylor[1] came to London with us and he has only just left me after about an hour's very interesting talk since Mr Sinclair[2] went off to keep an appointment.

Mr Welton met us here and gave us our tickets etc. We leave Charing Cross at 9.00 a.m. tomorrow and go via Dover, Ostend and Oberhausen. In St Petersburg, our address will be the Hotel de l'Europe for a few hours and in Moscow, from March 3rd, it will be the Hotel Metropole.

Before leaving Liverpool, I put copies of letters to your father, Joyce[3] and Miss Roby[4] into an envelope and posted them so that you might receive them by the 5.00 p.m. post and know exactly what I had done. I arranged with Mr Nash[5] to put the wiring in hand starting on Monday and finishing by March 7th

---

[1] A director of BI.

[2] Mr Sinclair was General Manager of the BI.

[3] Joyce Thomas, a barrister, who had been best man at their wedding.

[4] The owner of Craven Lodge, Rainhill, the house which Welbourn had just rented from her for £40 p.a. She lived in the other half of the pair of very large semi-detached houses.

[5] Mr R.P. Nash was manager of the electrical generating plant of the BI in Prescot, and of electricity distribution from it to Prescot and the neighbouring villages.

so that everything will be clear for Lowe[6] (or Swift) for making a start on March 9th. I asked Mr Nash to go round with you and decide the exact position of each light.

I also arranged that the three converted gas fittings should be done up at the Works (if and when necessary) and should then be put up in the three downstairs rooms similar to our present drawing room light.

When I have your letter, in the morning, I hope you will be able to give me some idea of what Mr Collingwood's attitude will be about releasing us. I have remembered today that he can hold us responsible for the rent up to July 31st 1909 if he likes.

I had my salary cheque and am sending it direct to the bank so that you can present your cheque at any time that you like. Now, please look after yourself and do not overwork and don't worry too much about the new household arrangements. Mr Taylor said tonight that I had left a very capable partner behind to run things in my absence.

Best love and kisses to you and the children

from your ever loving husband

Burke

Grand Hotel d'Europe
St. Pétersbourg, le March 2nd 1908
English Style
Feb. 18th 1908
Russian Style

Dearest,

We reached here about 2.45 p.m. after about 52 hours travelling straight through from London and two nights in the train. Tonight, we go on at 10.30 p.m. by the night train for Moscow and are due there at 10.00 a.m.

I wired you from Brussels on Saturday afternoon (5.30 p.m. Belgium Time) and sent you a p.p.c. of the Customs House at Wirballen on the Russian Frontier where we changed trains and had our baggage examined and our passports inspected.

We came from Ostend in the same train and only changed at Wirballen because the Russian Railways are of different gauge. I had a fairly comfortable sea journey from Dover to Ostend – near 3¾ hours. Saturday night was a bad one for me from the sleep point of view but yesterday (Sunday) I made full amends by sleeping two hours in the afternoon and practically from 11.15 p.m. to 9.10 a.m. this morning. The Russian train was heaps more comfortable than the Belgian or German one.

---

[6] 'Lowe the Plumber'.

The journey was through very uninteresting country, mostly flat or very gently undulating. The country round Berlin has a very slight sprinkling of snow and we did not really reach the permanent snow region until well over the Russian Frontier. On arrival, here, Mr Salter[7] and I came in a small sleigh to the Hotel. It was a novel experience. The cold is not intense here but I hear it is so in Moscow.

My first impression of St Petersburg is not a favourable one. This hotel, however, seems very comfortable and the people are obliging.

When we get to Moscow, I propose to send you a telegram announcing our arrival. Mr Sinclair is an excellent travelling companion.

I had a great surprise, on reaching here, in meeting my old friend Malek.

I must stop now. Please give the children my love and kisses and with much love to you from

Your loving husband

Burke

I want to hear what you are arranging about Craven Lodge.

I am told that letters get opened and sometimes do not reach destination.

Hotel Metropole	March 3rd 1908
Moskau	5.30 p.m.
Room No. 201	3 p.m. (English Time)

Dearest,

I have just wired you to say that we have arrived safely. We actually reached here at 10.45 a.m. after a not very comfortable night journey from St Petersburg. Since reaching here, I have unpacked, bathed, shaved, seen various people (including lunching with Mr Arthur Stanley – Lord Derby's son[8]) and have been fully occupied and seem likely to be for the rest of this week.

Mr Sinclair is wanting me now so I must stop.

Best love to you all from

Burke

---

[7] I know nothing about Mr Salter beyond what is in these letters.

[8] Lord Derby lived at Knowsley, just outside Prescot, which had been wired by, and was supplied with electricity by, the BI. The Hon. Arthur Stanley became a director of the BI in 1909.

Rainhill
MR 3
08
Received here at 5.18 p.m.

Handed in at Moscow 3 at 5.00 p.m.

To   Welbourn   Rainhill   England
Arrived safely   Welbourn

Hotel Metropole
Moscow, Russia   March 5th 1908

Dearest,

I am writing this in Mr Sinclair's room while waiting for our 8.30 a.m. coffee and rolls. We do not get our first proper meal until 1.00 p.m. I hope that I shall be able to satisfy myself on the chief points by tomorrow night but it seems doubtful if we shall get anything definite from the City Authorities before the end of the coming week. Friday, Sat. and Sunday are holidays and Mr Stanley tells us there are 70 saints' days + 52 Sundays which go clean out of every year as holidays.

I have not yet been out of doors so there is no news to give. I must go out today into *fresh* air and have exercise.

Breakfast now here.

Goodbye and love to you all

Your loving husband

Burke

Hotel Metropole   March 6th 1908
Moskau   Eng. Style

Dearest,

I am very pleased to have had two letters from you. Your letter of Feb. 29th reached here last night and of March 1st today.

We hear that there is to be a meeting of the *Uprava* (City Executive) next Tuesday March 10th and, thereafter, we shall *probably* know whether we stay or leave.

Yesterday morning I got out for about 40 minutes' walk and went round the enclosure containing the Kremlin. Today, Mr Sinclair, Salter and I went out for nearly an hour's stroll. Both these did me good.

We are being kept *very* busy with interviews and preparing for them and tomorrow (Saturday) we have two very important meetings at 11.30 and 2.0. We propose to go out to a winter garden place about 3 miles away for tea (tchi). I hope we shall have a complete rest (on Sunday) from work and see something from the tourist standpoint i.e. something which will be of interest to you.

All your arrangements about the new house are O.K. It means, no doubt, a lot of extra work for you. Presumably Lowe starts work next Monday.

I think it would be well for you to send to the furniture remover in Duke Street St Helen's and also to Turley to give a quotation for moving us. This ought to come out of the £30.

I hope, very much, that Lowe can find us a person to take Clarach[9] off our hands. Have you heard any more from Mr Collingwood, about it?

Must stop now. Mr Sinclair is waiting for me to join him.

Best love to you all from
your loving husband
Burke

Hotel Metropole   March 8th 1908
Moskau   Sunday

Dearest

Thank you for your letters. Three have reached me so far and Mr Sinclair has only had two letters from home. We are working today, I regret to say, and have just knocked off about 20 minutes before post time and I must send you a line. *I don't tell anybody* but I am getting heartily sick of Moscow and this work and want to get home. We get nothing definite and cannot before Tuesday. Mr S. can make no arrangements about leaving or staying. I am rather seedy today through loss of sleep and lack of fresh air – I have only been out for 2 hours in all since reaching here last Tuesday morning. We have done a good deal in the meantime.

Now we are off to a tea place 3 or 4 miles away with the express object of getting air and change.

The thaw set in yesterday.

At no time have I felt the cold although there were about 5 deg.F. of frost. There is very little breeze and the air is so dry.

I must now get this into the post.

Give my love and kisses to Edith and Tommy and much to yourself from
your loving husband
Burke

[9] The house on the Warrington Road, Rainhill, from which they were moving.

Hotel Metropole   Feb. 25th (O.S.)
Moskau   March 9th 1908
                                   E.S.

My dearest

Your letters[10] continue to arrive in regular order and No. 5 has now arrived today. I am very sorry that mine to you are so scrubby but I am doing the best I can under various difficulties.

By tomorrow night, we expect to know something definite as to our prospects and whether we stay or leave. Probably, Mr & Mrs Bullock leave for London tomorrow night as she has to undergo an internal operation if she stays here. He is a brother of the Prescot Bullock and is very valuable to us, here.

You had better keep Rotherham's cheque until my return. Will you please send my grandmother her 30/-, due March 1st, if you have not done so already? Her new address is in my address book.

I am going out for a walk before dinner to try to throw off the headache which I have which is chiefly due to liver and lack of exercise in this <u>hot</u> hotel.

Yesterday, Mr Sinclair and I went off for a 2-hours outing in a sleigh expressly to get fresh air. Will you, please, send me 5 5grain camomile pills for my liver at once? I cannot get them or Carter's Little Liver Pills here.

The sleigh ride was uncomfortable but novel and exciting at times. We had tea at a winter garden at Strelna and saw hundreds of other sleighs.

I do not tell Mr Sinclair so but I am heartily sick of this place and wish I could get away and home to you.

I do not think this letter will leave here for nearly 27 hours, yet. The postal arrangements seem very primitive.

Mr Herbert Scott is coming at 9.00 p.m. He is a relative of the late Mrs Hackworth[11].

Best love and kisses and tight hugs to you all from
Burke

Hotel Metropole   March 11th 1908
Moskau   12.45 a.m.

My dearest

I was so glad to have your letter last night and to hear all your news. I do so look for your letters and am very sorry I cannot reciprocate so fully. You see what the time is – I have only just finished work and have put in about 3¾

---

[10] All his wife's letters were destroyed with the rest of their correspondence.

[11] His guardian's wife.

hours since dinner. We are still on tenterhooks and may leave any day or be here indefinitely. It seems much longer than a week since we arrived. Important negotiations are proceeding with about as much speed as one would expect in a semi-oriental country. At least, I am weary of the whole business and would gladly pack up and leave this very day. Don't let this out to any <u>Works</u> people.

Young Herbert Scott came to see me on Monday night – on his 22nd birthday. He is a connection of the Hackworth family.

Please pay the £6-5-3 (?) due to Mr D. Munro of the Nat. Prov. Bank, Spalding on a/c of W. T. Welbourn's[12] Life Insurance and tell him briefly where I am.

I am glad to know that de Wynter has taken the house on terms so favourable to us. I thought Mr Collingwood would deal fairly with us.

Have you thought out where our stained glass can go? There are 3 pieces in entrance and bathroom. Plain glass will have to be put in by Lowe to replace the latter.

Have you decided yet on a date for moving? I think you will have Craven Lodge in readiness by March 23rd or 30th. Moving on a Monday or Tuesday would be best so as to leave the rest of the week for shaking down.

I am glad to hear that our friends are being so kind to you in my absence. You don't mention health so I presume you are all well. My tooth has not been troublesome but I have a cold in my head. I am feeling better since yesterday morning. The cold is not intense here and there has been a thaw on two days this week.

I really must go to bed now. Thank you for copying Aunts letter. I hope you are alright for money?

Love, kisses and tight hugs to you and the children from
your loving husband
Burke

Hotel Metropole   March 11th 1908
Moskau   10.30 p.m.

Dearest

Many thanks for No. 7 letter received this afternoon. Things are progressing and we expect some sort of an answer from the *Uprava* tomorrow and Malek to arrive from St Petersburg.

I think it not unlikely that we shall be able to make a satisfactory deal here although we may not get all we desire. I hope we shall obtain a fair

---

[12] His stepfather.

order for Prescot. We are hearing of other business also and are dealing with it. Business, here, is reaching a critical stage and in a week's time we ought either to be away or to be able to settle our plans definitely. I am very sorry that I cannot send you anything more definite than this – we are all in the same boat.

We went out to a neighbouring hotel for supper tonight for a change and to enable us to have a few minutes of fresh air and snow. Snow has fallen today rather thickly and there has been more wind.

The dining room paper which you have chosen will go very well with oak and will show off our pictures. It would be funny for me to come home and go straight to the new house. I hope to be home for the removal as I do not like the idea of you having it on your hands entirely.

I am so tired and head-achey tonight and intend to retire almost immediately.

My best love to you all

Your loving husband

Burke

Hotel Metropole   March 12th 1908

Moskau   10.10 p.m.

My dearest,

I am sorry to find no letter from you today. Perhaps the snow fall we have had, here, has impeded the trains. Things are moving here and Malek arrived about noon. We <u>hope</u> to have some definite news from the Moscow City *Uprava* (Council Executive) tomorrow and, if it is as we expect, then more or less protracted negotiations may begin. What the end will be and how long we shall still be here I cannot say – I wish I could. Tomorrow, I hope to get Mr Sinclair out of doors more. He nearly fainted this morning (don't mention this) and I feel sure it is due to lack of exercise, too much smoking and the heated rooms. We had a drive in a sleigh this morning to visit M. Chelnokoff, the Chairman of the Tramways Department.

There has been a little variety in getting some prices by telegram from Prescot to enable us to quote for some cables at Baku but it cannot lead to much of an order owing to the high import duty. We are getting a good deal of useful information and experience from our stay here and before we leave (whatever else happens) we shall, I think, have fixed up an agency and also seen some prospective customers.

We shall probably pass a couple of days in St Petersburg, on the way home, to see customers for our cables. The need of languages has been much brought home to me lately and I should like Edith and Tommy to speak fluently both French and German.

151

My cold is improving and I hope to have a longer nights sleep and to be in bed earlier as Mr Sinclair is out tonight

Love and tight hugs to you and the bairns from

your loving husband

Burke

Hotel Metropole   (Saturday) March 14th 1908

Moskau

My dearest

I do not know what has happened to the letters from England. This is the third day on which neither Mr Sinclair nor I have received any home letters.

Things have reached a critical pass here and anything may happen. If things go as I expect -- another week should see us away, possibly earlier.* A lot of fencing goes on and, although *we* are very busy, there is still no tangible news to send to Prescot.

* Don't build on this too much. It's all a guess.

Yesterday, I got out for about 1½ hours before lunch, went to the bank and then walked (briskly) to see the insides of the Cathedral and the Kremlin Churches. The former is a modern *very* handsomely decorated structure, in excellent taste; the decorations are paintings, marble.

In the Kremlin Church, the Czars are crowned. It is very old and very ornate. There seems to be massive panels of solid beaten gold. I only saw a bit of it but I am told that the value of gold and jewels in it is £4,000,000.

I hit on a service, fully attended, and heard some excellent singing by a male choir. I hope to get Mr Sinclair to them both, tomorrow, as a relief from business.

The Kremlin appears to be a large walled enclosure containing churches, law courts, palaces and barracks. In the square are a few hundred old cannon taken by the Russians at various times.

One of the entrances to the enclosure is through the Holy Gate – about 15 yards long – and however cold it may be, one has to go bareheaded so I avoid it as much as possible.

There are some large arcades here containing excellent shops. We have looked for some characteristic knick-knacks to bring home but have not yet discovered anything suitable and, at the same time, reasonable.

If you have not sent those pills, please don't trouble as Mr S. has a bottle of Eno's Fruit Salts.

I want your delayed letters so much, dear, and I want to hear how things are going at Craven Lodge and what further arrangements have been made.

Please give my love and kisses to Edith and Tommy and invite them to write me notes if *you* have the time to spare for it.

    Love and tight hugs for you from
    your loving husband
    Burke

Malek, now-a-days, sees far less of his wife and 2 children than I do of you.

Hotel Metropole   March 15th, 1908
Moskau

Dearest

I was so pleased to have two letters from you, by different posts, after the English mail closed yesterday and my letter to you had gone. My home news is now up to Tuesday the 10th (Letter No. 9).

Today is Sunday and we are having a day off. This morning, we walked up to see the open air market held on Sundays only. There are rows of stalls of merchants selling everything from rubber galoshes to jewellery and from curios to fur coats. We were out for just two hours. Also we got up later than usual and we propose to spend the afternoon quietly. I expect Mr Scott in to see me after 5.00 p.m. and before then I hope to have a snooze.

Today is very brilliant with a blazing sun making the snow glisten. There are 14 deg. of frost but no cutting wind.

Yesterday afternoon, Malek and I went out for about 2 hours and saw some of the old Tartar town and also climbed the bell tower in the Ivan Veliki and had a good view of Moscow. It <u>was</u> cold up there and we soon came down again.

Outside, we saw a curious ikon. From the front, one saw the Holy Ghost; from the right, the Father; from the left, the Son. It depends on where one stands.

I have bought 13 p.p.cs to bring home. They give a very good idea of some aspects of this City. I intend also to get for you a few samples of native work.

Letters seem to take, usually, 5 days including the day of posting.

Please thank Tommy for his letter and tell Edith I am looking forward to one from her.

Business is now decidedly on the move but is at a most delicate stage. Mr S. begins to have hopes that *he* may get the train from St. Petersburg on Saturday night next, but it is quite a Chateau en Espagne. I do not know whether I shall be able to come with him or not.

I am glad to hear that things are progressing so well at Craven Lodge. By the time you get this, I expect all workmen will have finished ready for us to move in. You do not mention what quotations you have had for the removal. It should be made quite clear to the Remover that he is responsible for all breakages and damages.

I propose to write to the Guardian Accd Insurance Co. notifying them of my absence both on a/c of Life and Accident Policies.

How are you fixed for money? If I should not be home by the end of the month, please ask Mr Kerfoot[13] to give you my salary cheque. I am sure Mr Varley[14] would cash it for you. Anyway, I hope to be home. I don't want to be stranded here.

Love and kisses to you and the children
Burke

Hotel Metropole   March 17th, 1908
Moskau

Dearest,

I am very sorry that I did not get a letter off to you by yesterday's post. We were very busy in the day before post time (3.00 p.m.) and did not finish until 8.00 p.m.

The Tramcar builders took Mr Sinclair and me to the Opera, last night, to hear a Russian favourite opera. The house is very fine and very large and tastefully decorated in red and gold. The singing of the principals was fairly good but the chorus was excellent. The dresses and scenery were fine. There was a full audience and among the audience was pointed out to us M. Sobnioff, a leading Russian tenor.

We got in at midnight and sat up with our hosts until 1.00 a.m.

Today, before lunch, Mr Sinclair, Malek and I went to a Russian Industries shop, run by the Grand Duchess Elizabeth, and bought various small presents for our wives and families. I have a few things which will be useful and ornamental as well as being inexpensive.

I have one more thing to get for you which will be useful and characteristically Russian.

In our pre-lunch walk yesterday, I took Mr Sinclair into the Kremlin Church where the Czars are crowned. We have not yet seen the famous painter's (Verestchagin) pictures. You will remember that he was killed on a battleship at Port Arthur while gathering material for further pictures of the war.

I received your letter No:11 yesterday bringing your news down to March 12th. This was a day quicker in transit than usual and I was pleased to get it. I

---

[13] Company Secretary of the BI.

[14] Manager of Parr's Bank.

154

have also heard from Joyce[15] today.

The tennis scheme is alright but I fear we shall not care much for the Shearars nor for playing gooseberry to Miss May L.![16]

Must stop now for post.
Love and hugs to you all from
your loving husband
Burke

Hotel Metropole   March 5/18th 1908
Moskau

The enclosed shows my name in Russian

My Dearest,
I have only had time in which to scribble a p.c. to you before the English post left at 4.00 p.m. Since then I have got your letter No. 14 of March 14th enclosing cutting about Col. Richard Pilkington.[17] He will be much missed in the public life of the district.

There seems no chance of Mr Sinclair or myself getting away this week, but Salter leaves on Friday night.

We had a most unsatisfactory round table conference with the *Uprava* today and I still cannot say whether we shall get any orders or not. I am not without hope that we shall get something, yet. This oriental bargaining and intrigue is most irritating to Englishmen.

About money – I am writing to Mr Kerfoot[18] asking him to send you my March salary cheques early in view of my unexpectedly long absence.

I have been out with Salter today to take him to a shop where Russian enamels and Caucasian silver work are sold. He has two very nice specimens – one of each.

The band, downstairs in the dining room, is playing the Tannhauser music. Malek left last night for St Petersburg, but I expect he will soon come back.

I, too, remember quite well our first meeting 15 years ago but I do not recall your greeting! I remember, quite well, how you looked.

It is now dinner time and I will finish this later.

---

[15] Joyce Thomas, best man at their wedding. Puisne Judge in West Indies.

[16] May Lowe never married. She was the village telephone operator. On one occasion a neighbour said on the phone, 'Be careful, May may be listening', at which she blurted out, for both to hear, 'No, I'm not!'

[17] Of the Pilkingtons Glass firm in St Helens.

[18] Secretary of the BI.

Later

The meals here are very leisurely functions. After ordering, from the printed menu, the first course arrives in about ¼ hour. Between courses, there will be an interval of 5 to 10 minutes. If one complains, the invariable answer is 'se chass' (that's what it sounds like). It means, literally, 'this hour' and corresponds with the Spanish *mañana* – tomorrow. A good but very noisy band plays during dinner and until about 3 a.m. The noise of it is so great that conversation is very difficult in the dining room – a large brilliantly lighted hall.

Our meals are:-

8.45 a.m.	Coffee, rolls and butter
1.00 p.m.	Lunch (3 courses)
4.30 p.m.	Tchi. Tea with lemon
7.30 p.m.	Dinner (4 courses)

This is quite sufficient in these heated rooms and with our small amount of exercise.

We see *The Times* and *Daily Mail* fairly regularly, but 4 or 5 days late.

I have been wondering about the garden at Craven Lodge. It is nearly time to put in sweet peas, wall flowers. I think it would be well to ask Miss Roby which is in now and then get the gardener from the Works (through Mr Nash) to put them in.

Much love and many kisses to you all
from Burke

Tell Tommy I appreciate his letter!

Hotel Metropole   March 6/19th 1908
Moskau

My darling,

Very many thanks for your letter of March 15th. Letters are now coming through in 4 days instead of five.

Things are getting critical here and we are promised/expect a decision from the *Uprava* on March 21st, i.e. two days' time. The upshot may mean immediate departure or another stay to pick up details of a contract. We have sent for Malek and he will be here again tomorrow. Today, we have only been out-of-doors for less than an hour when I had a quiet stroll with Mr Sinclair before dinner. I have been upset, internally, today which is very unusual with me. The pills came alright but I have not needed them yet.

I am sorry I shall not be at home to read the lessons on Sunday when the Bishop comes. Tomorrow, we are to go to see the Telephone people and Exchange here with a Swede whom Mr Sinclair knows and who is here from

Stockholm.

I am sorry to hear of Mrs Fred Marsh's further trouble. I sent her a p.p.c., a few days ago. It is now after 9.30 p.m. and we have only been up from dinner (the usual prolonged meal) about ¼ hour.

I intend to wire to you when I know what day I shall leave for home but there seems no chance of my being home for the removal to Craven Lodge. There are, I understand, only two good trains per week from St Petersburg to Berlin whence there are daily good trains.

Mr Sinclair is excellent as a companion and I am getting to know him so well on this trip. I hope it will bear some good fruits, hereafter!

There was a heavy thaw today but, tonight, there is frost again. There is really no news and little chance of getting information to send on to you as I get away from work so little, day or night. This will be ready for tomorrow afternoon's post at 4.00 p.m. It seems so strange to have only one post per day out of a city with 1¼ million people

I am sending a p.p.c. to Broomfield.[19]

Much love and kisses to you and E & T.

Your loving husband

Burke

Hotel Metropole   7/20th March 1908
Moskau 11.15 p.m.

My darling,

I was so pleased to receive, this afternoon, your letter No. 16 sent off on Monday last.

I am glad to say that things really are moving at last and I hope that we shall have a settlement tomorrow or Monday or at latest on Tuesday and that we shall be able to leave for home on March 28th and be home about April 2nd but only if things go smoothly. For downright slow torture, these people take the cake. I am sleeping well but Mr Sinclair has got the business on the brain now and has scarcely slept at all during the past two nights. The position is a very trying one for us all as there is a lot at stake not only in money but there is a national commercial fight in progress now which I cannot explain by letter.

The business is doing Mr Sinclair a lot of good from my point of view and I have told him so. It will make him understand better, in future, how times goes in negotiating orders.

Malek is here as representative of Dick Kerr & Co of London[20] who are

---

[19] A neighbouring house in Rainhill.

[20] The firm built trams and electrical machinery at its Preston factory which later became part of the English Electric Co. Ltd., itself to be absorbed by GEC.

partners with us in this fight. Salter is here in a manifold capacity as representative of Mr Arthur Stanley, as the holder of Bruce Peebles & Co's[21] Power of Attorney and as consulting engineer of the unformed Anglo-Russian Construction Co. All this is Greek to you but I hope to be able to make it plainer when I get home.

Mr Sinclair talks of returning via Stockholm and I may have to go with him but it would take very little longer than via Berlin, would be more interesting and might mean more business. One thing leads to another and by knocking about the world we pick up useful news and information. Besides the Moscow business, about four other things have turned up which may lead to business for us.

I sent a note to Mrs Fred Marsh today referring to her recent loss.

I think it would be well to get Mr Nash to have our new coal cellar filled up with large coal from Prescot Works. Will there be much left at Clarach? If so, the Prescot cart men would transfer it for you if you ask Mr Nash to arrange it. It will be funny for me to walk into a fresh house when I land back at Rainhill!

I have sent Frank[22] (a few day's ago) a p.c. conveying my farewells. You will not be able to entertain him before his departure from Liverpool, I think, in view of the removal.

I hope we (Mr S. and I) will be able to go to the English Church at 10.00 a.m. on Sunday. There is only one service on Sunday so I hear. We should like to have gone last Sunday and only found out, too late, about the one service *per diem*. I want to get him, afterwards, to see the Cathedral of which I told you and we still want to see the Virestchagin pictures and a local cable factory as well as the Telephone Exchange.

I have finished *The Tale of Two Cities* at last and feel I have now removed for ever the reproach of not having read one of Dickens' works, right through. It gets quite exciting towards the end.

I ought to stop now as it is late.

Much love and tight hugs to you and Edith and Tommy from

Your always loving husband

Burke

Hotel Metropole   9/22 March 1908
Moskau

My dearest,

Here is another Sunday and still neither Mr Sinclair nor I can make any

---

[21] A famous builder of power transformers.

[22] Frank Welbourn, one of three half-brothers with whose passages to Canada he assisted when they emigrated.

arrangements about leaving. The people here are hopeless from the business point of view. Several days ago, we were promised a written reply for yesterday and, when the time came, we were told that we *might* get it on Monday. When it comes it will possibly be only the jumping off point for further interminable negotiations and delays.

We rage and gnash and gnash and rage and are impotent. We would throw over the whole business but if we did – goodbye to our being taken as serious business people in Russia either in Moscow or elsewhere.

Malek came to St Petersburg 8 weeks ago, for 2 weeks, and has no notion when he will leave. Mr Sinclair has said, this morning, that he will stay another month yet, if need be, rather than that the business should suffer.

I have no doubt that you and Mrs Sinclair are 'grousing' at home but neither of you can realize at all what we are having to put up with, here. We are not having a holiday, by a long way. As you say 'Hope deferred maketh the heart sick'.

I wanted to go to the English Church today and wrote asking Mr Scott to call and take me but he has not come. It is difficult for you to realize the language difficulty here. One can hardly do anything without an interpreter. I am getting used to a few of the letters and characters e.g. I A K is 'Jacques', while

Barbara is spelled B A P B A P H A)

and pronounced   V A R V A R K A)

The difficulties are increased so much by letters in Russian having quite different sounds and meanings to those in French and English.

We went to dinner with Malek, at the Hotel National, last night. I like it so much better than this. It is quiet and no glare and no band and the service is so much quicker than here.

I spent three hours in Mr Sinclair's sitting room yarning with him over coffee and rolls and before he dressed. Coffee = КОФЕ.

I see *The Times*, *Daily Mail* and Paris Edition of the *New York Herald* most days but there seems to be some irregularity in arrival of the English papers.

I did so wish to be home yesterday. As I write, it is about 10.30 a.m. at Rainhill and I can imagine the flutter of excitement over the Bishop's coming. I hope you will enjoy it and that there will be a good congregation to greet him and a hearty service.

I have bought, here, something which you will like and which I intend to give you for your birthday so, meantime, you must please restrain your curiosity!

Much love and tight hugs for you and the children from

Your loving husband

Burke

Pl. tell Edith that I am still awaiting her promised letter.

Hotel National   March 10/23rd 1908
Moscou

My dearest,

You will see that we have moved from the Metropole to a fresh hotel – Hotel National – it is where Malek prefers to stay and it is much more to my liking than the Metropole as it is so much quieter and better conducted. I am very sorry that I have not been able to write to you today before post time. We have had a long day with one thing and another and the result from the B.I. standpoint is about nil. Your letter of March 19th contains a good grouse about my absence and Mrs Sinclair writes in similar strain to Mr S., I believe, although we have not discussed our letters directly. We are all in the same boat and we are grousing at this end just as much as you are and we dislike it. You are at home among friends and familiar surroundings and we are in this hopeless land of 'say chass' and 'na cha vo'.[23] We were promised a definite answer on Saturday and then it was to be today and still we have no answer. We live in hope and it is always 'tomorrow'. Mr Dixon came to St Petersburg recently only to sign a document. He arrived on Monday and was to leave again on Wednesday. They kept him three weeks! I would leave for home tonight, if I could, but Mr Sinclair cannot get on alone as he cannot make his own calculations and cannot write a decent letter without me. You must, please, keep this quite private, of course. I must stop now with much love to you and the children – you are all in my thoughts.

Your loving husband
Burke

Hotel National   11/24th March 1908
Moscou

My dearest

I have had no letter from you today and I am writing this hurried note for Mr Salter to take with him to post in London when he arrives late on Friday night.

The *Uprava* has now promised the B.I. the H.T. cables order value about £32,000 but we cannot definitely accept it until they settle with Dick Kerr & Co as we stand or fall together. A Russian engineer leaves tonight for London to examine dynamos of D. K. & Co's make and probably he will be at Prescot on Tuesday or Wednesday next. *Really and genuinely*, I am sick of this waiting and hope to be able to persuade Mr Sinclair to let me come home. He told me a

---

[23] When his son visited Russia 43 years later, he said that he only needed to understand one word, 'na cha vo'.

few days ago that Mrs Sinclair really put him under my charge because of the state of his health. It is not safe for him to take a bath without my being near at hand. It gives me a feeling of responsibility for him which makes it difficult for me to press to leave him alone – 3 days from home.

We wired to Prescot today notifying our change of address and asking that all concerned should be notified so I hope Mr Kerfoot has sent you word by Mr Nash.

Two days hence, you should be at Craven Lodge. I am sorry I shall not be at home to take the burden of this off your shoulders. I must stop now as there are visitors come into our private sitting room.

My best love and kisses to you all.

Your loving husband

Burke

Hotel National   12/25th March 1908
Moscou 11.00 p.m.

My dearest

Since writing to you this afternoon Mr Sinclair and I have had a serious talk about various matters with the following result:-

Unless something develops to keep him here he will leave Moscow on Friday, St Petersburg on Saturday and reach London later on Monday night. On Tuesday night he will try to see Mr Taylor and other interested parties in London and then wire me whether I am to stay on or leave Malek to struggle on alone. We expect that I shall be told to return home and, if so, I expect I shall not get a train from St Petersburg until the following Saturday and reach home on Tuesday April 7th. If this occurs, then probably, Mr S. or I would have to return in about a month's time to sign the formal contract and agree the specification etc.

I told Mr Sinclair that I wanted to be able to let you know something definite about my return as you were making yourself ill owing to the uncertainty.

March 13/26th 1908

There are no developments worth mentioning in the situation today. Things have gone very flat.

Tomorrow, I go to see some copper works about 8 miles from here. In the evening. I expect I shall have to pack Mr S. off on his way home. So far, he has not been able to secure a sleeper on the train.

Must stop now. Mr S. wants to go to dinner. It's very cold here today.
Best love to you all
your ever loving
Burke

Hotel National   14/27th March 1908
Moscou   11-10 p.m.

Dearest

Thank you for your p.c. of the 23rd. I hope you got through the removal yesterday and will be straight by Sunday, or nearly so, and will like the new house. You see the time at which I am writing? It is the first time in the day that I have been able to sit down. I have had a long busy day and, tonight, Mr Sinclair has left for St Petersburg and should be in London on Monday night and at the Works on Thursday. If you care to go along and see him in the afternoon I am sure he will be pleased to give you first-hand news of me. I *expect* now to leave for home on Wednesday or Saturday of next week and will wire you definitely later on. We have had a staggering blow tonight just before Mr S. left in the shape of a second (secret?) telegram from London to the City Council which seems to have completely undone all we came out for which may send us home minus any orders. It is too disgusting to write about.

The weather is very cold here again as there is a wind. I had to go out to inspect some works today, for Mr Sinclair, about 2 miles beyond the suburbs. It is a snowbound *country* still although the streets in the City are getting fairly free of it. I will finish this tomorrow.

Saturday

It is a lovely morning and the sun streams in on me as I write. I have to see Mr Alex Watt (our English merchant helper) at 11.30 a.m. and at 4.00 p.m. I expect a telephone message from Mr Sinclair from St Petersburg. In the interval, I propose to make an effort to see the Verestchagin pictures in the Tretaikov Gallery. Mr S. went away, after all, without seeing them or the Cathedral.

I cannot say where is the best place for hanging your portrait.[24] So much depends on the way the light comes in from the windows. Probably it will go in the study as the picture (qua picture) is too large for the breakfast room.

An important letter has just come from St Petersburg for Mr Sinclair. I have

---

[24] A fine portrait painted by Elsie Gregory, his cousin. She was hung regularly in the Royal Academy.

opened it and must deal with it at once.

Much love to you and the bairns from
Your loving husband
Burke

I EXPECT to be able to telegraph to you tonight saying when I shall be able to leave for HOME. BW

Hotel National   15/28th March 1908
Moscou

My dearest

You sent me a few days ago a letter from a man named Havern (of Sheffield). I remember his previous letter which I tore up and this one suffers the same fate. It is only a betting man's offer to wire me the names of horses to bet on.

About Joe Scott – I really have nothing for him and, anyway, I am not anxious to have him again. He took to drinking, I believe.

I am glad you enjoyed hearing the Bishop and Mrs Knowles last Sunday. I expect Herbert Scott tomorrow morning to take me to the English Church, here.

I am disappointed that I have no news to wire you, tonight, about the date of my return. Mr Sinclair telephoned to me at 4.00 p.m. today from St Petersburg but he had discovered nothing there throwing any light on the telegram from London which has upset our plans and prospects and is 'a stab in the back' and, apparently, undoes all we have done during the past month and makes our time completely wasted. This blow in the dark has quite upset Mr Sinclair and I have never seen him so thoroughly angry before. I cannot very well explain our business here by letter (for obvious reasons connected with the P.O.). It must wait until I get home. We have had a rough time, had (within an ace) gained our minimum demands and expected 'Peace with Honour' in a very short time. Now, it appears to have been swept away and, in the absence of explanation, it seems like TREACHERY from the least expected quarter.

I am much amused with Tommy's comment on Edith's German songs!!

I have seen very little, so far, of Moscow. Of course, constant intercourse and meals with Mr Sinclair and evenings in his sitting room have been the means of drawing us together but he is a great talker and takes up almost all of one's time. I was taken up, practically all the time, with him and, as you have seen, my letters to you have had to be written at odd times in a scrappy way.

However, this afternoon, after early lunch, I made a dash for the Tritiakov Gallery. It is large and filled with modern Russian pictures with few exceptions.

163

The chief ones are those by Verestchagin who was already well known to me by name as his pictures were exhibited in London some years ago and created a sensation. He lost his life on Admiral Makharoff's flag-ship at Port Arthur when it was destroyed by the Japanese. He was on board with the object of collecting impressions etc. for paintings. First of all, he has on show about 130 designs, mostly small, during his second journey through Turkestan 1869–1871 – then another 130 (about) in oils during the same trip. Then come 75 studies during a trip to India. The most memorable pictures are 6 in number and are episodes of the Turco-Russian War, 1877/8. They are never-to-be- forgotten pictures, large in size and grimly realistic in detail, especially 'Après l'Attaque' and 'Skobéleff à Schipka' and 'Les Vaincus'.

The gallery contains about 2,000 pictures in all. Some of them are fine in conception and treatment. Especially a portrait of Count Tolstoï, 'An ill-assorted marriage', a cornfield, some paintings of forest scenes, a scene outside the Kremlin. A few of the 'subject' pictures are *ghastly* in realism.

I hope you have got through the removal. If I could have said when I should be home, I should have asked you to postpone it for a short time. You were quite right in getting Lizzie and Willie to help.

15/28th/3/08

Our interviews are naturally slow as Mr S. and I can only speak English. We have an excellent interpreter, Mr Alex Watt, an English merchant here, who has been mixed up in this tramways contract and who has given us a lot of time. He is cool and clear-headed and knows the local ropes.

Your letter of last Sunday, March 22nd, posted on Monday morning received today only is now, I think, fully answered and I will put this aside until tomorrow.

Sunday

After coffee and rolls and honey in bed, and a warm bath, I got up about 9-10 a.m. Mr Scott came about 10.40 a.m. and we went together to the English Church. Mr Wybeigh – the clergyman – is not very inspiring. We had four hymns and I was rather amused when two ladies turned round to see who was singing behind! One of them was a married lady – who might be Mary Clarke's twin.

When I got in, Alex Watt was waiting for me. We had a quiet lunch and stroll together and now he has gone home. I wish I were at home with you! Its not yet 3.00 p.m. and I do not know what to do with myself for the rest of the day in this outlandish place.

Malek telegraphs on a message received from Mr Salter from London to the effect that he is as much in the dark as we are but that he would see Mr Stanley today. I hope to hear sometime tonight or tomorrow and also to hear when Malek will return here.

I want to take this to the post now.

My best love, many kisses and tight hugs to you and the children
from your loving husband
Burke

Hotel National   17/30 March 1908
Moscou

My darling,

Since I wrote to you, early this evening, I have had an avalanche of correspondence from you, *by one post* – 3 letters posted on March 24, 25, 26 and a p.c. dated March 25th.

I also had, by the same post, a letter from Mrs Fred Marsh and one from Joyce.

The visit to the Kremlin Palace today was most interesting but there is much more to see than one can properly assimilate in one hurried visit. We saw lots of guns, pikes, shields, jewels, vases, dishes, china, gilded carriages, Czar and Czarina's crowns and coronation robes etc. The palace consists of the new part – about 60 years old – and the old part 400 years old. The modern part consists of huge white and gold well-proportioned rooms chiefly arranged for reception purposes at Coronation times. There is much gilding and the floors are very elaborately done in inlaid wood. In the largest room, 23 different kinds of wood are used for the floor. There are the gilded chairs for the Czar Czarina and Dowager Czarina to be seen.

In the old part of the palace, the rooms are small but elaborate of their kind. In the largest one, the Czars eat their first meal after Coronation. Napoleon occupied these quarters after he reached Moscow.

I have received cheering news tonight about our business. I could have the cable order still but am in honour bound not to accept it until our partner gets his order also, unless I get a telegram from Mr Sinclair saying he has arranged differently in London.

I have written several letters tonight including all the Insurance Companies notifying our change of address and telling them to acknowledge receipt to you. Did you hear, some days ago, from the Guardian Assurance Co. Liverpool giving me permission to be abroad, under my accident policy?

I am head-achy tonight partly through sightseeing today with my visitor and partly through need of opening medicine which I have now taken and from which I await results!

The verse you quote is very *à per pro*. I want to return to Prescot with this cable order, very much, after so much effort, patience and money and thought have been expended over it. *Personally*, there would be no loss of prestige in coming home without the order but, for Mr Sinclair, it would be a disheartening incident and for Mr James Taylor, also, and for their sakes I hope to bring it off, now. Apart from that, I have now a £100 at stake, promised by Mr Sinclair in the event of victory. I hope this does come to us as it will comfortably pay for our removal and leave something over.

I am sorry you have had so much worry with the local tradespeople. They are a trying lot!

I notice that you have definitely accepted 'Craven Lodge' as the new abode's name instead of 'Clarach' so I have given that name to all the insurance people concerned.

Have you seen the result of the Peckham Election? Wasn't it a splendid win for the Unionists? Joyce had a hand in it.

I see *The Times* here and, tonight, I have been reading last Friday's issue. It came through in splendid time.

I will leave this now and will send a note to Mr Collingwood.

Tuesday

Today, I have done some business – not much – and seen a picture show. The only picture which I really liked could have been bought for 700 (100?) Roubles and I enclose a p.p.c. of it.

I want this to catch the post so I will write again tonight.

Much love to you all from

Burke

Hotel National   17/30 March 1908
Moscou

My dearest,

Two days have gone by without my hearing from you, presumably due to the removal at home.*

I have had a busy day due to an Anglo-American from New York turning up today, quite unexpectedly, with a letter of introduction from Mr Dixon who is in St Petersburg and who expects to be here on Wednesday or Thursday.

*I have just been called away to the telephone and hear that some English

166

letters are now *en route* from the Metropole.

I have had little business to do today and so I spent some hours with this Mr Wigglesworth who is some sort of cousin of Dr Wigglesworth of Rainhill Asylum. It's a small world! He spent over £6 in souvenirs. He arrived this morning and left at 6.00 p.m. tonight for St Petersburg.

This morning he bought his souvenirs and then we went to the Cathedral Church at the Kremlin, did the Armoury and went through the new and old state rooms in the Palace. It's very interesting and very head-achey.

After lunch, we went to the Cathedral of St Saviour and then he bought more souvenirs and a lot of p.p.cs. and had tea and a rest with me and then left on his journey back.

Our lawyer has gone to St Petersburgh tonight and will not be back until Thursday. It is possible (*and I am trying*) that we may get matters provisionally fixed up so that I may leave on Friday night and be in London on Monday night. I shall be very disappointed if I cannot. I think it is certain that Mr S., or I will have to return later, for a short time.

The telegram arrived from London yesterday which helps to clear up the mystery here but I fear its effect has been to delay matters and so my return. I wired to Mr Salter today intimating my intention to leave this week with a view to expediting matters at the London end.

I must stop now.

Best love and tight hugs from

Burke

Hotel National   18/31 March 1908

Moscou

My dearest,

There is no letter from you today to make up, I suppose, for the big bunch which arrived last evening.

I have just had a telegram from Mr Dixon saying he will be here on Thursday morning from St Petersburg.

The special picture show at the Historical museum today was very dull. There were many paintings of amateurish merit, only. A few pictures were good and the one I liked best was the study of the boy of which I sent you a p.p.c. As one would expect, there were several war pictures depicting fighting between Russians and Japs. In all, the Russians were getting the best of the conflict!!

There was also a fair number of the modern type of picture – paintings of nude, or nearly so, women. Some of the attitudes in which they were done were far from graceful.

Two of the pictures which were most attractive were typically Russian. One was of Russian country people at a fair. The other of country children going down a road. Both were very bright in colouring. The girls wore brightly coloured clothes. This, I am told, is a characteristic of the Russian country-women when in public, on holiday.

A few of the portraits were excellent.

This afternoon, after dealing with my correspondence, I went to see the Mussky Tram Depot but it was not very new or interesting.

The snow and wet are fast disappearing from the streets and it is getting more comfortable to walk about. Sleighs have disappeared, generally, in favour of wheeled vehicles during the past week.

The works' people do not appear to have notified you of our changed address. Our telegram said "Inform all who may be interested". Their collective imagination does not seem to have risen to including wives as there has been a letter from Mrs Sinclair, addressed to him at the Metropole Hotel, which I have had to return today.

I am feeling better tonight since my opening medicine acted. It has relieved the pile also. By the way, I hope there will be no scarcity of hot water when I get home after my long journey. I fancy we shall have more than we did in the old house.

Tomorrow, I hope to see one or two other museums here. Besides the pictures, I had a look in the Historical Museum proper today but I could not appreciate the old stones etc from Greece. They are beyond me!

I have started, tonight, on the first chapter of *Diana of the Crossways* but I do not know how far I shall get. I remember, with amusement, from time to time, Tommy's comment on Baba's German songs:- 'Fräulein, ... I'm *sick* of it!'

I am awaiting a critical telegram from Mr Sinclair either tonight or tomorrow morning. After that comes and after Thursday's interview with the lawyers, I expect to be able to decide definitely when I shall leave here and whether I come straight home or via Odessa.

Wednesday

Before I was up this morning I had a telegram of 73 words from London from Mr Salter. It will help to clear the air. I now await one from Mr Sinclair and do not now expect it before 3.00 p.m. owing to the 3 hours difference in time between here and London. I intend to wire you when I can definitely fix my departure.

Best love and kisses and tight hugs,
Burke

Hotel National   March 19/April 1st 1908
Moscou

My dearest,
Today, I have had your letter written just before midnight on March 27th and your p.c. of the 28th. You are quite right in getting in all necessary help for getting the new house shipshape. I *don't* want to come home and find you fagged out with doing my proper share of the removal as well as your own. I am sure you quite understand that. You are evidently much in love with the new residence! I have heard that the nursery, breakfast room and study, and kitchen are *nice*, each in turn, but I hear nothing of the drawing room and other apartments. By all means, have our bedroom floor stained all over as you have made up your mind that that is best. I hope we shall be able to go barefoot occasionally without having a shock! I still remember my linoleum-covered bedroom at 45 Denton's Green Lane when I got off the skimpy rug at the bedside, in the winter, and that's about 10 years ago. Rugs, of course, are much easier, I should say, from the servants' point of view. How often does the staining need polishing over? We ought to be able to get two sufficiently large rugs for not more than 30/- each, I should think.

With regard to lights – my idea was to have 'Osram' lamps in drawing room, study, kitchen, our bedroom, nursery and Fräulein's[25] room *after* we had used up our 'Clarach' stock of lamps. I hope you have left behind the fittings which properly belong to 'Clarach' and the lamps for them? Is de Wynter taking over our metaphones? If not, they should be taken away.

I don't follow your remark about a letter from Mr Berry asking me to see his cooking stoves. Is he A. F. Berry of the British Elec. Transformer Co?

I am so wondering what tomorrow will bring forth and whether I can then arrange to leave for home. You know as well as I do that I would willingly pack up and leave for *home* and you and the bairns by the very first train. I am somewhat afraid I may have to make a choice between inclination and duty and stay behind after all until Malek can come here permanently from St Petersburg to represent the combined firms.

I have, again, been killing time by sightseeing today. This morning, I went to the Musée Roumiantsov and saw lots of pictures of various schools and countries – most of them I do not remember nor was interested in. Perhaps the most striking room was one containing a large painting of the Baptism in Jordan by John the Baptist. There were a large number of studies in the room evidently made by the painter for the composition of the big picture. In the Musée there are a lot of books, dressed models of various tribes, e.g. Caucasians,

---

[25] Fräulein B.E. Roth was a mother's help with them from 1907 until the outbreak of war in 1914.

Laplanders etc.

This afternoon, I went for half-an-hour to the Musée Polytechnique but it would need a week with a guide-book to absorb all there is to be seen. The collection is evidently used for the purpose of illustrating lectures from the variety of the exhibits. I also went in the wonderful church built by Ivan the Terrible. It is really 11 small churches under one roof and is very weird. It is only used now on the saints' days of the saints whose names were given to the 11 miniature churches. It's nice, in a way, to see these things but, for me, it is a weary killing of time. Tomorrow, Mr Dixon is to be here. That will make a pleasant change.

I am getting on well with *Diana of the Crossways*. It becomes quite readable even for an outsider like me.

Have the children had an 'April-fooling' today?

POST OFFICE TELEGRAPHS

Rainhill
Ap 2 08
Received here at 4.2 p.m

Handed in at   Moscow 2 at 3.36 pm

TO Welbourn Rainhill England
Expect arrive Tuesday   Burke

(Editor's Note: Welbourn was on his way to St Petersburg in order to obtain a contract for tramways, in which he was successful.)

Wet in London

Hotel Victoria
London
4-6-09

My dearest,

I am beginning this en route to London.

I caught my train at Edge Hill. The Sunbeam man met me alright and took my bicycle for overhauling. He said they had a letter from their works acknowledging receipt of order for your bike and saying it will be ready for despatch on Thursday or Friday next. I had to stop here as the train was too shaky.

I have been busy counting money, reading various business papers and am now at Stafford (11.10 a.m.).

I hope I shall see the Gregorys[26] and Mr Hackworth[27] tonight and say good-bye to Janet[28].

My train NORD EXPRESS leaves at 9.00 a.m. tomorrow from Charing Cross to Dover – then cross to Calais and then 2 days in the train except for occasional halts at wayside stations. I suppose my breakfasts will be *café-au-lait* and rolls for the next few weeks and not the substantial English breakfast.

Later

I found Mr Sinclair in London and had a final talk with him both about Russian and Canadian business. He sails on June 11th with Mrs Sinclair. She is not at all well and has been living on a milk diet.

Mr S. has kept me later than I expected and I shall not have much time left for saying goodbye to Janet and also seeing Mr Hackworth.

I will try to send you a p.c. both from Dover, Calais and Liège. I leave Liège at 7.00 p.m. tomorrow and imagine (although not certain) that I shall have some time to wait there.

Goodbye, dearest, and please keep cheerful and improve in health while I am away. Best love to you and the dear kiddies from
your loving husband
Burke

en route Dover 5-6-09

Very many thanks for your letter and enclosures. I have written a hurried note to uncle Walter[29] telling *I* think the decision abt. Broombank[30] a very wise one – so I do!

I think it might be well to let Dr Knowles arrange for an oculist (*not* Jones) to examine your eyes and find out whether your glasses are the right sort. It might be that your present ones have served their purpose and should be replaced with more permanent ones

So many people are going to the Continent that 2 trains are required. I am in the first one. I saw aunt[31] and Janet last night.

Love Burke

---

[26] Cousins.

[27] Welbourn's much-loved guardian.

[28] Janet Gregory was a younger sister of Elsie, who had painted his wife's portrait. Welbourn spent much time with the family as a young man.

[29] Walter Appleyard, his wife's uncle, a director of Bassett's sweets. Mayor of Sheffield 1916/17.

[30] Joseph Appleyard, his father-in-law, had died at Kobe 10 February 1909. Broombank, Sheffield, had been his home. Welbourn was an executor.

[31] Welbourn's beloved aunt Emily Gregory, mother of Janet.

My dearest,

The enclosed stamped p.p.c. will show you that I tried to carry out my intention of sending you a line from Calais and did not succeed. There was such a rush that I only got into my train while in motion after getting the stamp at the Telegraph Office.

I think the boat must have been rather late as we have done nothing but 'rush' ever since. We left Calais about 12.45 and actually got to Liège one minute early. I had just comfortable time there to change trains only and now, after dinner, we have crossed the frontier into Germany at Herbstthal and have suddenly gained in time – it is 9.30 p.m. here while English time is 8.30 p.m. and you are, I hope, on the point of going to bed.

So far, I have had variety on the journey. From London to Dover there was a very smart lady, American I think, who smoked cigarettes and was apparently going to Paris.

The crossing was fairly smooth and I had no qualms. There was a good fresh breeze and I kept warm by walking up and down all the time. The crossing took 1 hour 20 minutes by the S. S. *Dover* – not a boat designed for comfortable travelling.

From Calais to Liège, I had 5 Scotch people who were very sociable. We discovered two mutual acquaintances. They have gone to Cologne in Germany for a holiday.

Now, I am quite alone in a compartment by myself and seem likely to be so all the way to Wirballen at the Russian frontier where I expect to post this tomorrow evening and you will get it probably on Wednesday. I *am* missing you tonight, dearest, and so much wish I could have you here and give you some tight hugs and kisses.

I have had two interruptions – first the *Douane* man to examine my luggage. One bag was not opened at all and the other just had the lid raised. Also, I have had a ticket collector – a smartly dressed soldierly sort of man with nearly white hair – I thought at once that he had been in the army and, probably, through the Franco–German war.

I did not remember the interesting country which is on this side of Liège for about ¾ hour's ride. It is very similar to that between Buxton and Matlock. There is a much-winding river at the bottom of the valley, with a good cycling road and wooded hills on both sides.

Last night, I got to bed about 11.00 p.m. and slept well till nearly 6.00 a.m. I got up at 7.00 a.m. to shave and bath and already I feel I need another one. It is, in a way, fortunate that the sun is not shining much as it makes the train cool. I am, unfortunately, right over the wheels and I fear it may interfere with my sleep although I am tired. I have not looked at my business papers and do not propose to do so until Monday.

The Gregorys had a fire about a week ago and did about £10 in damage. Janet got her arm rather badly burnt. She is pleased with her vases.

Please let me know the result of your *Echo* advt. for a housemaid. I am not at all sorry that Alice is going. She has been a continual source of worry to you and has not repaid the trouble you have taken with her. Please do not let her take away that grey coat nor my sailor hat.

I hope you will like to read the enclosed cutting from today's *Times*.

I like the decided business-like tone of your mother's letter. I feel that the decision to leave Broombank and cut down expenses is a very wise one. I have no doubt that Harry[32] will arrange the furniture storage for her.

I quite agree with you that Mr E. was most unwise in his remarks – if he really made them in the spirit in which they were received.

Mind you see an oculist *quickly* if your eyes go back or do not improve by June 11th. Tell Dr Fred[33] not to arrange for Dr Jones.

Sunday afternoon June 6th 1909

I was in bed nearly 11 hours last night and slept really well for which I am truly thankful. The bed was quite comfortable and easy although over the wheels.

We left the rain behind at Berlin and now we are getting warm. The air is quite hot. I did not feel quite up to the mark this morning so I took some Kutnow before lunch and now I feel better already and propose to have some tea soon. I have read the day's N.T. lessons and also looked through Printer's Pie. I do not find the latter very entertaining but I am keeping it for Malek.

I saw Cologne last night by dark but could see the Cathedral quite plainly. This morning I had a good view of Berlin. It seems a well-planned, clean looking City with good buildings. I saw a lot of people off on an excursion on small steamers on the river (?Spree).

Elsewhere, I have seen Germans fishing and cycling. Also, two fine storks. I wonder if they were carrying babies to their destination! Tell Tommy and Edith I have seen storks like those on their magic lantern.

The country I am now going through – Konitz to Dirschan – is distinctly wooded and in places it is really forest. There is an excellent road which looks good for cycling.

---

[32] Harry Appleyard, his wife's eldest brother. He was Secretary of the family furniture firm of Johnson & Appleyards Ltd., Sheffield.

[33] Dr Fred Knowles, their doctor and secretary of their tennis club. He brought all four of their sons into the world.

It is now about 1.15 p.m. English Time and I expect you are starting dinner and, after a rest, will take E & T to the children's service.

How much smarter and more orderly everything and everybody seem here than in France or Belgium!

We are still going ahead famously and seem to reach the various places ahead of scheduled time. I do not find postal boxes at the stations and have quite concluded to await arrival at Wirballen before posting this long (for me) letter.

I hope Mr Gull has been able to get through this morning's services alright. If you see him, please remember me to him.

Getting it posted at Dirshan.

Love Burke

Hotel de France
St Petersburg
June 7th 1909 (E.S.)

My darling,

Here I am once more in this benighted country feeling alone and lonely. I have just telegraphed you at 3.15 p.m. (1.15 English Time) saying I have arrived safely. There is no letter awaiting me from Malek so I have wired him at the Hotel National, Moscow to ring me up at 8.00 p.m. tonight.

It was fine on arrival here but it is now raining hard. The whole place is *en fête* – I do not know why. I saw something in the London papers last week about the Czar coming here to unveil a statue and I saw a statue with scaffolding round it on my way from the station.

This is a quiet clean hotel – quite homely and with no glitter. It is also in a fairly quiet street. My room is 11 and, as far as my French carries me, I gather that the manager proposes to move me into a better room later. There is nothing to grumble about in this one except that it is on the third floor and there is no lift.

With my French, I have just managed to order some tea and bread and butter to be brought to me in my bedroom where I am writing this.

There are three men here to whom I have introductions but I do not wish to see them until I have seen Malek or, at least, spoken to him.

Opposite is a very fine new granite building which is not finished internally. There is some good carving in granite. It might be a Bank when complete.

I am glad to be out of the train once more. I found it very slow and stuffy although I had a compartment to myself all the way from Liege. Such excitement! I was called to the telephone and, of course, thought it was Malek. When I got there, a mistake had been made and someone else was wanted.

I want to catch the outgoing English post now so I will stop.

I hope to hear from you tomorrow or, at the latest, Wednesday and then daily but, dear, don't try your eyes by attempting *long* letters.

It is fine again and I propose to go out for much-needed exercise.

Much love, dearest, to you and the children from

your loving husband

Burke

POST OFFICE TELEGRAPHS

Rainhill Ju 7 09

Office of Origin and Service Instructions

Petersburg

Handed in at 3.18

Received here at 3.34

TO Welbourn Rainhill England
Arrived safely Burke

Hotel de France   May 26/June 8th 1909
Renault

My dearest,

I have some news of a vague character of Malek. He telephoned last night from Moscow after I had gone to bed and now I have put in a telephone call for him and hope to speak to him myself.

I had an excellent night's sleep and feel better for it. I had *café-au-lait* with rolls in my room at 9.00 a.m. After breakfast, I went for a good long walk. First, I went to get some literature at the English Library and then went a long way along the Bank of the Neva and, incidentally, went into two of the big and beautiful churches that Malek introduced me to, last year.

In the Czar's Commemoration Church, I heard some good singing by a male choir in harmony and saw the blessing of some babies by gorgeously-robed priests. Some of the babes were given something to drink from a silver cup by means of a spoon and then yelled vigorously. Babies seem much alike all the world over! One babe was comically dressed. It had a white close-fitting head dress and, over it, a Cambridge blue jockey cap.

After this, the priests went down to the railed enclosure at the other end of the Church and then I left.

There is a very large open space near this church. It looks like a cavalry exercise ground. On it, I saw a lady bicycling and, clearly, she was a beginner. She was so funny. She was dressed in black except for a metal buckle on her belt. She wore loose-fitting knickerbockers and a loose-sleeved tight-fitting blouse. I have only seen a cyclist clad thus about twice before. One in London at the height of the cycling crazes, about 14 years ago, and once in Paris.

The day is a lovely one – blue sky with sunshine and a good breeze. I think there must have been heavy rain in the night. Outside, a man is watering the street with a hose pipe. Do you remember it, in Paris?

Many of the streets are paved with wooden blocks – this shape (a hexagon is sketched here) – evidently cut from tree trunks as in Winnipeg.

I was interrupted here to receive your welcome letter of June 5th posted at 9.45 a.m. received here June 8th at 1.20 p.m. This is much better than the 4 and sometimes 5 days to Moscow last year. Very many thanks, dear, for writing so promptly. I am glad you put 'Russia' on the envelope as I find there are other St Petersburgs. I am pleased that you have decided to have a *thorough* rest while I am away. I am hoping to find you getting on and to have made substantial progress in my absence. I hope you won't go too much 'on the bust' when your new bicycle arrives!

Please give love, hugs and kisses to the children and tell them, from me, to give some to you for me.

Much love, dearest, from
your loving husband
Burke

Hotel de France   9 Juin 1909
Renault

My Dearest

Things are beginning to move now. Malek telegraphed last night to say that he cannot come here until Saturday and, today, Mr Riches has been to call on me and introduced his wife. There is a vague invitation to lunch in the air. R. knows Mr Sinclair and has a great respect for him. Also, I had a letter of introduction to him.

I am expecting Mr Dixon's friend sometime today.

I did not sleep so well last night. I cannot get my bowels regular yet although I walked miles yesterday finding my way about the City. This afternoon, after lunch, I propose to do some miles more if the weather keeps fine. At present, it is rather overcast and cool weather.

This morning, I went to the English Library and got a sort of self-educator for Russian. I got it, for the alphabet chiefly. I am in the 'Tommy' state of spelling out the names on the shops and advertisements.

An elderly gentleman has just walked in and I recognize him as the proprietor of the Hotel National of Moscow.

These hotels cannot compare in comfort with the English ones. My room is clean and airy and high up and it costs 4 Roubles (say *8s. 6d.*) a day. I am told I should have to pay twice that at the Hotel d'Europe.

It is so funny here to go to bed by daylight. It was still quite light at 11.15 p.m. last night when I turned in. I believe it never gets really dark during the night here at midsummer. I imagine we are here about on a level with the North of Scotland.

I hardly expect to receive a letter from you today as there is no post out from Rainhill on Sunday morning. I am anxious to hear, dear, how your eyes are and whether you are seeing an oculist this or next week?

So far, my personal expenditure has been *6d.*

This hotel is quite near to the Czar's Winter Palace – about ¼ mile only – and nearly the same distance from the NEVA. This river is broad – about 600 yards – and keeps the air cool. It is quite a busy water-fare.

With much love to you all from

Your loving husband

Burke

I have seen some of the poorer class children in trousers to their ankles. They look so quaint!

Hotel de France   May 28/June 9th 1909
Renault

My darling Wife

Although I cannot be with you, I feel a great desire tonight to write you again although I only wrote to you for this afternoon's post. I feel that I want to keep in close intimate touch with you and not let these enforced absences come between us, in any way but, rather, draw us nearer together.

This trip to Petersburg is not to my liking and I am not deriving the slightest pleasure from it but, being sent here on duty, I feel I must do my best for the B.I. My time is not fully occupied until Malek comes next Saturday and it seems so funny after the very busy time which I have had for months past.

Today, I finished lunch by 1.00 p.m. and then went out for about 4½ hours walk making acquaintance with the various tramway routes with the aid of a map. I came home quite footsore and weary.

Mr Borsdorf came to see me about 1.15 and stayed 20 minutes. He is coming to dinner tomorrow evening and to have a good business talk.

I have had a letter from Malek tonight in which he says he thinks I have come out here 3 months too soon. I do not think so but we shall see. I recognize that there is a great deal of work to be done here and how long it will take largely depends on Malek and his business people here. He seems to be very busy in Moscow and says he must return there at the middle of next week. I hope nothing will prevent my getting through my share of the work in a fortnight after his arrival. It is now 10.15 p.m. and I will put this aside until tomorrow.

Since dinner, I have been reading (in French) *Serge Panine*. It is most exciting.

Thursday 5.20 p.m.

I have not tried to do so much today and, instead of walking entirely, I ventured on a tram part of the way while looking over tramway routes. I now have a very fair idea where the various trams run to and expect to have a good grip on them by the time Malek arrives.

While out, this afternoon, I saw various smartly dressed men, in uniform. They wore fezzes and I should say they were the Turkish Ambassador and his Embassy Staff. Probably they had been to see the Emperor or some important Minister of State.

Thank you for your letter which reached me before I was up this morning. I do not understand why your mother finds it possible to stay on at the house. I am sure she cannot do so on her income without having to scrape and pinch.

Today, I believe, is the day for Mrs Nash's nurse to appear. I hope they will not have a long and weary time of waiting! I hope she keeps well and cheerful. Let me have the news as soon as there is an arrival (or two).

I have some work to do before Mr Borsdorf comes to dinner so I must close this now, with much love and hugs to you and our children.

Your loving husband
Burke

I intend to write to Janet in a day or two so that she may hear before her wedding.

Hotel de France   May 29th/June 11th 1909
Renault

My dearest,

Very many thanks for your long letter written on Sunday and Monday last. I had not heard about the visit, tomorrow, of the Czar and his family and I see no signs of decorations.

There is an Italian here, with a Russian name – Prince Tronbetzkoi – who is the man responsible for a bronze statue of Czar Alexander III on horseback which has been unveiled by the Czar just before I came here.

It is much criticized as a work. I like the late Czar's figure but the horse is appalling. The Prince is said to be an amateur only and not a properly-trained artist-sculptor.

It is so funny to see, in the streets, here, officers dressed very much in the style of the illustrations to *Vanity Fair.*

The public gardens are beginning to look well; the tulips are at their best and in a variety of colours, red, white, yellow and variegated. The trees are backward compared to England and are not yet fully in leaf. I am told that it is an unusually late spring.

After dinner, last night, Mr Borsdorf drove me out to see the sunset from one of the Islands (I forget which – the names are appalling!!). It was a beautiful evening, *tout le monde* was there in carriages and on foot. The trees, lakes, rivers and lovely sky made a beautiful effect altogether. There were many sailing boats and some rowing boats on the river but most of the sailing boats were laid up for the evening. The sun set at 9.15 p.m. and we walked about during that time. Afterwards, we drove to Krestovski Island and went to the garden there for some time to see how the Russian Public spends its evenings. There was a sort of semi-open air entertainment going on in one part – cinematograph, trick cycling and so on. In another place, also a variety show entirely under cover. Here were dancing, singing, gymnasts and so on. There were negroes doing cake-walks, English, Parisian, Austrian artistes but, on the whole, it was feeble.

In another part of the grounds was a large brightly-lit restaurant for suppers and it had an orchestra.

When we drove home, it was still comparatively light and about as dark as it would be at all. The light is something like that just after dawn.

I forgot to say that we passed the residence of Count Witte, an able statesman who made the Treaty of Peace at Portsmouth (USA) with Japan, and M. Stolypin the Premier. The latter lives in one of the Imperial Palaces. It is not very large but looks a lovely summer residence in a large garden.

I had another excellent night's sleep and did not go out until about 11.00 a.m. and then stayed out for 1½ hours before lunch.

I expect Malek tomorrow about noon and then the serious business will, I hope, begin.

With many loves, hugs and kisses to you and the children from your loving husband

Burke

Hotel de France
Renault

May 30/June 12th (Saturday) 1909
10.00 a.m.

My dear Wife,

I am starting this letter to you now as Malek will be here this morning and then I expect not to have much free time.

I have had a nice long letter from you this morning posted last Tuesday. You say I had an interesting journey. I tried to make it so by letter but, really, it was very boring alone and with no interesting country to look at from Saturday evening until Monday afternoon. I hope Malek and I will be able to arrange to return home together. On the way out, we stayed, for a few minutes only, at Koenigsberg where Miss Chamberlain's friend lives. The train runs into a terminal station and if you faced the engine on going into it, you continue your journey with your back to it.

Last evening, I only got back to the Hotel at 7.00 p.m. after an investigation, to the far end, of a suburban steam tramway. It goes into a very interesting suburb of wooden houses – evidently summer residences. The last ½ mile or so is simply a road cut through a forest – but there is practically no undergrowth.

At the far end, is a *huge* new granite building. I must find out what it is but I think it is the Politechnic Institute. Lots of people travel on this line.

After I had finished dinner at 8.00 p.m., I sat down in the small entrance hall and chose p.p.cs. to bring home. Two of them, I have sent to Edith and Tom and one to Mrs Thomas who has written me a friendly note.

Also, I wrote my letter to Janet last night – a chatty letter which will also do for aunt and, perhaps, help to cheer her up on losing Janet. I have not written to Glinton yet but I wrote only a week ago.

I must write to Mr Sinclair in Montreal. He asked me to do so. He and Mrs Sinclair were to sail yesterday for Quebec.

The waiters here are mostly Tartars by birth but they seem a fairly obliging set of men and youths.

It seems so curious to be suddenly cut off from current English news. E.g. the 2nd Test Match was to begin on Thursday morning. I suppose it will be Monday next before I know the result of the 1st day's play, when, in England, the final result will be known and much ink has been spilled in discussing it. I wish it had been possible for you to come here with me, dear, but I am quite sure that the long fatiguing journey in stuffy carriages would have completely bowled you over.

Even I, who am used to travelling, find it trying and it took me a few days to get over it.

The big new granite building opposite is to be a Bank. The builder was engaged to Mr Borsdorf's niece but she has broken off the match.

I have finished *Serge Panine*. It was most exciting but the ending was not at

180

all what I expected. I went to see Mr Borsdorf yesterday at his house 'MOIKA.110'. It is a flat with about 6 rooms and a bathroom. It costs £140 a year with servant and wood for fires but no lights. There is about the same 'effective' room as at Clarach, Rainhill.

    With much love to you all from
    your loving husband
    Burke

Have the 'storks' come to Mrs Nash yet?

Hotel de France   May 31/June 13th 1909
Renault

Dearest Edie,
    Thank you for you p.c. this morning (Sunday). Malek arrived yesterday and we spent the afternoon in opening the ball.

    Malek thinks there is nothing likely to detain us here after June 23rd or June 26th so I ought to be home on June 26th or June 29th. I do not, however, wish to say I shall, too definitely, as anything seems possible in this 'se chass' country.

    Malek and I went out to the Aquarius Garden last evening, after dinner. There was a band and an *excellent* open-air performance. The performance consisted almost entirely of acrobats, gymnasts, strong men, ventriloquisms and that sort of 'clean' variety show. There were some really strong, muscular men and woman showing what they could do. One popular turn here is for one man to stand on his head on another man's head

    so:- [sketch]
and then the man who is on his legs walks up an upright ladder and comes down on the other side. I saw it, also, at the Krestovsky Garden.

    We left at 11.00 p.m. and walked home and went straight to bed. This morning, I got up at 9.15 but had my early tea rolls and marmalade in bed at 8.20 a.m. At 9.15, I had a hot hip-bath in my room. This costs, I believe, about 7½d. – 30 Kopecks. When I have a bath in the bathroom, it means lighting a fire specially and costs 1R 50K or say 3s. 1½d. It is too much.

    I have had a jar of Crosse & Blackwell marmalade got in for my breakfasts. A 1 lb jar and that is on my bill at 1R 50K also!!

    Evening dinner is 1R 50K and they give about 6 courses. The meals are cheap but my room, which is on the top floor and not a big one, costs 4Rs, say 8s. 4d. a day.

    Of course, one cannot drink the water here and so I have a large bottle of Appollinaris water in my room for teeth-cleaning purposes, another 1.50!

Yesterday was quite hot with bright sunshine. This morning, it seems cooler and somewhat overcast.

What I find trying here is the absence of plenty of stewed fruit and it is not very safe to eat fruit from the shops so it resolved itself into a ½ dose of Kutnow every day.

Malek is very excellent company and both he and his wife are thoroughly sick of his vagabond life of the past 3 years. He would much like to have a settled job.

Mr Marsden sends his news-letter to me here now and has twice called but both times has found me not at home.

I am glad to hear your eyes are improving and that you can do without glasses. That seems to me to be an excellent sign of returning health. I do hope you will steadily refuse to be drawn into overdoing things – household and otherwise.

Much love to you and the bairns
from your loving husband
Burke

Hotel de France   June 1/14th 1909
Renault

Dearest,

Thank you very much for your long letter of Thursday last enclosing your mother's letter. It was nice to have such a long letter and to hear all the news but I do not want you to tire yourself with correspondence. It is becoming very evident, from your own letters, that you are already attempting too much in the way of visiting, receiving visitors, etc. and then this servant hunting and the letters connected with it are just too much.

I hope that Janet Rimmer will turn out a success. If so and if she will do her work well without worrying *you*, then I do not grudge the extra wages.

I am glad to hear that Fräulein is being so useful to you.

Yesterday was very hot. In town, it was a sort of steamy-heat so Malek and I went out into the country by electric tram and had a long walk among the 'Islands'. There is open sea – 'the Baltic' in the distance, plenty of creeks, trees, and really radiant green such as one sees in Ireland. We walked miles and only got in about 8.30 p.m. The exercise did me much good judging by 'results' this morning. Yesterday morning, we went for a short walk but it was too hot and we turned in to see the pictures in the big Alexander Museum and then came back here to lunch and had it in the open air in the Courtyard.

We had dinner in the open air also after getting back last night. I slept well after so much air and exercise and got up promptly at 8.5 a.m. had my bath and breakfast and am now waiting to begin the real business of the week. I do not think it will be of any avail for you to post any letter to me from Rainhill after 9.45 a.m. on Saturday June 19th. If we can get away, we propose to leave here a day earlier than the Nord Express and spend a day in Berlin so as to break the journey and have a quiet night's sleep and also to see that City. Malek finds, as I do, that the continuous travelling without a break takes the stuffing out of one too much in this summer weather. With the sun pouring down, the carriages get so hot and stuffy. I shall be very glad to get home again to the bosom of my family!

I must stop now. A man has telephoned to say that he is coming to see us.
With much love
from
Burke

Hotel de France   2/15 June 1909
Renault

Dearest,

Thank you for another nice long letter. I hope you will be successful in getting a good maid now that Janet Rimmer has cried off. I trust that all this writing will not injure your eyes. I am quite sure that you ought not to write when you have any headache at all.

Yesterday was bitterly cold here. We spent all the afternoon until about 7.00 p.m. on business and after dinner we went for a stroll round before bed. We went to see, again, the much-criticized new monument to the late emperor. The horse is extra-ordinary. The figure of the Czar, I like. It gives an impression of strength.

This morning we have been able to do no work. It is now nearly 2.30 and we have been waiting for our man since 11.30. It's the usual way in which time is frittered away in this "se chass" country.

There is a strike here of the tramway men and only a very few trams are running. It is a harvest for the droshky drivers who are doing a thriving trade. There is no dis-order in connection with the strike so far as one can ascertain. The streets are curiously quiet, without the trams.

This morning, we went for a walk and included a tour through the rest of the Alexander Museum. We did the lower portion for which we had not time on Sunday. It is not so interesting as upstairs. There are lots of portraits, sketches, ikons and so on. There was, however, one marble figure of a reclining female which I liked immensely. I do not remember ever seeing a piece of sculpture which I liked so much.

Please thank baba for her letter. Its surprisingly well composed and written. I did not know she could do anything so well.

There are quite a lot of English speaking people here today. It is warmer in the sun, today, but still far from hot. I am glad to think that I may be able to leave here a week today. Malek returns to Moscow tomorrow night.

With best love to you, Edith and Tom
from your loving husband
Burke

Hotel de France   3/16 Juin 1909
Renault

My dear Wife,

I was very pleased to have your letter of June 11th yesterday morning and your p.c. of June 12th in the afternoon announcing the end of Mrs Nash's waiting! I expect Estelle will be tremendously pleased with her baby sister when she has had time to realize her existence and when she has been allowed to nurse her, under supervision. I hope Mrs Nash is going on O.K.

I wonder if your mother is still with you and whether she has seen Dr Fred. I hope he can do something for her?

Has your bicycle arrived and have you tried it? I hope it is a success and does not look funereal.

Have you had any tennis yet? I suppose not as you have had your hands full in other directions and have suffered with headaches.

Our man rushed in, breathless, yesterday about 2.45 p.m. to say he could not see us until 1 p.m. today. This is a 'se chass' country, as I have remarked before! We went, therefore, to examine another long tramway route along the Schlusselberg Road. We went there by a river steamer which we managed to find by trial and error. The first steamer which we entered took us in the wrong direction and we had to get out at the first stopping place and walk back to our starting point. Our next trial turned out right and we had an hour's journey on the *Neva*, on deck. It was just about as cold as one could stand for the time. We then walked a little distance and came home by the very slow-going steam tram. I have quite a collection of tram tickets for the children, from that ride. We got in about 6.45 p.m. and after a wash and change we went out for dinner at the Medrade Restaurant near here. In the season, it is very fashionable but it was almost empty last night. The cooking was better than here and there was almost continuous music from a string band of violins, guitar, mandolines and so on. We stayed and talked there until nearly 10.30 and then came back here, *tired* and found Mr Marsden at supper. He kept us up until after midnight. We nearly yawned him out, I fear.

184

I asked Malek if he would like Frau's sister[34] but he says they have given up governesses and sent the children to a kinder-garten. I suppose Mrs Nash would not take her? It would settle Frau to have a sister near. I believe Watkin Oppenheim would *consider* it. He said as much, some months ago, when I told him about Fräulein. He thought he would like to have a similar arrangement.

Your letter of June 12th has just been brought to me. Many, many thanks for it.

With much love and hugs and kisses for you and the two children from
Your ever-loving
Burke

Hotel de France
St. Petersbourg
Thursday 4/17 June 1909

My dearest,

I am writing this in my bedroom before going downstairs to begin the day's work. I have just received your letter of last Sunday in which you tell me of Estelle's departure to live with her baby sister. It must have been an exciting 36 hours for R.P.N. – go to London, have a baby, have a sister married and then the journey home and the excitement of seeing his wife and infant.

I suppose Janet's wedding and first night are nearly over now. I hope she has had some sleep and rest!!

I am glad you are having fine weather. Here, except on the day of arrival, I have not seen any rain although there have often been thickening clouds and I believe rain has come at night. The cold snap has gone and yesterday was quite warm again. Our man did not turn up yesterday until lunch time. Afterwards, we had a taxi-cab and went round to see the generating station and a sub-station and then came back and worked until about 6.00 p.m. in my room. Malek packed and then we had dinner at the Café de Paris and had a stroll. After this (10.00 p.m.) I walked to the station with him about 1½ miles as he was leaving for Moscow and does not return here until about Sunday. I left him before his train went and then walked home and went to bed.

I have to stay in for two telephone messages at 10.00 and 1.00 today and I do not yet know what my programme is to be except that I have plenty of writing to do.

I am *very* pleased to hear you have definitely got a maid and one whom you know something of and are prepared to like. I must stop now. It is later than I thought and I must go down to await my first telephone call.

---

[34] Had they found a position for her, she might not have married Julius Streicher, the Nazi Jew-baiter.

With much love and various thousands and millions of love hugs and kisses to you and the children from
your ever-loving husband
Burke

Hotel de France   5/18 Juin 1909
Renault

My darling wife,
I have been very pleased to receive today your and Tommy's letters of last Monday. Fräulein's help is very apparent in the letter even to the 'woves' (loves). I didn't know she had developed a sense of humour.

I spent a good deal of time, yesterday, going round the tramway system and in making estimates. I did not finish for the day until 8.45 p.m. and then had supper in the open air in the hotel courtyard. I wrote to Malek, finished my book – T*he Royal End* by Henry Harland and was in bed about 11.15 p.m. and slept *well* until 8.10 a.m.

Yesterday, Mr Kamenetzky, who splutters through a good deal of English, took me to lunch at the Restaurant Contant in the open air and, tonight, he is taking me to dinner somewhere in the suburbs after more tramway inspection work.

I am expecting Mr Riches – an Englishman to whom I had a letter of introduction – in a few minutes but he is not staying for lunch, I believe.

Mr. Borsdorf speaks English very fairly. When a young man, he spent 3½ years in business in London. He has asked me to go to dinner at his summer residence on Sunday. It is about ½ hour away by rail. I do not know if I can go yet as I expect Malek back on Sunday morning, from Moscow.

The weather has changed a good deal this week and I am told that it is very characteristic of St P. all the year round. On Monday and Tuesday, it was bitterly cold. Wednesday was very hot. Thursday and today are lovely sunny spring days with a good breeze which is not, however, at all bracing. As in all these continental towns, I find the glare from the houses and pavements rather trying.

The tramway strike is still on and prevents our getting information as quickly as I should like. More trams are running today with the help of Politechnic students and so on. There is some talk of deporting for 3 years to their home villages the ring-leaders of the strike movement. The City is losing about £2,500 a day in revenue.

I have been to the Banque du Nord this morning for money on my Letter of Credit. It is a slow business and took me ½ hour to get £25. I do not know what I should do without my smattering of French. It is very valuable.

I have been out, also, and bought you a small silver bracelet to match your Caucasian belt. I was tempted to get a neck ornament but refrained.

I want to go to the Fortress of Peter and Paul this afternoon before I go out with K. It is one of the things to see. Yes – I feel I am getting to know the 'lay of the land' here very well. The systematic investigation of a long tramway system is a splendid way of learning a city. I know of nothing to prevent my leaving here next Tuesday morning and I expect to be home sometime on June 26th.

A few million loves, hugs and kisses to the bairns and much love to you from your loving husband

Burke

Hotel de France   6/19th Juin 1909
Renault

My dearest,

Very many thanks for your letter of June 15th which came last night. I got it about 10.00 p.m. This is unusually quick. I expect you posted it at 9.45 a.m.

You enclosed a cutting about Mr Gull wanting help from a curate. I do not think he will get it from his parishioners until he gives up his workhouse duties which take him away from us and take his strength and, in any case, I think his Easter Offering will have to go if we find a curate. People, now-a-days, have so many expenses that they *cannot* comply with demands like this at a moment's notice. I imagine that £5 a year would mean a good deal to the Taylors[35] when the children cannot, now, have proper skating boots.

I have just been speaking to Malek on the telephone at Moscow (400 miles away). He arrives here early tomorrow and, after lunch, we are to go to Mr Borsdorf's country residence. A great step forward (towards home) has just been made in that I have ordered our tickets to Berlin for Tuesday morning next. We are due there about 7.15 p.m. on Wednesday and propose to sleep there and see the City and come on from there on Thursday evening. This should bring me to London at 7.15 p.m. on Friday week and should be much less tiring than coming straight through without any break.

I have sent p.p.cs. to Mrs Knowles, the Marshs, Misses Windus[36], Mr Hollingworth and Don John[37] today. I thought the Misses Windus, in particular, would appreciate the attention and it might help to cheer them up.

I am very pleased you like your bicycle. I feel sure you have tried it, by now.

---

[35] Neighbours in the village.

[36] When Welbourn married, he was in digs. with Miss Windus, of Lyon House, St Helens.

[37] J.M. Donaldson, a close business and personal friend. He was referred to from Canada as 'Donaldson'.

I suppose he did not say when mine would be ready? I will send them a p.c. only saying I want it home by June 26th certain and then, perhaps, we can have a ride together.

Last evening, about 5.45 p.m., we started off to do more inspection work and finished at 8.00 p.m. Then we had dinner at the Restaurant Earnest in the suburbs and came home by 10.00 p.m.

In the afternoon, I had nothing to do so went to see the Sebastopol panorama – very good and realistic – and, afterwards, went to the Czars' burial church inside the Fortress of St Peter and St Paul. It is a very rich affair. Lots of gilding and probably a ton of silver made up into wreaths.

Today, I have had a visit from Mr Borsdorf, before I was out of my bedroom, and have to see him again this afternoon. I propose to spend the morning quietly. The sun and hot pavements and the glare are very tiring.

I am much looking forward to being home with you and the children and often wish I were with you.

With much love
from
Burke

Hotel de France   7/20 Juin 1909
Renault

My dearest,

I have no letter today so far but I expect everything is undergoing rather a close scrutiny owing to this supposed attempt on the Czar in the Gulf of Finland. Only very hazy reports are obtainable here and I expect you know much more about it in England.

We have had a sell! There is no sleeping accommodation obtaining before Friday next so we are travelling in what Malek calls cattle-trucks and intend to leave here on Tuesday morning as planned. Malek has turned up alright this morning, from Moscow, and seems as cheerful as I am at the prospect of returning to the bosoms of our families, this week.

Yesterday afternoon, Mr Marsden came to call on me at about 10.00 p.m. I went to his apartment – office. He has a Bechstein and played Chopin's first Polonaise to me and then we went through the Mikado and I left him about 11.45 p.m. quite cheered up by the music. His wife is a great invalid and lives about an hour's journey away at the seaside. He has asked Malek and me to go out there to dinner with them tomorrow.

I am quite looking forward to going into the country, this afternoon, to the Borsdorf's. I am so tired of this relaxing air here and *never* having an appetite. I suppose that is why the people, who can afford it, live outside the town during the spring and summer months.

After early dinner last night, I went by tram to the Finland Station and then walked out to the end of a tram route, which goes into the country; it was after this that I went to see Mr Marsden on my way home.

I have actually seen rain again. The rain fell heavily at 8.00 a.m. this morning and the air seems fresher. I fancy a storm has been hanging about for some days.

I have a full day in prospect for tomorrow and shall have to bestir myself early.

I quite forgot to write to the Sunbeam people about my bicycle. Will you, please, just send them a p.c. when you get this?

I finished a most amusing book yesterday. *Salthaven* by W. W. Jacobs. I am bringing it home for you. It really is very laughable and is quite in Jacobs' best style. You remember the *Lady of the Barge.*

With much love to you and Edith and Tommy

from you loving husband

Burke

Hotel de France   8/21 Juin 1909
Renault

Dearest,

I have been delighted to have two letters from you and the snap-shots which are excellent. Tell Tommy that his photograph just confirms what I have often said to him viz:- that he is a roly-poly. Edith's photo quite does her justice as a merry healthy kiddie.

We went out to the Borsdorf's yesterday and although it was very wet, it did me a lot of good. My appetite quite returned with the country air and I enjoyed a meal for the first time since coming here. The meal was real Russian:-

Sarkoust – i.e. hors d'oeuvres.

Cold fish

Asparagus soup with toast and cheese

Cold Ham with French Beans

Another dish

Hot chicken and salad

Chocolate blancmange

Coffee

Fruit

The bread was of the English variety and delicious. The coffee with cream was excellent.

The summer bungalow (called a *datcha*) in which they live is of wood and a curious little house in a village where many people go for the summer only.

After dinner, the rain cleared up and the men went for a good long stroll. We saw 7 excellent tennis courts (not grass) and went through a public park – the Schuvaloff – given by the statesman of that name, who represented Russia at the Berlin Treaty Conference about 1876. It is quite unlike anything I know in England. It is really walks cut through forest with small lakes, a church and summer houses. It is very big and contains some tall trees – pines and firs and white birch. The Birch trees are very graceful. The ozone from the pines after the rain was very refreshing. Mrs Borsdorf was most nice and kind. She is a tall stately lady of about 50 – a second Mrs Marsh – and cultured. She speaks Russian, German and French with equal facility and speaks a little English and understands it quite well. The Borsdorfs are really Germans.

There were another married couple there – the Bentines. The man was a second Alfred Rawlinson – all alive and doing silly things which made us laugh. We came back to Petersburg with them.

We still have not got our railway accommodation for tomorrow but the hotel manager personally has taken the matter in hand and I expect something will be found for us. A good deal can be done in this country with the assistance of a few roubles. We propose to stay at the Hotel Continental in Berlin from Wednesday evening to Thursday evening, this week. I should arrive in London at Holborn Viaduct Stn. at 7.15 p.m. on Friday.

Much love from
Burke

It is no use writing again until I get to Berlin

Continental Hotel   Berlin, N. W.
L. Adlon H. Klicks   Neustadt. Kirchstr. 6/7
                                     June 24th 1909

Dearest,

I arrived here safely last night with Malek after a very hot and uncomfortable journey of 33 hours and we were very tired and liverish.

Two of his directors are at the Hotel Adlon and we are to see them this morning about this Russian business.

We expect to leave here tonight and I expect to reach London at 7.15 p.m. tomorrow (Friday) to go up on the midnight to Liverpool if I can get a sleeper on the train and be home to breakfast on Saturday.

Please do not make any programme for me for Saturday as I am sure to be tired after this long journey of about another 33 hours from here.

I am writing this before having my bath so that I may post it when I go down to breakfast. We have to arrange about sleeping accommodation on the train yet. There may be some trouble about this as the trains are *very* full going West.

I am so looking forward to being home with you all, again.

Much love,

Burke

Letters written to his wife by B. Welbourn AKC MIEE, aged 36/37, Contracts Manager of the British Insulated and Helsby Cables Ltd., when travelling on business for it to Constantinople and Sofia in 1912 and 1913.

(Editor's note: Mr Dane Sinclair, the BI's General Manager, had visited Turkey in 1909 to negotiate, together with the National Telephone Co., a contract with the Ottoman Telephone Company for a telephone system for Constantinople. In 1912 a team of BI Engineers visited Constantinople, and finalised a contract to supply 80 miles of underground, and 70 miles of aerial cables.)

> Constitutional Club
> Northumberland Avenue, W.C.
> March 12-1912

Dearest,

I am sorry we had such a very hurried parting this afternoon.

I got to London much earlier than I expected – only about ¾ hour late. I had the compartment to myself from Crewe to Rugby. I am glad to find a room reserved for me here for two nights.

I saw Mr Beavis[1] immediately on reaching here. He gives a *very* bad account of aunt Emily's health. He has not been able to see her yet – the nurse only left yesterday. He seems doubtful whether I shall be able to see her when I call tomorrow. She was getting over the attack, which Fred told us of, but had a relapse.

I have posted my article to the *Electrician*[2]. I do not know whether they will pay for it even if they accept it.

I am writing to thank Mrs Nuttall[3] for her letter and then I want to go to bed as I am really tired.

Much love to you all

from Burke

---

[1] Accountant for the estates of Welbourn's father and grandfather.

[2] According to his account book, he was paid £1. 0s. 0d. for his 'tarif article'.

[3] A neighbour who owned a billiard table, and kept cars.

192

Constitutional Club
Northumberland Avenue, W.C.
13-3-1912

Dearest,

Thank you very much for your warm-hearted loving letter. We need such as there is much misery in the world. This must be a brief note as I have had much to do today and cannot have dinner before going to meet Mary and Norman[4] to help them in their problems.

I have not been able to see aunt, but she is improving. She has been frightfully ill this time – I do not think Fred[5] understands how bad the relapse was.

Poor Elsie[6] – I have had a very painful talk with her, today. She and de Silva are separated, *permanently*. Don't, on my account, write to her or anyone about it or even mention it. I will write to you more details, soon, when I have digested the matter. I am to try to see her again on my return to London and it is left to me to tell Fred. Aunt does not know, yet.

Give much love for me to the bairns and yourself and take plenty of rest.

I am going direct to C. without breaking at Vienna. It can't be helped.

Burke

POST CARD
(Buckingham Palace)

14-3-1912
Just leaving Charing Cross for Dover
etc and my 3 days journey.
I saw Uncle Toby and Aunt Mary last
night and gave your messages.
Uncle Toby is probably going to Chili.
Much love to you all
Father

Miss & Master Welbourn
Craven Lodge
Rainhill
Lancashire

---

[4] Norman and Mary Beavis. He was possibly a relation of the accountant, she the younger sister of Welbourn's wife. He was an engineer with Sturtevant, ventilating engineers.

[5] Fred Gregory, her son, who worked in the BI.

[6] Elsie Gregory was Aunt Emily's eldest daughter, the same age as Welbourn. She painted the portrait of his wife.

en route Calais-Brussels
14-3-1912

Dearest,

Thank you for your letter in London before starting. We had a comfortable sea journey but this train is frightfully jolty. I have had a sleep since lunch and feel fresher. I had a very full day and slept badly so I needed this nap.

I saw Mary and Norman after their dinner for about ½ hour. Mary looked tired out after her day's shopping with Miss Tyzack. Norman has decided to go to Chili if they will take him. His proposer will now send on full particulars to New York and he will probably have a cablegram in 10 days or so. Before going, he would have a month in Manchester at the Westinghouse works and would like to have a week-end with us. Mary and Madge had been to Surbiton[7] and found all well as could be expected. I arranged for Norman to see Flanagan tomorrow night. Tell the children I have just seen some cows drawing a plough near the French-Belgian Frontier. We are now to have our baggage examined at Blandain – I am not sure whether it is Belgium but I presume so. I have 2 hours to wait in Brussels for the Vienna train. I shall appreciate the break as I did the fresh air in the Channel for an hour. There is a notice in the carriage in 4 languages

Défense de Cracher – Niet spueven
Verboten zu spucken – It is forbidden to spit.
also *Défense de fumer – Niet rooken.*

The customs man has just been and taken my best French as follows:- *Je n'ai rien à declarer – il n'y a pas de tabac.* He smiled and departed and did not rummage in my bag.

I sent a card of congratulations to Wilf[8] and also a card to the Vicar saying that obviously I could not attend the Committee meeting on Friday evening but telling him to push ahead with the work.

Already I should like another bath and cannot have one for nearly 3 days! R-Murray came to lunch yesterday and seemed very fit.

I will give some news about Elsie on p.3 but I think you would be wise to destroy it after reading it.

With lots of love to you and the children
from your loving husband
Burke

---

[7] Welbourn's mother-in-law when widowed had moved there from Sheffield.

[8] His wife's favourite elder brother; the occasion being his promotion to Captain in the 2nd Battalion East Surrey Regiment.

Péra Palace Hotel   March 15-1912
Constantinople

Dearest,

We have just left Regensburg. After passing the Customs examination of luggage last night, at Herbstthal, on entering Germany, we had to put our watches forward one hour to Mid- European Time. I was very tired and went to bed before 10.00 (English Time) and had an excellent night getting up about 8.15 a.m. much refreshed.

So far, I have this compartment to myself and so I managed to get a *petit bain* by means of my wash-basin. After shaving, I had *café-au-lait*, fruit, curious tasting jam which looked like pulped apricot, rolls in paper bags bearing the name of Max Schäffer of Wuerzburg where we stopped about 6.00 a.m. I cannot make out whether we came through Bamberg[9] or not. The route is Frankfurt, Würzburg, Fürth, Nürnberg etc. I could see very little of Nuremberg because of the mist and certainly I saw nothing picturesque. Some miles from there, I saw two fine sights. In each case, a castle on a knoll surrounded by houses on the slopes.

There is no sun – there has evidently been heavy rain and there is still some mist. We are nearing the Austrian Frontier now and enter the country at Passau – after another Customs exam. By the way, 2.00 p.m. in Constantinople is 12.00 noon in England. This is more cheerful – the sun is now shining. We have left the forests and now are riding over a plain with few trees. I slept so well last night that I knew nothing of the stoppage at Cologne or of the ride along the Rhine Bank until we got to Mainz – which is a very big station. In Brussels, yesterday, I did nothing except get tea at a small confectioner's and then stroll round for ¾ hour. After that, I went and waited for this train. The city was *very* full of people.

Such numbers of these smaller village houses look more picturesque than comfortable. There seems more roof than house. I fancy this must be a prosperous part of Germany, because there are so many new-looking houses.

Will you tell the children that I see such numbers of boxes – like letter boxes – fixed on trees and roofs outside houses? I suppose they are for the birds to build in. Outside one small house there were five boxes in one tree and two in another.

I want to post these notes at the Frontier as I think there is a chance, then, of their reaching you on Sunday morning.

I am wondering so much if this man is worthy of Elsie and will really make

---

[9] Fräulein Roth, their governess, came from Bamberg.

her happy. I forgot to tell you that aunt's complaint is angina pectoris but the doctor says she may live for years yet.[10]

With much love to you all

from your husband

Burke

Péra Palace Hotel   March 16th 1912

Constantinople

Dearest,

I hope you will get the letter which I gave to a man to post for me yesterday at I think Passau where luggage was examined. I also sent a p.c. to Mr & Mrs Callum asking for the labour rates for the 3 following pole lines: Bradford, North Wales and Newcastle Co. Please ask Mr Nash to find out if he got it and, if not, ask him to forward them to me *at once.*

This railway travelling is agreeing with me fairly well. It is a leisurely performance averaging about 30 miles per hour as in Canada. Also the weather is cool. I think it must have been the great heat both in Spain[11] and Canada which made me so tired in travelling. Going to and from Madrid, also, the French part of the journey was done at about 65 m.p.h. I should say.

I had a good sleep yesterday afternoon and a fairly good night also – I felt *very* fit after dinner last night. I want a sharp 2 mile walk now to freshen me.

We are under a System once more. Immediately after leaving Vienna, last night, my passport and railway tickets were demanded, as in Russia, and I have not seen them since. We left Hungary in the night and have been travelling across Servia until 1.00 p.m. when we crossed into Bulgaria at Pirot. We leave it about midnight and pass into Turkey at Mustapha Pacha. Another customs exam! and at midnight, too!

In Servia, the language clearly resembles Russian – at any rate, the characters seem identical and it is quite like old times to be spelling out the names of stations. During lunch today, we passed along the bottom of a gorge alongside a very muddy fast-flowing stream. The mountains on either side of us rose up high and precipitous and were almost bare of vegetation. It was impressive for ¼ hour. The scenery is constantly changing. At times, we are in the mountains – at others, on a plain. Now, we are on a plain with mountains near by. Some of them are sprinkled with snow. It is a bright sunny day and the air is very good whenever we stop and get a breath of it for a few minutes, as at Nisch and Pirot.

---

[10] She died 10 February 1938 aged 85.

[11] There are no letters, and more surprisingly, no ppc from this trip.

196

Yesterday, we ran alongside the un-navigable part of the Danube for miles. There was some beautifully wooded country as we approached Vienna but I could not see much of the City as the darkness came on rapidly.

This is clearly a much less advanced part of Europe than the country in Belgium and Germany. The country is less well cultivated, the people are poorly clad and there is seldom a house with an upper storey. Some of the people are picturesquely clad and I have seen a few officials about with swords and revolvers (in their cases). The houses remind me of the pictures of the East especially when there are sufficient to form a village. Mostly, they have red tile roofs. Many are whitewashed – many appear to have wooden frameworks plastered over with mud. I judge this from the buildings in progress. Some houses look more like cattle hovels, to our ideas. In Austria, many of the country farms appeared to be built on the quadrangular plan – house and buildings surrounding a square. There are many picturesque scenes of children out tending the small flocks of sheep etc.

This is the Near East – the storm centre of Europe. You may remember that the King and Queen of Servia were murdered about 7 years ago and the present King is not supposed to be too secure on his throne. Bulgaria declared itself an independent kingdom about 2 years ago and is supposed to be much more stable and to be governed by a strong man – King Ferdinand.

We have just stopped at a little place – Tzaribrod – and changed our watches to Eastern European Time. On the platform, two soldiers in big grey coats and with swords walked up and down to keep us in order, I suppose. There were some picturesque gentlemen about – one old man in a sheepskin coat over a surtout. He had close-fitting trousers and soft boots of cloth which tied on and round the leg by thongs. Most of the men wear sheepskin hats. I suppose the costumes will grow in interest as I go Eastwards.

The next important city is Sofia where I hope to be able to post this. This is an uneventful journey – there is no-one to speak to and there are not many people on the train. There is no daily paper and I don't know whether the coal strike is settled or not and how things go at home. I expect to hear from you on Tuesday when the English mail comes in.

In my hurried departure, I forgot to pack your and the children's photographs, as I intended, and they might miss me if you sent them, on receipt of this.

I hope Lowe has made good progress this week and that the grate will turn up soon so that he may finish with us before getting his head full of Church cleaning business. Do you know yet the total result of the Church appeal? When I left, it was £143 – with £5 still to come from Mr Baxter.

I hope you are looking after yourself and taking plenty of rest – don't let all the spring-cleaning worry you too much. You know you have not yourself only to think about and to nourish.[12] I have not written to my mother yet. I find it

---

[12] Their son Fred was born 12 October 1912.

very difficult to write in the train, to work or to read. I have not read a line yet of either of Mrs Hyde's books which I have with me.

Tomorrow, on reaching Constantinople, I intend to send you a wire but I expect it will not be delivered to you until Monday morning.

With much love to you and Edith and Tom. Tell them I will send a few p.p.cs. from Constantinople if I can.

Your loving husband
Burke

Péra-Palace Hotel
Constantinople
March 17th 1912

My dearest

I arrived all safe this morning at 10.17 a.m. but only got here about 6.45 p.m. as our Agent, Mr Seager, and his assistant, Mr Martin, met me at the train and took me straight to the office, then to lunch and then home for afternoon tea at Mr Seager's at his house in Bebek, a suburb up the Bosphorus. Afterwards, we walked round to Mr Martin's to see Mrs M. and get the view of the Bosphorus etc. Mrs Seager 'expects' almost at once and Mrs Martin in July. The Seagers have five sturdy youngsters already – they speak English, Turkish and some French. Mr & Mrs Seager were both born here and have lived here nearly all their lives. They tell me that the English colony keeps severely aloof from the Turks and Mr S. says he has only once or twice even entered a Turkish home. They also hold aloof very much in business.

The Martins are both English and were married last July. I did not get my telegram off to you this morning. By the time I got through the Customs examination, got my passport back and so on it was quite clear that you would not have got it by 10.00 a.m. at Rainhill. I will wire you tomorrow morning.

This is a fine new hotel but, for me, there is the continual language difficulty. Most of the people here speak French fluently – the hotel belongs to the French company which manages most of the good sleeping car and restaurant car business on the Continent. I have a small room on the fourth floor at 13.00 francs a day (about 10/6). There seem to be few people here – I am told that the war is upsetting business etc.

The City has changed very much since I was here 18 years ago with Mr Gregory.[13] There are now many paved roads and there are some horse trams and motor-buses of a decrepit type. A big electricity scheme is being carried through and there are to be electric trams and telephones. The city does not seem to me to be so attractive as when I saw it last. I am perhaps older and

---

[13] His uncle Henry, husband of Aunt Emily.

more critical but I think the sun was from the wrong quarter and angle as I saw none of the lighting up of golden minarets which attracted me so much before, in the early morning.

There were four Americans at the table next to me, at dinner, tonight. They were busy comparing their sight-seeing notes.

I did not have quite so good a night's sleep in the train last night as we had to wake up at the Turkish frontier about 12.30 a.m. to have our hand-baggage examined and hand over our passports.

I hope you will get the three letters which I have posted to you *en route* – at Brussels, Passau and Sofia.

Tell the children I have seen numbers of lamb – several of them quite black. Yesterday, I saw a man with a big black lamb curled round his neck. The big sheep are either dirty white or very brown. The plum trees here and right across the Continent are in very profuse full bloom. If there is no early frost, there will be a fine crop. In places here, the air is heavily perfumed with the scent of the bloom.

I learn here with much regret that the Coal Conference, under Mr Asquith, has failed and that he has announced legislation to deal with the difficulty. Unless the strike is settled this week, the country's outlook will be serious. I understand that the archbishops have appointed today for special Intercession and I suppose you have had the special service at our church at Rainhill. This seems a curious Sunday for me – never mind – keep your pecker up – I hope to be home again in about two weeks if all goes well – there is much for me to do here in the interval.

With much love to you and the children from
your loving husband
Burke

Péra-Palace Hotel
Constantinople
18th Mars 1912

My dearest,

No letter has arrived yet from you and so I have no news of you later than Wednesday. I fully expect one or probably two letters to come on the Orient Express train tomorrow morning. I wish you were coming by it, too.

After making enquiry, I find there is another way from England by going overland to Marseilles and thence by boat – 3 days' sail and 1 day train from Calais. Say, 5 days from Liverpool.

I went to bed in good time, last night, slept well and, this morning, had a much needed hot bath – the first for four days.

Today has been a busy one with a good deal of walking. This is *very* tiring to the feet as the roads are so badly paved. Also, it is quite hot in the sun but one cannot discard a coat as the air is quite cool in the narrow shaded streets.

I am sending a p.p.c. to the children shewing the Bridge of Boats which is near Mr Seager's office. The approach to it is about as crowded with people as any spot which I have seen. It is quite as busy as the Mansion House in London. It is certainly more picturesque as most of the men wear the red fez. I find that a good many women are not covering their faces now but this, I believe, applies to the lower classes. The middle and upper class women are heavily veiled with black silk veils so that the whole face is hidden. Mr Seager says the highest class women do not veil the eyes. I will send a p.p.c. to the children, soon, to shew what I mean.

We have seen various people today – the officials of the Telephone Co. and a director, H. L. Webb, who is staying here. Also we went to see Mahmoud Chukin Bay – a big municipal official. Also the secretaries of the Tramway and Electric Light companies. All this was by way of skirmishing to get the lie of the land and feel my way. I have, of course, had long talks with Mr Seager who has practically given up the whole day to me and will, I fancy, be able to do very little other business while I am here. Tomorrow, we have to interview all sorts of people at the Custom House, Quay offices and so on. One things seems clear and that is that the Turk is much like the Russian and won't be hurried!

I hear, today, that Mr Asquith has to introduce a bill to settle the miners' minimum wage question and that it will take 8/10 days to get through Parliament. I suppose this means that the mines will not be fully at work again until about Easter.

With lots of love to you and the children
from your husband,
Burke.

I am sending a few p.p.cs. to friends

POST OFFICE TELEGRAPHS

Rainhill
MR 18
12

Pera   Handed in at 10.40 a.m.   Received here at 11.33 a.m.

TO   Welbourn   Rainhill   England
Arrived   Safely   Burke

Péra-Palace Hotel
Constantinople
20 Mars 1912

My dearest

Tomorrow, I am going to stay for the rest of my visit with Mr Bigland, the Contract Manager of the Telephone Co., at Bebek – a healthy suburb – and I am arranging with the Post Office to send my letters to me c/o Walter Seager & Co., Tchinili Rihtim Han, Constantinople.

I do not think it will be safe for you to write to me after Saturday.

I find this hotel is in a noisy street, there is not enough air and I shall be in congenial company. Bigland is stepbrother to Rigby Swift M.P. for St Helen's and cousin of Alfred Bigland M.P. for Birkenhead. He is going home to London in August to be married.

About New Brighton – I think I should arrange for 3 weeks stay certain from the Saturday before August Bank Holiday. I leave the terms to you to arrange but I should think you would get comfortable quarters at 21 to 25 shillings per room per week. We want to have enough left for a week's holiday together about November. It is very kind of Mrs Hyde to go with you. Have you told her the 'news'? Today, I felt very headachey after an indifferent night and got Bigland to take me by steamer down the Bosphorus until we could see the Black Sea. We touched at a landing place – Cavak – on the Asian shore. The fresh air blew away most of the cobwebs for me. We were away for about 5½ hours. Incidentally, I was looking over the routes etc to be covered by the Telephone work for which we are to quote. We expect to have a similar expedition tomorrow in the Scutari direction and shall go past Leander's Tower. Scutari is where Florence Nightingale did her great nursing feats during the Crimean War about 1854–6. You may remember that she was known as 'the Lady of the Lamp'.

I am not having any time yet for detailed sightseeing but I may be able to see the Sultan in the Salamlik procession on Friday.

This is a difficult place to estimate the cost of work for – the Austrian engineer of the new Electric Light Co. tells me his trenching costs fully twice what it would cost in any other part of Europe. For my own (and the B.I.) protection, I am getting a quotation from a native contractor for a large part of the work.

I have written to Mr Cramp at once – the letter was evidently from him. I will send a p.p.c. to Mrs Fred Marsh.

I must go and pack and get to bed earlier than last night if possible. It is now nearly 10.00 p.m.

With very much love to you all
your loving husband,
Burke.

Dearest

I wrote 3 p.p.cs. last night for today's post and I am now snatching a few minutes out of this busy existence to send you a short letter. There is no letter from you today but your letter of March 17 came yesterday with Edith's. It is quite a good letter and she had quite a good shot at 'Rhododendron'.

After yesterday's wet, the fine weather has returned again and the sun is blazing away. I am not feeling too fit – for 2 or 3 nights, I have not slept very well although I have had my window wide open and a running brook outside to lull me.

The Binns family at Bebek are cousins of Mr Seager and Mr Bigland is living there. They are quite nice sort of people but I should get very weary of Mrs Binns who chatters incessantly.

My papers from London have still not come and I cannot possibly get them until Monday I fear. If they come then, the earliest date for my leaving will be Wednesday evening and I should probably get home about 11.30 on Sunday evening if the trains have resumed regular running by then. Tomorrow morning, we go to the non-conformist Church at Bebek and in the afternoon we go sightseeing.

On Monday, I expect a long day – going to the Islands to see where the submarine cables are to go and to see some more of the Telephone territory.

I have some 'bites' – I think one is a flea and the rest mosquitoes. People sleep under mosquito nets in summer.

If I have to come here again, as seems likely, I think I shall go to Marseilles and then by sea.

Much love
Burke

Mr Seager just come to take me to the boat for home.

Bebek 24-3-1912   (Post-card of Mosquée et l'Hippodrome, Constantinople)

It is again a very lovely morning – plenty of
sun and blue sky – and clear atmosphere.
Bigland has gone to the R.C. church and we go   Mrs Welbourn
to the Nonconformist service in a schoolroom   Rainhill
shortly. This afternoon, we expect to see this   Lancashire,
mosque from the outside at close quarters.   England.

202

It's the only one in the world with 6 minarets
but there is one at Mecca with 7. Most mosques
have 4, I believe. The postal arrangements are such
that I do not know when this will actually leave here.
From the minaret the muezzin calls the people to
prayer so many times a day. Love – Burke

c/o Mrs Binns
Bebek – Bosphorus
Constantinople
24-3-1912

My dearest

It is a lovely Sunday morning but so strange to be right away among strangers. You would much enjoy the novelty of a week or two in this Eastern city etc but the walking entailed through the absence of trams and the bad paving makes one very weary especially when the sun is hot. I don't think you would be able to stand much of it. There is easy boat communication across and along the Bosphorus and Golden Horn by steamer and rowing boats but that does not help in the city.

Yesterday, we had a pleasant interview with Evien Bay the chief engineer of the Turkish Govt. Telegraph Dept. He is quite a nice man and seemed very unaffected and friendly. The new G.P.O. is a very palatial building with much white marble about.

We also had a very useful interview with a Scotchman who runs the Turkish Govt. gas works for Péra. He was a most decided 'character' who suffers much from 'swelled head'.

The telephone people here are particularly nice – the gen. manager used to be under Mr Sinclair[14] and knows him well. He has given me some useful help.

In Bebek is one English Colony – composed mostly of aunts, cousins etc who inter-marry and are nearly all related to one another. Seager married his cousin and has 5 bonny children but he says it has always been a great anxiety to his wife and himself lest they should have trouble with their children. He says some other cousins who married here never were able to raise a child over 3 years old.

At Moda, on the opposite side of the Bosphorus, on the Asiatic side, there is another English Colony mainly composed of the Whittall family. The old lady patriarch died a few weeks ago leaving over 200 descendants behind – some of them do not speak English now.

---

[14] Mr Dane Sinclair, General Manager of BI. He had been in Constantinople in 1909 trying to develop telephone business.

Tomorrow, I expect to go to look over the ground at San Stefano and on Tuesday (instead of Monday) go with Bigland to the Islands to see where the submarine cables etc are to be. This will be a long day and probably I shall not be able to get a letter off to you. The postal business is difficult – there are British, German etc. Post Offices because the Turkish postal arrangements are (or may be) primitive. It will probably be of no use writing to you after Tuesday and I hope to be able to wire to you on Wednesday saying when I shall leave for home. I could not have got along so quickly as I have, had it not been for Seager. He knows so many people and the ropes and speaks English, Turkish, Greek and French.

As I write someone in a neighbouring house is playing 'Songs without Words' etc -very well too.

With very much love to you and the bairns

from your loving husband

Burke

Is the spring cleaning nearly finished?

c/o Walter Seager
Constantinople
25-3-1912

Dearest

To shew you how erratic the post is:- Your letter of March *18th* (a week ago) arrived *today*, your letter and p.c. of the *19th* and your p.c. of the *20th* arrived *yesterday*. Thank you very much for them all.

Things are moving slowly but to my annoyance, the papers are not yet here from London nor my telegram from Prescot about them although I wired on Friday afternoon. My hopes of leaving on Wednesday evening are slowly evaporating and I begin to fear it may have to be Friday. Anyway, before you get this I hope to have sent you a telegram telling you definitely when I leave.

I am glad to hear of the progress being made in the spring cleaning etc and I sincerely hope, for your sake, that it is now about done with. I fear you will be 'fed up' with men for a time. By the way, Mr Bradford's letter has not reached me. I expect you will enclose it with your next letter.

I shall be glad to get away from here. This stuffiness is making me tired even though I have the 40 minutes on the water morning and evening to and from Bebek.

Bigland is a very good fellow and a most cheerful Roman Catholic. He is most anxious that I should call on his fiancée and her people in London. She and her mother are coming here on a visit next month and the wedding is in London on Aug. 25th. He is most kind in taking me about when Seager cannot.

He gave up all this morning to taking me to San Stefano and tomorrow he gives the whole day to go to the Islands.

Yesterday, we made up a party at the house and came in to see the mosques of St. Sophia and Sultan Ahmed – the latter is comparatively new (1614). We could not see the underground 1001 columns. A man told us that the keeper had gone to the war and had taken the key with him! Sounds Irish, *n'est ce pas*? Bigland is Irish, has a keen sense of humour and was much amused.

The service yesterday morning was conducted by an American on Nonconformist lines. There was a very small congregation but the singing was hearty. Bigland took me over his house yesterday. It is of wood, with plenty of rooms but each one is about as big as a large cupboard. I don't know what they will do with any babies if there are any.

I find I am beginning to understand French when I hear it spoken!

With very much love, dearest (and to the children) from

your loving husband

Burke

Splendid Palace
Prinkipo
le 26 Mars 1912

Dearest,

Today, Bigland and I left Bebek by the 8.15 a.m. boat, in the heavy rain, and just had time to charge into the boat at C. for this island and landed here at 10.40.

We had a walk on the island and then came here for lunch which is over at 12.45. We now have to wait until 5.00 p.m. for the boat back to Constantinople and what time we shall get home I don't know. The telephone is to be brought to these islands – Proti, Halki, Antigoui and Prinkipo – the last being the most important and nearest to the Asiatic coast. This island has some excellent houses and hotels on it and is a famous summer resort. I can see this section of the work will be difficult for us as a good deal of cable has to be laid under the sea. If we get the whole order, I think we shall have to send out at least four superintendents to manage it and probably I should have to come out two or three times.

I am still without my further papers from London and I do not yet know if I can get away tomorrow night. I think, however, it is almost certain to be Friday night before I can leave. In that case I should not get home until Tuesday next or even Wednesday if Mr Sinclair is in London. I want to get home to you and the bairns --- I am tired of this and feel tired as I have to get up about 7.10 each day and seldom get to bed before 11.00.

I am writing to you here as there will not be time in C. on the way back and, as it is, I do not think it will leave until tomorrow night and reach you on Sunday or more probably Monday. I hope the train service will have improved when I get home again. The newspaper accounts of the strike – as published here – indicate that the strike is not yet settled. It would seem that my original estimate of 6 to 8 weeks for the strike to start, run and for the mines to get into swing again is not going to be far wrong. The damage will be incalculable to England.

I am now going to send the children a p.p.c. from Asia – I expect they think I am a wonderful traveller – don't they?

With much love to you and them

from your loving husband

Burke

c/o Mrs James Binns
Bebek – Constantinople
March 27th 1912

My dearest

Thank you for two letters received together last night. I fear that Oppenheim & Son[15] will not get the papers from the Bank without the official receipt for them which I have – anyway, I do not mind if it has to stand over until my return. I have been over to the Asian side again today and did not return in time to send a letter by the mail tonight. Stanley Binns has come home and says no letters have come to the office for me today.

I fully expect to wire you on Friday that I am leaving that night at 7.15 and should be home sometime on Tuesday if Mr Sinclair does not ask me to stay in London to see him. My address on Tuesday morning will be: c/o B.I. & H. Cables Ltd., Lennox House, Norfolk Street, Strand, London W.C.

I had my hands *full* last night – just as I was dressing last night after our late arrival home from Prinkipo, Bigland rushed into my bedroom with a letter from his lady breaking off their engagement and really giving no substantial reasons. He is quite mystified. After a long talk, we went out and sent a telegram to her brother asking if it would be of any use for him to come to England and talk things over. He is 39 and she is 35 and there is an idea that she is scared at the thought of having babies at her age. They had taken their house here, fixed the wedding date in August etc. etc. It is a stunner for him. He only came here, with her full consent, to improve his position and to enable them to marry earlier and in greater comfort. He is now anxiously awaiting a telegram.

I hope you have bought your Eau de Cologne which I was to have got before I came away. Please do if you have not done so already. I have thought of it,

---

[15] His solicitor.

many times. I expect to bring something home. I hear I have a present of Loucooms awaiting me at the office. Apart from a fez or a narghili, there seems to be nothing very distinctive to get here as a souvenir.

The weather has been wet and cold for two days and the people here are horrified when I tell them how infinitely I prefer it to their hotter weather.

Will you please send my grandmother two 15/- P.O.s and a brief letter telling her I am away on the Continent on business?

With lots of love and kisses to you and the bairns

from your loving husband

Burke

I hope Tom will like his letter and Edith her p.p.c.
I am not physically tired tonight but am <u>very sleepy</u>.

(Editor's note: At this point there is a fine puzzle. In his eldest son's picture postcard album is a ppc dated 30/3/1912 with a British ½d. stamp on it, addressed to Master Welbourn, Rainhill, Lancashire England. the postmark saying 'London W8, 7.30 pm April 1 12'. Welbourn refers in a letter above to writing cards for the children. Did he get the date wrong, and give it to someone returning to England to post? London was at least 3 days by train away, with no flying. It is also puzzling, since it implies that cable laying had commenced.)

ppc showing a fine castle called Roumeli-Hissar   30/3/1912

Roumeli means European. There is also Anatolie-Hissar (meaning Asiatic-Hissar) across the Bosphorus. The submarine telegraph cables are laid between the two villages, and start from the foot of King Darius' Tower which you see on this ppc. At this point the current is very swift and is always in the direction from the Black Sea to the Sea of Marmora, the Dardenelles, and then to the Mediterranean. there are lots of porpoises in it. Very much love from Father.

c/o Walter Seager & Co.
Constantinople
6-4-1912
8 p.m.

My dearest,

Thank you for your letters received yesterday (Sunday) and today. Seager went to town yesterday, got the letters and sent yours to me by his young son. This morning, on reaching town, I went straight to the British Post Office and sent you two days' letters and also one for the children.

We have had a long and late sitting today negotiating with the local contractor and are now at a critical stage of our negotiations. This will last certainly until Wednesday. Things are going favourably, so far.

So far, I have not been able to find anywhere for Mr & Mrs Greenwood[16] to live when they arrive next week. I have been quite busy on the subject.

Tomorrow, I am seeing the Revd Robert Frew in regard to finding suitable lodgings for our jointers when they arrive and believe I am to meet him at the Club de Constantinople – the Pera quarter.

Tonight, we lost the usual boat home and had to drive the whole way. It was an uncomfortable proceeding – three were on a seat barely capable of taking two.

Dinner is very late tonight fortunately and it has enabled me to have a bath. At 9.00 p.m., at Seager's, is the first rehearsal of the coming Amateur Theatricals 'Facing the Music'. (I had to break off here for the evening meal which was not over until 9.00 p.m.).

Mrs Binns has just been in telling me that if necessary, she will take in the Greenwoods, on their arrival, for a month or so, so that they will not be stranded.

I have now got over the first drowsiness caused by this air and am really feeling very well. I have not had to wear the glasses much today – that is a good sign for me.

I am glad to hear that you have, at last, had some much-needed rain. I am hoping to see the garden quite refreshed when I return. I learn today, that Mr Watson, the general manager, is expected back here on May 14th so I hope to leave on the following Friday.

There is news here today that the Italians have blockaded the Island of Rhodes – I wonder if this will postpone the opening of the Dardanelles.

With best love to you all

from your loving husband

Burke

(Editorial note: clearly some letters are missing at this point, since Welbourn has returned to England, and in the next letter is starting another visit to Constantinople.)

Constitutional Club
Northumberland Avenue, W.C.
29-4-1912

My dearest,

It is now 7.45 p.m. and this is the first moment I am free since reaching

---

[16] Mr Greenwood was one of the superintendents in the Contracts Department.

Euston at noon. Busby met me with his car, brought me and my baggage here and then took me to our London Office where I was kept going fully until 1.30. I had lunch with one of my visitors and was back by 2.10. I had a hurried chat with Mr Walton who has to face his operation for appendicitis at once, after all. At 2.30 I was with Gill and Cook, etc. and we had a conference on Constantinople matters until 4.50 when I left to meet Murray here at 5.00. We walked up to St Pancras and then I got back about 7.15. Now I will wash and have a meal and then I propose to retire early as I am tired and want a good rest before starting the long journey tomorrow early.

Thank you very much for seeing me off at Prescot this morning. I do hope you were not tired out, by the evening, as the result? Tom looked especially fresh – I hope he will write me one letter while I am away and Edith at least two.

There has been a little rain here and the weather is cool and cloudy. I travelled down this morning with a "rubber" merchant who told me of a mutual acquaintance who went down on the Titanic. He was a well-to-do bachelor who did a good deal of social work among youths etc. He had with him a man whom he was taking out to give a fresh start in America.

With best love to all
from
Burke

Constitutional Club
Northumberland Avenue, W.C.
30-4-1912

Dearest,

Just a line before leaving to send my love and greetings to you all.

It is a beautiful sunny morning for the start of the long journey and it should be a good omen.

Burke

30-4-1912   CARTE POSTALE
                    (Paris – La Gare de l'Est)

This is the station which we are about   Mrs Welbourn
to leave for Constanza etc.   Rainhill
We are going strong and have had no   Lancashire
adventures. Much love all,
Burke.

1-5-1912   Salzburg
Just stopped for a few minutes. We have   Mrs Welbourn
been riding through this beautiful scenery for   Rainhill
some hours and are now about 5 hours from   Lancashire
Vienna. It is quite cool here and the hills   Angleterre
are covered with snow.
Love Burke

1-5-1912   Vienna
We have just driven across Vienna and   Mrs Welbourn
passed this magnificent Opera House.   Rainhill
The drive has quite freshened me after   Lancashire
nearly 24 hours in the train. The air is   Angleterre
still quite chilly.I have no paper and
envelopes and have not been able to
get any so far. Hope all well at home.
Best love, Burke

en route Bucharest
May 2nd 1912

My dearest,

I did not bring any writing paper with me nor have I been able to get any on the train. I sent various picture post cards from Paris, Salzburg and Vienna and I hope these have reached you quite safely.

First of all, thank you for my pen and your letter which came just before I left London on Tuesday. Bunn[17] was seen off by his father and brother who had taken him, on the previous night, to see 'Bunty pulls the strings'. We are not appreciating Podmore as a travelling companion. He is an unattractive type of pert provincial Sheffielder who wears two rings, a big watch chain with a medal, then a scarfpin and so on and he pronounces 'sugar' – shugger – which you so strongly object to. He has also made very unfortunate remarks about other travellers on the assumption that they did not understand English!

We crossed the Channel alright but B and I were not too happy as there was a good deal of rolling and sometimes the spray came on the top deck. There were long waits at Dover and Calais but we reached Paris to time and had a good walk before leaving again. I took them round by Notre Dame and the

---

[17] N.K. Bunn, a superintendent in the Contracts Dept., who had many years' experience in Brazil for the BI. He later became Welbourn's deputy and then successor as Contracts Manager. He could be a most amusing man.

Tuileries Gardens and along part of the Rue St Honoré. We had China tea at a confectioners and unanimously voted it poor stuff! Except at breakfast on the train, I am keeping off coffee! In Vienna yesterday, we made up a party of four and drove across the City to the other station. It was a refreshing change. For some hours yesterday, we ran along a range of snowclad mountains. I think they were the Bavarian Alps and the boundary of the Austrian Tyrol. During breakfast today, we came through the Iron Gates in the Balkans but it is not nearly so impressive as the similar pass on the southern route via Sofia. We do not see so much of the Danube on this route, but this morning we ran alongside it for some miles where it is quite wide. Afterwards we had a slow climb up a hill and at the top we could see where we had come lower down.

At present, the country east of Craiova is not very interesting but I am, as a whole, much more impressed with the civilisation in Roumania than in Bulgaria and Servia. There are better houses and better clad people here. The trees etc do not seem more appreciably forward here than at home. I think this must be because the weather is still so chilly. I expect we shall find things very different in Constantinople which is much further South. We leave the train tonight at Constanza and go down the Black Sea by steamer. I hope to send you a wire in less than 24 hours telling of our safe arrival. I hope you are taking lots of rest and keeping yourself fit and well for your coming responsibilities!

With much love to you and the children

from your loving husband

Burke

c/o Walter Seager & Co.
Constantinople
May 3rd 1912

My dearest,

Here we are again and very thankful to be at the end of that long and weary journey.

It *was* nice of you to think of writing to me so that your letter travelled with me. I received it about 2/3 hours after my arrival. I sent you a telegram quickly "Arrived safely" and I shall hope to hear, in four days time, that you got it alright. Seager's telegraphic address is:- 'JOLLY Constantinople'.

Bunn and I are tired and want a good night's sleep ashore. I had quite a good long sleep on the boat last night while crossing the Black Sea. I was in bed by about 12.45 a.m. and did not get up until 9.40 a.m. The sea was quite calm and we had no trouble from mal-de-mer. The weather is abominably cold here, still, and cloudy and here am I with only one thick suit which I can wear and two thin summer suits which are useless. Fortunately, I have one spare winter vest and I expect I shall have to buy a pair of pants. I was sorry that Bunn should arrive here on such a cloudy day by sea as he saw the City under a very bad aspect and his face looked glum but I think he is cheering up. Seager and Bigland met us at the boat with their respective Ravasses to look after our luggages and get it through the Customs and then they took us straight off to lunch at the usual place – the Double D – a quiet restaurant run on simple French lines.

Bunn and I are very 'fed up' with Podmore – unless he changes into a gentleman etc. I fear there will be some friction, one day. I don't know what his company was thinking about in appointing such a man. Bigland is just the same and I have arranged to see him and have a chat, tomorrow. He is in charge while Douglas Watson, the general manager, is away in England settling up his affairs and arranging for his wife and family to come out here.

It is expected here that the Dardanelles will be cleared of the mines so that the straits can be re-opened for shipping on Monday. Meanwhile the Bosphorus is a sight, with all the held-up shipping. Seager says he has never seen such a sight before and never expects to see it again.

Those Guardian Insurance premiums can await my return – I had remembered that they would fall due in my absence. I hope you have had satisfactory letters from Mr Kerfoot and Mr Kitchen about the endorsement of cheques and warrants?

I cannot, at this moment, think of any way in which I can help Mr Tunstall to obtain employment but I will bear him in mind. It would help me if I knew what he could do. Does he want work as a canvasser for orders or would he do clerical work and what has his past experience been? Also, presumably he wants to live at home.

I hope Dutton has come from the Works to cut the garden etc. Will you please ask Miss Longton about the purple rock?

Dinner bell!

Much love to you all

from your loving husband

Burke

<table>
<tr><td>I have no p.p.cs. yet to send</td><td>c/o Walter Seager & Co.
Constantinople
May 4th 1912</td></tr>
</table>

Dearest,

Thank you for your long letter received this afternoon. As Seager is so interested in shipping and in view of the recent Titanic disaster I read out to him the extract which you gave me from Percy's[18] letter wherein he described his experiences among the icefields and icebergs. It will have made an indelible impression on his memory, I expect. I am sorry to hear about Betty's trouble.

---

[18] Percy Appleyard, one of his wife's younger brothers, was in the Merchant Navy.

Will there be any difficulty about making her right until she has another child?

Did Harry[19] tell your mother what his new business venture is and what are his prospects in it? I should be glad to hear of his finding really congenial employment so that he could have an additional inducement to settle down in England.

I am glad to know you are resting while you can. Keep it up. Bunn and I came out yesterday and today by the 4.30 boat instead of the 5.55. Both of us feel so tired in this air – it always takes some time to get used to it. My head and eyes were very tired tonight on arrival home and I went to sleep or almost so before having a hot bath and now feel a good deal fresher. Incidentally, I washed my head to get rid of the accumulated dust during travelling and now my head looks the usual wild mass.

I quite agree about the value to the B.I. of your shewing off the electric stove. You might throw out a hint to our friend R.P.Nash that he should forget to put in the new meter for some weeks longer.

Have you had any rain yet to lay the dreadful dust and give the needed refreshment to the garden and fields? Here the weather is still cold and the wind is from the North. However, we live in hope. The sun came out for a few minutes today but did not disperse the grey clouds. A curious thing is that so few porpoises are to be seen. Perhaps they do not like the cold. The cormorants have departed for the summer since I left here, 5 weeks ago. That is one notable change. Another is the wisteria and the Judas trees which are in full bloom. The Judas trees on the hill sides have rather the effect of purple heather, in the distance.

We had a full busy morning and, from my point of view, an anxious one – re-opening our negotiations with the local contractor who will probably do the trenching and pipe laying here for us. Tomorrow, being Sunday, we hope to have a rest. Bigland and Podmore are coming to dinner and I expect we shall have an afternoon stroll. I am rather afraid that this cannot leave until the evening of the 6th unless I can find someone going to the City who will post it.

With much love to you and the children from your

ever loving husband

Burke

c/o Walter Seager & Co.
Constantinople
May 7th 1912

My dearest,

Thank you very much for your letter last Friday. I am glad to hear that my telegram reached you so early as 3.35 p.m. on that day. Evidently it only took

---

[19] Harry Appleyard, his wife's eldest brother.

about two hours to get through to you. I expect you will be getting my first letter from here and also a p.p.c. of the S. S. *Principesa Maria* – the boat on which we came here from Constanza which is in Roumania, at one of the mouths of the Danube. Have the children located it yet?

Did I tell you I heard a nightingale, two nights ago? I have never heard one before and I am most distinctly disappointed. Seager says they get much finer later in the summer and also that the trill is then much more prolonged and that, often, half-a-dozen will sing, at the same time, with beautiful effect.

I am sorry to hear you have been so much worried about that ... in Prescot. It may be that the chemist had an accident – they will happen to us all, at times, you know.

With regard to Dutton, I don't think much of him, as you are aware. I only arranged for him in desperation, at the last moment, as Willie Harris was not available and as Miss Rawlins' man did not turn up. If you are able to find another better man who will do temporary jobs, as required, and without having a permanent engagement, please send word to Mr W. Callum via Mr Nash to stop Dutton from coming again at present.

This morning, we were out on the Golden Horn examining lighters (or barges) in which to carry our drums of cable from the ship to the shore as required. We found some very suitable ones – better ones than I expected we should be able to obtain.

I do not see much opportunity of sight-seeing, this time. We have two things in view. Seager proposes that we should have a half-holiday on Friday (the Mohammedan Sunday) and go for a row up the Golden Horn.

Bigland has invited us to lunch with him at Moda, at the hotel at which he lives, on Sunday, and we have accepted.

Did the clock-cleaner make any suggestions as to the best way of keeping our clock clear of dust and in good working order? The wooden case is awfully poor and ill made and ill fitting for such a good bronze exterior.

I have had a notice, via the Works, of my re-election on the Manchester Section Committee and, together, Bunn has had notice of his election as an Assoc. Member of the Institution.[20] Things are going on, slowly today but, tomorrow, we expect an important meeting and things should then move briskly. I sent off 12 p.p.cs. this morning and propose to send some more soon to your mother and mine.

With much love to you and the bairns
from your loving husband
Burke

---

[20] The Institution of Electrical Engineers of which Welbourn was a Member (in 1995 parlance, Fellow). Associate Members then were the equivalent of Members today.

I hope you are taking full care of yourself – don't go cutting the lawn or doing anything heavy of that sort.

c/o Walter Seager & Co.
Constantinople
Sunday night May 5 1912 10.15 p.m.

My dearest,

Before retiring for the night, I want to begin this letter to you. I wrote a note, this morning, to Edith and Tom and have enclosed it with my letter of yesterday to you. That letter is still unposted as I have not discovered anyone going to the City in time for today's outward mail. Going to the City is a much more formidable business than going to Liverpool from Rainhill.

After breakfast, Bunn and I went for a stroll along the Quays and then came back for Church at 11.00 a.m. There was a very small congregation for the service which lasted only a full hour. There was an excellent address from the American lay preacher whom I heard when here before. Bigland and Podmore came for dinner and tea. After dinner, Bigland and I had a good walk on the hill behind the house and then along overlooking the Bosphorus and were out for about 1½ hours. He says that Miss Bodenham has written expressing a desire to return a writing case which she had given him and which he had returned to her and also asking him if she may send him papers and magazines! He is nursing the hope that she is relenting already!!

The day has been a very beautiful one – plenty of sun tempered by a breeze, plenty of blue sky and blue water. The view over the Bosphorus into Asia was perfect and I could not but wish that you could be here with me to enter into the enjoyment of it.

After a long and merry tea party, Bunn and I took the men down to their boat for Kadikeny (the ancient Calcedon) and then we had another stroll terminating with a call on Mr Seager from whom we borrowed *The Times*. I had a peep of Mrs Seager and the 3-weeks' old baby, this morning, on the way to church. S. says that Master John spends all his time between sleeping and crying and that he is quite different in behaviour from his other 5 bairns. Bunn, Seager and Bigland are all interested in postage stamps. Bunn shewed me his collections last night and also gave me some spare, used and unused, S. American stamps which the children will find useful some day, I expect. There seems to be a lot more in the hobby than meets the eye!

I want to go to bed now to rest as I expect a very busy and anxious week ahead. Goodnight, dearest.

With much love to you all
from
Burke

c/o Walter Seager & Co.
Constantinople
May 9 – 1912

My dearest,

I hope my letters are getting through to you alright and regularly as I am posting/writing to you every day. I *expect* to be able to leave here on May 18th (but I might leave on the 16th) so I do not think it will be safe for you to write to me here after May 14th.

Today is another bitterly cold one and there has been a little rain but not much. Tonight, the wind is high. Bigland came here for tea this afternoon before going on to direct the rehearsal of 'Facing the Music' which he is helping to get up to assist in raising funds for the Bebek School.

Please thank the children for their letters which came today. I hope they have had my joint one to them?

I will write to them again soon. I have had very little time yet for sending them p.p.cs. Please thank them for all the watering which they have done in the garden for me. I hope we shall have some results through it.

Have any of the tadpoles lost their tails and turned into frogs yet?

We were to have gone to the Asian side this afternoon but there were various unavoidable changes and, in the end, we postponed the visit until tomorrow. We want to find out the best place for landing the submarine cables. Owing to the cold weather, I expect our half-holiday trip up the Gold Horn will be 'off'.

I am keeping clear of the Turkish coffee. I don't like it and it does not agree with me. I am having to eat such a lot of fruit, lettuce etc. as well as taking medicine to keep me all right.

There was an exciting report here last night that the Turks had captured 1,100 Italians and 6 guns on one of the Islands which the Italians have landed on not far from the Dardanelles. It is thought that they would not be able to keep their prisoners as they could not feed them long and they could not get them away owing to lack of transports and a protecting fleet. The Dardanelles are still un-opened and the large amount of shipping is therefore still at anchor off the City, opposite to Scutari.

I shall be glad to get out of this place and be homeward bound to you, once more.

With much love to you all from
Your loving husband
Burke

British Insulated & Helsby Cables Ltd.
c/o Walter Seager & Co., Agents
Constantinople
le 9 Mai 1912

Dearest,

Thank you for your postcard of last Saturday. I am glad the rain has come at last. It will make a huge difference to our garden and the countryside. We had a very full day, yesterday, and I did not get my usual free time in the evening for writing to you.

We had our final interview with the local contractor yesterday and made our bargain – I think it is a good one. I am now awaiting his written confirmation so that I may see a lawyer and get the draft contract prepared.

We find it frightfully difficult to sit down and do one thing consecutively here. There are so many interruptions and so many things to be thought of and planned in a short time. Things are shaping very well but everything takes time in this country – not your time but the time of the place.

Today is again cold with a grey sky. Yesterday was a *perfect* day for seeing this City. There was bright sun, cool wind from the West which blew the steamer smoke away from the City proper. When I walked to the boat at Bebek yesterday morning I felt at peace with the world and longed for a day's holiday in which to enjoy the beauties of this Bosphorus country. Now, today, there is this complete change and I am glad to have my warm clothes.

Last night, we went to Mr Seager's, after dinner, for a chat and to see the baby – No. 6, they call him. He was very much awake and had been for hours. He is just a month old with a very strong back and neck. He is giving all of them a lively time, so far.

I have arranged, at last, for Mr & Mrs Greenwood to go to the Maison Binns next Tuesday on their arrival. I expect I shall have to be out about 6.15 that morning to go and meet them on arrival, give them breakfast in town and then take them to Bebek.

I must close now – with much love to you all
from Burke

I have not yet heard from Tom or Edith.

British Insulated & Helsby Cables Ltd.
c/o Walter Seager & Co., Agents
Constantinople
11-5-1912

My dearest,

I have a few minutes breathing space now – at least, I think so. This is a terrible place for interruptions and one never can be sure of being able to do anything continuously.

Thank you very much for your long letter yesterday – yes, I hope to leave here on Saturday next, if not earlier. There is still no definite word from Mr Watson, the general manager of the Telephone Co. saying when he will arrive but it is expected that he is leaving London today and will arrive on Tuesday. I have not heard either from Greenwood as to what time and day to expect him and his wife but I hope it will be Tuesday. I wired him a few days ago to say I had arranged for his boarding on arrival.

Yesterday afternoon, although cold, we had our half-holiday and went in 2-pair oar caiques, rowed by men in wonderful uniforms, from the Pontoon Bridge, close by here, to the Sweet Waters of Europe where the Turks go for their country outing on their Sunday afternoon (i.e. Friday). It is very unexciting and the country is a long way from being either beautiful or interesting. The journey by boat up the Golden Horn took about an hour each way. At the Sweet Waters, we had tea, nuts, oranges and country cakes, listened to the native music (?) and singing, were *pestered* by beggars – chiefly Gipsy women and children – and finally got home at 7.30. After supper, we went to Mr Seager's brother-in-law's house – Mr & Mrs Robert Rowell – very nice people – and had a quiet game of bridge and then went home to sleep very soundly after the long spell of fresh air. We met a Mr Biggs – a much travelled Englishmen – at the Rowells. Bigland was my companion in the caique each way. He has Miss Bodenham on the brain. It is telling on him very much and he looks thinner and aged. At times, he looks quite careworn and so tired – in other words 'broken'.

This morning, we have had an interview with the lawyer about making the contract for the underground work and have to see him again this afternoon. In the interval, we have to turn into French some notes which I had made in English for his guidance. Tomorrow, we go to Bigland for lunch at the house where he is living in Moda. It is really Kadikeny (the ancient Calcedon) and when it became fashionable, years ago, to live in Moda, it was said to be *à la mode* – hence the name.

You do not make any mention of the Tricity Cooker – other than the demonstration of it to your callers last Monday week – so I assume it is going alright. If that iron gives much more trouble and the new flexible and new connector from the makers does not cure it, I think we must just use the flat iron only and heat it, when necessary, on one of the Tricity hot plates. It would be safer and possibly not more expensive than as now and it would certainly be much more reliable.

The cold weather still continues here but there are some good flowers now out including the Rose of Sharon and some honeysuckle. The wisteria is nearly over.

218

I will enclose a note for the children's special benefit.
With much love, wife mine,
from your loving husband
Burke

c/o Walter Seager & Co.
Constantinople
11-5-1912

My dearest,

I am hastening, at the first opportunity, to comply with your request in your letter received this afternoon and sent off last Tuesday.

I have the *Churchman's Almanack* with me – I thought you knew. Please read the second lesson for the evening service. At present, I find St. Paul's explanations and commentaries very illuminating and worth reading. Sometimes, he is very obscure and sometimes he makes remarks about women which seem to me to be gratuitous and out of place in the Bible. I suppose it shews he was a very human man, at the bottom.

Well, I hope very much that I shall be able to start off on the return journey to you and the bairns, this day week. In that case, I fully expect to be with you on the following Wednesday evening. I should try to catch the train which would get me home about 7.30 p.m. and this time I hope there will be no coal strike and no 10-hours' journey from Euston. I did get tired of that long long weary journey coming on top of 3-days from here to London.

I am glad to hear you have found the baby basket along with other treasures in my wooden box in the attic. Please take care of the cash box which was also in it, containing foreign coins etc.

Apart from occasional remarks about feeling tired and having sore eyes, you do not tell me how you are, dearest. I hope you are not overdoing things. Please take very great care of yourself for my sake and for the sake of the little one whom we are expecting in a few months' time.

I am keeping very well except that I have been much worried by constipation. This is not due to coffee drinking and I am eating quantities of fruit, lettuce and so on. Tonight, Bunn and I bought a bag of cherries at a shop but, apart from being quite clean, they are not yet very tasty or big. Usually, I only eat meat once a day.

I am glad to know that my pencilled note from Pitesti reached you alright. I sent you a good long letter today and also tired my hand by printing a long joint one to the children. I have ready for them a p.p.c. each to post tomorrow. I am sending one, as you wished, to Percy and am also sending one each to my mother and yours.

I shall be able to post all these tomorrow, Sunday, as we have to go to the

Bridge from here to get the boat for Moda where Bigland is living.

The rain has come tonight and at present, it is raining more heavily than I have seen it here before.

Keep your spirits up dearest I hope to start for home soon after you get this. With much love to you, dear wife, and to our bairns from
Your ever loving husband,
Burke

(The name is written here in Turkish)
BRITISH INSULATED & HELSBY CABLES Ltd.

Tchinili Rihtim Han
Galata
Constantinople
May 13th 1912

My dearest,

What do you think of our company's name in Turkish? Read from right to left.

We had quite a refreshing day, yesterday, with Bigland and in cheering up that lonely man. I fancy we did some useful work although we had to miss church for it. He met us on arrival at Kadikeny Landing stage, took us through the town part to the shore for a little while until lunch was ready at 12.45. In the afternoon, we engaged a two-pair oar rowing boat and went out on the sea for two hours and took turns in rowing. The sea was very smooth and clear. We rowed right over the wreck of a sunken grain steamer and could see it quite clearly on the bottom. The smell from the rotting grain was unpleasant and we soon withdrew. We saw much more shipping, than we knew of, waiting for the re-opening of the Dardanelles. Did I tell you that we saw the Turkish Navy last Friday when we went up the Golden Horn? It is a disgraceful collection of out-of-date and largely useless battleships. We left Bigland at 6.00 o'clock and by good luck caught a connecting boat at the Bridge and were home before 7.30. After supper, we had a little music and I sang 'Margaretta' and 'Ora Pro Nobis'. The collection of music at the *Maison* Binns is very limited.

I have a letter from Greenwood saying that he and his wife arrive here at 7.47 a.m. tomorrow so I must be up about 6.00 a.m. in order to meet them. As things go here, I expect I shall do no real work tomorrow until the afternoon.

Today, there is a letter from Mr Watson to Bigland saying he has not left London and is not leaving today so it seems that I shall not see him here at all. I am sorry about this. It may mean that I shall see him in London.

Bunn has not been at all well today but after dosing him with brandy, an hour's sleep and then tea, he seems nearly alright again. I fancy it was acute indigestion. We had to postpone one visit to San Stafano.

I am glad to hear that Edith's teeth questions are going on alright. I hope the attention her and Tom's teeth get, now, will save them trouble in the future.

Yes – Bunn and I are staying at Mrs Binns' and when Mr & Mrs Greenwood arrive tomorrow, the house will be very full until my departure. It is a considerable fag to have such a long way to go, twice a day, but the ride along the Bosphorus is very refreshing and sometimes it is a very cold ride even when the sun is shining.

I enclose a letter from Ida[21] which I have answered affirmatively. I expect she will want us to put her up for one night and to see her off by the boat – if she goes via Liverpool. I have told her to write to me at home. Please find out from Mr Kitchen what my Deposit and Current A/cs stand at.

With much love to you all
from your loving husband
Burke

c/o Walter Seager & Co.
Constantinople
16-5-1912

My dearest,

Before post time today, I only had bare time in which to send to you and the children p.p.cs. Yesterday, we had a very full day and in the evening, I went to dinner with Mr & Mrs Martin near here. He is our engineer at our agency here. He is a nice young fellow and has a very sensible capable wife. They expect their first baby about 2 months hence. They gave me a well-cooked simple 3 course meal – the pudding was their last Christmas pudding. Afterwards, we sat in the dark on a rough terrace in their garden on the hillside. The atmosphere was too hazy and full of smoke for us to see far or clearly. We heard a nightingale very occasionally but I am not more impressed on further acquaintance. We saw two *glow worms* and actually caught one of them. It looks like a centipede about half-an-inch long. I came back about 10.15 and they brought me to shew the way. It is a very indirect route from their house and, in the daylight, it is perilous enough and, in the dark, it is absolutely dangerous for a stranger. Martin struck a series of matches to shew me the way. I was really too sleepy last night to enter at all thoroughly into conversation. The weather has suddenly turned *HOT* with a south wind. In 2 days, I have been able to change from my thickest things into my thinnest.

I am sick at heart at not being able to leave on Saturday as I had expected and so get home to you when I had led you to expect me. We had a long interview with the first lawyer today and afterwards, over lunch, with the local

---

[21] Ida Welbourn, a half-sister who emigrated to Canada, and later became a much-loved matron of a hospital in California.

contractor. If everything now goes well, I think I can get away on Tuesday.

Today is a genuine Turkish holiday and the natives are at play. Mr Robert Rowell asked me to go on the 2.45 boat and join his wife and some friends for a climb up the hillside at Candilli which is opposite to Bebek on the other side of the Bosphorus. Mrs Rowell thoughtfully brought afternoon tea for the 3 businessmen who had come straight from the city. She had it in a Thermos flask. It was quite hot and most acceptable. We had about 2½ hours there, examined the observatory, saw some Turkish soldiers at firing practice and saw quantities of wild flowers such as daisies, vetches, wild sweet peas, white and red horse chestnuts, laburnums, wild thyme and sage, may blossom etc. Bigland was here when I got back. He had called for tea on his way to Mr Seagers'. They are rehearsing their play again tonight. Mrs Robert Rowell was very interested in the story of the Rogation Days originating here owing to an earthquake. She could not recollect hearing of any special earthquake at that early date.

It *would* be most useful to me, now, if I could speak French at all fluently. Most of these people here speak it and 3 other languages besides. I hope Tom and Edith will realize the need for languages before they get too old to acquire them easily. Sometimes, I can understand nearly all the French I hear and at other times it does not sink in at all. Today is one of the *dies non*.

I am very pleased to hear that you are sleeping better and are now feeling so much better.

With much love to you all

from your loving husband Burke

16-5-1912

I am sending this now as I shall not	Mrs Welbourn
have time to write a letter before post time.	Rainhill, Lancashire
It is now HOT here and my thin clothes are	England

at last usable. I am going down the
Bosphorus now with an Englishman. This is a
Turkish general holiday but it does not seem to
affect the English Community very much except
that some are taking a short half holiday.
Love from Burke

c/o Walter Seager & Co.
Constantinople
19-5-1912

My dear wife

Thank you for your letter. I wired to you yesterday (through Mr Seager) that

I fully expect to leave on Tuesday. Today I have sent to you from Bebek via the Turkish P.O. a p.p.c. to say I expect to reach London next Friday evening but that I am not sure when I can get home i.e. whether it will be Friday night or Saturday. I think it advisable to send you similar news via the British P.O. to make sure of your getting the news correctly. This letter cannot however leave until tomorrow when I go to town. I am very glad to be in sight of leaving here – I have booked my berth on the train!

Last evening, we *had* to go for the evening to Mrs Walter Binns – it was another peep behind the scenes of Cranford! If I had to live in this country permanently, I do not think I should want to settle in Bebek.

This morning, we are going to church and this afternoon, we shall probably go for a walk with Mr Martin and then go home with him for afternoon tea. His home has a very nice atmosphere.

Yesterday, I was in Pera with Bigland and when passing the Club, he took me in and gave me tea.

I think my most anxious work is nearly over and that Tuesday will see the end of it, here, for some time to come. I am rather anxious about the first interview with Mr Sinclair on my return when I tell him of all the arrangements which I have made while here.

The heat here has moderated and now we have a fresh breeze to temper the sun.

Thank you also for your letter of the 14th. I hardly expect to hear again from you before I leave.

The Dardanelles was actually opened yesterday, I believe, and the first ships left here yesterday morning and were to go through the Straits, this morning.

The shipping was a great sight yesterday. All ships (60) under orders to go were flying the Blue Peter at the main and had their other code flags out to denote their order of sailing.

Must close this now and go to church. Bell just stopped.

Much love to you all from
your loving husband
Burke

19-5-1912 Sunday
I am writing this through the Turkish   Mrs Welbourn
P.O. at Bebek to let you know I expect   Rainhill
to reach London next Friday evening but   Lancashire
I am not sure that I shall be able to get   England
home until Saturday. I will also write
through the British P.O. tomorrow to
make sure of your knowing my movements.

223

Weather has gone very breezy now – it is
very changeable.
Love from
B.W.

(Editor's note: The following letters are from the following year.)

en route London
June 4-1913

My dearest

I am sorry that Fred took the parting so much to heart today that the elders could not properly say goodbye – or do you think he was frightened only?

I have arranged my notes and lantern slides and feel ready for the fray tomorrow![22] I am not worrying about the encounter but I shall be glad when it is over, all the same.

There is a very talkative man in the carriage and it is difficult to go on writing when he keeps chipping in. Did I tell you what a very kind and appreciative letter I had today from Mr Larke of Rugby about my paper? He cannot come to it himself but is sending his chief assistant.

I think I told you that I am meeting Mr Hunter[23] on business tonight and have invited him to dinner with me at the Club. Tomorrow evening, I dine with the Institution of Mining Engineers at their Annual Dinner at the Waldorf Hotel at 7.30. While in London, I have a good deal to do – I want to see Aunt Emily and Mrs Thomas and also do various B.I. work including seeing Messrs. Nisbett[24] & Sinclair. I cannot see any idle time before departing on Saturday. By the way, I leave Charing Cross at 9.00 a.m. and travel via Calais, Paris, Vienna and Budapest to Sofia. Mr Green is to accompany me as far as Vienna and share my compartment and then he is to join me in Constantinople. He has not been abroad before and I shall have the amusement, I expect, of putting another *very* provincial through his first Continental experiences. I hope he wont commit similar *faux pas* to the other man!

I expect the dress rehearsal is in full swing – if it is fine. Here (Stafford) the roofs are quite wet. I hope all will go quite well tomorrow and that Edith and

---

[22] Welbourn, B., 'Insulated and Bare Copper and Aluminium Cables for the Transmission of Electrical Energy, with special Reference to Mining Work,' *Trans. Inst. Mining Engineers* Vol. XLV Part 5 (5 June 1913): 658–780.

[23] P.V. Hunter became Chief Engineer of BI's great rivals, The Callender Cable Co. Ltd.

[24] Mr G.H. Nisbett was Engineering Director of BI.

Tom will enjoy themselves. Who looks after Fred for the afternoon?

I hope you will find money matters alright. I paid in £37 to your a/c besides what I gave you. If you need more, I am sure Mr Kitchen[25] will let you have it. I have arranged with the B.I. to pay my next salary cheque straight into my account at the Bank. I meant to leave a rent cheque ready for Miss Roby – this must now await my return. You might see her sometime and tell her in advance that it may be 10 days or so late – it is due on July 1st.

I cannot think of anything else which I have overlooked in the scurry of the past week. I am starting with new shaving soap and toothbrush so please don't send these articles from the bathroom.

I am not looking forward to this trip (strictly *entre nous*) but I must put my back into the Bulgarian business to support Mr Sinclair Kerfoot hinted today that there is a good deal involved in this journey, for me! It is a bit ambiguous but we shall see.

With much love to you and the bairns from your loving husband
Burke

You keep the flag flying at your end while I do the same at mine!

I am staying here

Constitutional Club
Northumberland Ave, W.C.
London 5 6/13

My dearest,

I hope the bairns have had a successful afternoon and fine weather for the Fête and that all went well. It has been fine and quite warm here.

My paper did not get a fair chance – only 40 minutes in all – as so many people wanted to talk about laying coal dust by mixing stone dust with it. It will perhaps come on again at Manchester in the Autumn.

Thank you for your note – I am very pushed tonight, too.

With much love to you all from
Burke

Constitutional Club
Northumberland Avenue, W.C
London 6 6/1913

My dearest,

Thank you very much for your brief note which I have just received on coming in after having supper with Aunt Emily. She seems quite bright and

---

[25] Their new bank manager.

comparatively well. Doris[26] sang some songs for us in French and she wants to know the exact name, price (if possible) and the publisher of the book of Elizabethan Love Songs which I have.

She also wants to know where this quotation comes from:- 'Storied windows, richly dight, casting a dim religious light.'[27]

Can you tell her? A p.c. will do, in a few days. Elsie seems to have given a glowing account of Fred and of Yvonne[28] and of the Derby baby. Whelan brought me a set of proofs of the snapshots and will also let you have some, next week. The proofs are poor but those of Fred came out best. Frau will like to have this odd one of herself. The one of her with Fred (both all smiles) is better still.

Hugh[29] *is* marrying the H-less girl and Elsie departs next week but I have no other particulars.

I had tea with Mrs Thomas who looks much better but is evidently quite blind now. Joyce and Bea came in after a motor ride to see some of the racing at Epsom. Did you read of the sensational Derby and the suffragettes outrage? It will be surprising if she does not die.

Aunt Emily asked me to give you her love which I now do. I enclose two other things which I think you may like to keep. I have already returned a Harrod bill which I think you sent me by mistake. Have you yet asked Liberty & Co. to refund your 5/-?

It has gone wet and cold here too.

Much love from Burke

Constitutional Club
Northumberland Avenue,W.C.
June 6th 1913

My Dearest

Thank you for your letter and enclosures. I am sorry the children had such a disappointment yesterday through the rain – I suppose the powers that be will try to arrange something else so that the children will still have an opportunity of giving their complete performance.

The pairing off of the young people is very amusing and shews that Nature does not regard single blessedness as the normal state of things!

I hope the taxi arrangements worked out alright yesterday?

The dinner last night went off alright but there was nothing exciting or very amusing. There were various eminent people there including the Master Cutler

---

[26] His cousin Doris Gregory, later Lady Jephcot, wife of Sir Harry Jephcot, Chairman of Glaxo.

[27] Milton: *Il Pensoroso*

[28] Another Gregory cousin.

[29] Another Gregory cousin.

(J. R. Hoyle) who spoke. Mr John Robinson of Haydock, who is closely associated with Mr Part[30] , was at my paper and also at the dinner. Mr Robert Nelson was also there.

An old assistant – Charles Stewart – was at the dinner and came here with me for 20 minutes while waiting for his train, afterwards.

My address for some days will be at Hotel Bulgaria, Sofia and afterwards
c/o Walter Seager & Co.
Tchinili Rihtim Han
Galata Constantinople
Please don't forgot that 2½ d. stamp is necessary on a letter.
Please keep these enclosures until my return.
I will try to send you a line before leaving.
With much love to you all
from Burke

I was quite jealous that you all should have the enjoyment of Fred and it should be denied to me.

> Constitutional Club
> Northumberland Avenue, W.C.
> 7 /6/13

Dearest,

Just a line before leaving Charing X to thank you for your letter and to say *au revoir*.

Will you please tear out each day the page in the *Telegraph*[31] which deals with the Balkans–Turkey business and enclose it with your letter? Usually it is almost impossible to get accurate information on the spot.

Much love,
Burke

CARTE POSTALE

Calais 7/6/13	
Just reached here after a not altogether	Mrs B Welbourn
satisfactory crossing! Weather cold –	Rainhill
high wind. Soon leave for Paris	Lancashire
Love Burke	Angleterre

---

[30] A colliery director who lived in Rainhill.

[31] During and after World War One they took *The Times* and *The Liverpool Post*.

CARTE POSTALE

Paris 7/6/13

We find it warmer here than in London
but it is quite cloudy. We had such a hunt
but finally found some drinkable tea at an
exorbitant price. It was very acceptable.
We are just leaving the Gare de l'Est on
our long journey. Much love, Burke

Mrs B. Welbourn
Rainhill
Lancashire,
Angleterre

en route Munich
Sunday 8-6-1913

My dearest,

Here we are in sunshine and in sight of the snowclad Alps of the Austrian
Tyrol. We are also an hour in advance of English time – it is M.E.T. (mid-
European Time). The Germans seem to be making the most of their fine
Sunday and are out holidaying in their Sunday best.

We left Paris at 7.13 last evening after spending 2 hours in the City. I took
Mr Green for a walk past the Opera House to the Tuileries Gardens and then
along the Seine embankment. He seemed to enjoy his first peep at Paris. The
Tuileries Gardens are not looking at their best yet nor did I see any sparrows!
Paris seemed *full* of people. The pavements were very crowded.

Neither of us slept well and I am sick of the travelling already. Green leaves
me at Vienna late this afternoon and I continue alone to Sofia where I am due
about noon tomorrow. He goes on tomorrow to Constantinople via Bucharest
and Constanza.

I am very amused with Toms early and poetical attentions to Elizabeth[32]! He
seems very constant in that quarter.

I will let you know as soon as I can about my movements – probably by
telegraph occasionally. I must close this now as I think we are just entering
Munich where I want to post this.

Much love to you all
from
Burke
Pl. enter this bill for me.

Vienna
8-6-1913
Sunday evening

My dearest,

Mr Green has gone – he stays here for a day and then goes on to C. via
Bucharest and Constanza. I go on and hope to be in Sofia by noon tomorrow.

---

[32] Elizabeth Brewis, a girl of his own age.

We have had an uneventful day. Neither of us slept well and so I propose to avoid coffee tonight. It made me feel quite cheap this morning and I did not feel right until after the noon meal and a sleep. I feel alright now and am going to have dinner in about ¾ hour.

The weather is hot and bright here but not unbearably so. I have been very surprised at two things today – the desertion of the country and absence of motor cars. We have only seen one car and that was an old one standing at the roadside. Until we got to the suburbs of Vienna we saw very few people out of doors except 3 or 4 lots at work in the fields. Hay making seems to be general in Germany and Austria and other crops look well advanced and healthy. There seems to be however exceedingly little fruit on the wayside trees. You remember how laden the trees were at Sobernheim[33]?

We have seen a few football games in progress; it looks so HOT in this weather.

I have been longing today to be at home with you all to enjoy our comparatively quiet and cool Sunday – this is such a rummy way of spending the day.

Last night, I got to S. John III.21 and propose to go on from there tonight.

I understand that the railway is *not* open from Adrianople to Constantinople so I may have some weary journeying to do to get through yet.

I hope to post this in Buda Pest tonight.

With very much love to you all including Fred from

your loving husband

Burke

en route Sofia

Monday June 9th 1913

My dearest,

I hope you have had the p.cards from Calais and Paris and Salzburg and will also get the 2 letters posted *en route* – one from Ersekujvar (instead of Buda Pest). I cannot remember where the other was posted – I gave it to the dining car attendant.

I had a mild surprise in Vienna – Mr Caspar joined me there and is travelling with me. I expected to find him in Sofia. He also has a secretary named Craddock going out with him for the new trading Co.

Today we are having a thin time. The weather is hot and travelling is therefore not comfortable. In addition, owing to the Balkan troubles, the railway arrangements are all upset and instead of getting to Sofia before noon *today* we are not likely to get there until *tomorrow* morning. The prospect of another night in the train is not cheerful.

---

[33] In the Pfalz, where they had holidayed together in August 1909.

I begin to understand the meaning of the phrase a nation under arms. We pass trains full of troops and, at most stations, we see troops bivouacked with piled arms. Most of them are not in uniform. The railway line is guarded at all important points such as bridges and tunnels. Men on the train are excitedly discussing the situation. We spoke to one Bulgarian – evidently well informed. He says it is all a game of bluff – very much what we were told in England.

The fields do not seem neglected in this country, i.e. Servia. Hay harvest is in full swing – the cereal crops look good – there are people at work in the fields, chiefly women, girls and boys.

I am told that the Servian and Bulgarian armies are encamped on opposite sides of the frontier but we are unlikely to see all the tents etc owing to darkness. It is much to be hoped that this fair country is not to be devastated with war although a good many people seem to think it might be best to settle now and perhaps for all time the mastery of the Balkans. If anything should happen, you need not be uneasy about me. There are two railways out of Sofia to ports on the Black Sea and also, on one of them, one can get to Bucharest and so to C. via Constanza.

I took care to get a passport from Sir Edward Grey[34] for Travelling in Europe before I left. I intend to send you a telegram from Sofia on arrival but you may not get it if the censor is active or if the lines are full with diplomatic and press messages.

I'm slowly melting and would give something for a warm bath as I have not had one since Saturday morning. Please tell the children that I have seen numbers of puppies and one beautiful young goat but not a single cat. I hope to get this posted at NISH, this evening.

With much love to you all from

Your loving husband

Burke XXXX – two for you and one for each of the bairns.

Grand Hotel Bulgarie Sofia
10 Juin 1913

Dearest,

I am beginning this note immediately after late breakfast. We got here about 3.45 a.m. (15½ hours late) and went straight to bed and I have had about 4 hours of sound sleep. Since then I have had a grand *bain* with all the ceremony that these foreigners attach to such an event and I feel much cleaner. This hotel is opposite to the Royal Palace but I have not seen much of it yet because of the big acacia trees. King Ferdinand appears to be in residence as the Royal Standard is flying at the top of the mast. There seem to be big public gardens

---

[34] The Foreign Secretary.

opposite, also.

I have not been out yet and cannot say whether the Hotel looks as important as it does on the picture above – possibly it does, judging by the price of this room (18 francs).

I sent you a telegram at 10.20 a.m. (8.20 Rainhill time) – Arrived – so that you might know I am here and I hope it will reach you today. My letter from Servia (to be posted at Nish) was not sent. W. Caspar advised that it was almost useless to post it because of the censor. He thought you would probably not get it so we are to see what can be done here about getting the Bulgarian censor to frank it through. We found a lot of soldiers at Sofia station on arrival – some sleeping on the platform and some walking about. Up here, I have seen no warlike signs yet except that a British military attache is staying here. We saw no big guns being moved on the railway, anywhere. Our train was searched last night by the military near the frontier presumably to see if any Servians were trying to flee their country. My passport seems to be quite in order and has been returned to me today, already. My trunk is not here yet although the hotel man came to see me about it over 2 hours ago. I must go and root out Caspar now. The English letters are not yet in – I expect they are being censored also.

Much love from
Burke

POST OFFICE TELEGRAPHS

                                        Rainhill
                                        JU 10
                                        13
Sofia 10th   Handed in at 11 a.m.   Received here at 4.55
            To: Welbourn   Rainhill   England
                  Arrived

                                    Grand Hotel Bulgarie Sofia
                                    11 Juin 1913
My dearest

Thank you very much for your kindly thought in sending a letter by the same train to greet me on arrival. For outward letters, there are censor difficulties at present and the result was that my letters of Monday and yesterday would only leave here today while this can only leave tomorrow morning. I am afraid that I can only write generalities because of his mightiness, the censor!

I meant to tell you before, chiefly for the children's benefit, that I saw an aeroplane flying on the outskirts of Vienna on Sunday evening. Tom will be interested to know that it was a monoplane – and it is the first one which I have seen. The others have been biplanes. Then, in that wonderful gorge through which the railway passes in the Balkans, near Nish, and of which I told you last year, we saw a living monoplane – a big eagle on the wing. It looked a magnificent bird and it appeared to be swooping towards some objective – not aimlessly flying.

We did some skirmishing yesterday and today the serious work begins (at least I think so). I have yet to discover what points of difference there are here between the Turks and Russians and these people in business methods. I am told that they compare very favourably – we shall see.

The hotel seems very full of people and the prices are war prices. Staying here are the British Military attache Lt. Col. Lyon and also the German military attache and his wife. I saw them dining together in the garden last night. The Belgian Minister or Consul (I forget which) is here and he was lunching yesterday with a Turkish cavalry general who lives here and who was made a prisoner at Adrianople. He is on parole and has one Turkish and one Bulgarian soldier to attend him, presumably as personal servants.

The regime in the City is severe – all theatres and cinema shows are closed and all cafés have to close at 10.00 p.m. instead of about 2.00 a.m. as usual. I am impressed with this City – there are big straight streets – well paved. The principal buildings are quite modern and a good many more big blocks are being built. I am told that the city proper has been built in about 20 years. I have only seen electric light – there appears to be no gas. The electric tramway work seems to have been done well – the rails are British and the points and crossing come from Hadfields. There is also a telephone system on which the open wire work looks quite good. On looking into the telephone directory, there are, so far as I can understand it, about 1200 subscribers already.

The chief item of news here yesterday was that the Czar of Russia had telegraphed to King Ferdinand and King Peter saying that he would arbitrate on the Bulgarian–Servian dispute (over conquered territory) provided that they would forthwith demobilize their armies. I expect you know more about it from the *Daily Telegraph* than we do, here.

I am pleasantly surprised to find that there is no overwhelming heat here yet – there is, at times, quite a nice breeze. The city is on a plateau and one side, quite close, there are mountains from which all the snow has not yet disappeared.

How many new words (!) has Fred used during the past week? and has he yet forgotten me altogether?

With much love to you all
from Burke

Grand Hotel Bulgarie Sofia
11 Juin 1913

Dearest,

I expect to leave here for VARNA next Monday June 16th and my address there will be c/o Hofmann & Co Shipping Agents. I expect to go to Constantinople from there and I do not think it will be of any use to write to me again except c/o Walter Seager & Co at Constantinople until I give you an address. I think if you post again about June 18th it will be quite soon enough. I intend to telegraph to Prescot and ask them also to let you know.

In haste.

Burke

Grand Hotel Bulgarie Sofia
Room No. 2
12 Juin 1913

My dearest,

There was no letter from you yesterday and I put this down to Sunday postal arrangements in England. I am hoping there will be one or two letters from you today whenever the post comes in.

We are not excitingly busy – the day does not seem to begin until about 10.30 a.m. and then about 12.45 comes the interval for *déjeuner* until about 2.30. The evening meal is too late for my liking. Last night we went with two doctors to a Bulgarian restaurant about 8.30 but the placc was closed at 9.00 p.m. in accordance with the police regulations so we did not get much of a meal. I hear that the chief reason for all this early closing is that experience of all wars has shown that the soldiery gets its passions aroused during war and so it is necessary afterwards for a time to remove temptations and let them live a very quiet life. We saw General Ivanoff quietly at dinner in the restaurant with one or two other officers. Such a democratic thing would scarcely be possible in London or America. Such a hero would have been annoyed by a mob applauding or staring him out. He looks a very unaffected elderly man with iron-grey goatee beard and a moustache. Caspar says that he has seen Ministers dining with the people just in the same way and no one seems to take any notice.

It is probable that, when we leave here next Monday, we shall do so by motor car and have a 400 odd kilometre drive to the coast. It is said to be a beautiful ride via Philippopolis and Stara-Zagoria and for part of the way the road goes through the Bulgarian rose fields where oil of roses are made. The ride will take two days and I expect it will be a very tiring and dusty one.

One of the doctors referred to is Dr Augeloff – head of the Bacteriological Laboratory here and he is to show it to us today. He remembers, slightly, Dr. Roth.[35]

---

[35] Uncle or father of Fräulein B.E. Roth, their governess.

Roses seem to grow here to perfection in the open – I have not seen many gardens yet but those I have seen have had beautiful roses. There are a few beautiful trees in the garden of Dr Daneff the new prime minister.

I fancy there was rain last night. This morning, the sky is quite overcast. If fine this morning, I am invited to play tennis at the Club here – there seems to be some keen players. I shall welcome the exercise which I am needing but I do not know whether I shall be able to give any grand exhibition of English tennis.

There is very little news here of importance in regard to foreign affairs – I expect we shall have to await the English newspapers and get news at least three days late.

May I give you a word of advice about the Hoylake preparations? Don't leave all your packing to the last moment! If you are sending some trunks in advance, send them about 5 days early if possible. I think they will go via Chester. It might be well to put a number on each label and let Mrs Jones know which number is to go in which room – it may save a lot of transferring on your arrival. I hope all things are going straight? Is your mother still with you and have Mary and Norman returned from Lyme Regis and settled down to a regular life now?

Please give my love to the bairns and say I hope they will get the p.p.cs. which I sent yesterday – I hope you have had from Mr Nelson a set of prints from the snapshots which I took?

With much love from
Burke

Grand Hotel Bulgarie Sofia
13 Juin 1913

My dearest

Thank you very much for your letters. A p.c. and 2 letters came yesterday and one letter today enclosing the D.T. cutting.

Things are beginning to move here but owing to our having to wait for a man from Newcastle who is due next Monday night we cannot leave here until Tuesday. Yesterday before *déjeuner* we went to look over the Bacteriological Institute and saw microbes under the microscope etc. and saw how the cultures are made etc. It was all most interesting. In the afternoon, we made an expedition by motor car to see the hydro-electric works in the mountains where current is generated for power and lighting in Sofia. The mountain scenery is very beautiful. We passed the remains of an old mountain fortress – *circa* A.D. 800. There is very little of it left. The electricity works were very interesting and instructive.

On our return about 6.30, we went to the Baths and had a short Turkish bath and a swim – the new baths are quite elaborate and extensive. This morning, we have spent in interviewing people and we have the same programme for this afternoon. The weather is cooler after rain in the night. The news has reached here of the murder of Mahmoud Sherkel Pasha in Constantinople. I have been expecting it for some time. The murder of Nazim Pasha some months ago was sure to be revenged. Mahmoud was pointed out to me last year – he was a fine looking man of much bigger stature than most Turks and he had a good military bearing and looked self-controlled.

I am sorry to hear of Percy's failure – I hope he will not develop into a hanger-on at Claygate[36] now that Mary has gone.

I suppose you are allowing Tom and Edith to act next Monday? Please give them my best wishes for a happy afternoon. The Certe. from the Urban Electric Co. should be carefully kept for me. Your surmise is correct – about 4 years hence, I hope to convert the Certe. into cash. I will look into that 13/10 on my return – I do not know what it is. If you get your bank books made up to date, you will probably find it has come alright.

Thank you for giving me the gist of the special M.U. address – I must talk to W.G.S.[37] about what is wrong with Christianity. There is surely something wrong when such *hatred* can exist between Bulgarians and Servians who profess to be Christian nations. I saw the Servian Minister to Sofia last night – in repose, his face has a very worried look. He must be having an intensely anxious time.

Fred and the chicken bone must have been very amusing – has he any more teeth yet?

Much love to you all
from your loving husband
Burke

Grand Hotel Bulgarie Sofia
14 Juin 1913

My dearest,

Yesterday, after working all day (as work goes here), an engineer, whose name I do not know came and fetched me to play tennis at the Club and we had some good hard doubles from 6.00 to 8.00 p.m. I was very pleased to find that I could hold my own with these men. There was only one set in which a lady played – she could speak some English and she stays sometimes in England at Windermere, Buckingham and London. She plays a fair game. Some of the tennis which I watched is of the amateurish order. It is funny to hear all the

---

[36] Where his wife's mother, Mrs Appleyard, lived.

[37] The Revd W.G. Swainson, who had read mathematics in Cambridge, was the new vicar of Rainhill. He was Fred's godfather.

scoring etc called out in English – vantage out, deuce etc etc. It makes it quite easy to follow the game without knowing Bulgarian. As a matter of fact most of these people speak also both French and German. I am pleased to find that I understand a lot more of the French which I hear and I can sometimes make myself understood – which is a great advance for me. A literary man, who spoke some English, was introduced to me. He knows Shakespeare, Scott, Dickens etc and has translated one or two plays into Bulgarian – particularly Arnold Galsworthys *Strife*. I gave him the *Grey Lady* to read. While we were playing tennis, two military aeroplanes circled around the City for fully an hour – one biplane, one monoplane. The latter came right overhead once and fairly low down. The aviators were splendid and the aeroplanes were very steady. I have been asked to play again tonight and intend to go as I was needing hard exercise.

Mr Caspar and I had supper last night with an Armenian and his wife whose house is in Hesketh Park, Southport. The name is something like this:- Kouyoundjian. They have two boys at Mr Harold Taylor's Preparatory School at Freshfield and besides they have two boys and a girl. He is staying here on business. He and his brothers have big Stores here and elsewhere in Bulgaria and appears to be very prosperous but unpretentious.

The weather is cool this morning and the sky overcast but I expect it will clear up again as it did yesterday. I am expecting the mail soon and hope there will arrive a letter from you. I hope the Weds *Times* will also come and have in the Eng. Supplement a notice of my Al-Copper Paper.

I forgot to tell you about the beautiful rose garden which I saw in the public park which adjoins the Tennis ground. The roses looked beautiful. By the way, the tennis courts are not of grass but of very fine gravel rolled hard and they are very fast and true and the balls bounce high. It is somewhat trying for the feet. I wish you could be here to play on them too and I fancy you would appreciate all the sunshine more than I do. The children would soon get brown here – I think I am browner already.

With much love to you and the bairns from

Your loving husband

Burke

Grand Hotel Bulgarie Sofia
Sunday
15 Juin 1913

My dearest,

I have sent you a telegram this morning asking you to write to me at VARNA Post Office. We do not leave here until Tuesday and I expect we shall reach Varna Friday or Saturday so there will be ample time for a letter to reach me there. I will try to arrange also for my letters to be forwarded to Constantinople if they arrive after I have left. I had a second motive in telegraphing. We had a considerable earthquake here about 11.40 a.m. yesterday and there are reports of considerable damage at Tiruovo and other places in Bulgaria. I thought you would understand from my wire that I am alright. When the shock came, I was reading *The Times* in my bedroom while waiting for Mr Caspar. I soon tumbled to what was happening. The whole building swayed about for some seconds – people rushed out into the open air – *tout le monde* was there in the street. Tales soon got round – one said that a man had died of fright in a Bank – another that the tower of the Turkish mosque had fallen. In the evening came stories of the collapse of a big school at Tiruovo and the killing of hundreds of children and also of the sinking of a whole village with the appearance of hot springs. *The Times* correspondent lives here and naturally he was quickly out for copy. I find that the Eng. Supplement of *The Times* of last Wednesday has an abstract of my paper and also a favourable leaderette on it.

Yesterday afternoon we had a long expedition by motor car over very rough roads to the State coal mine at Peruik. It was a very jolty business and Mr Caspar, who weighs nearly 19 stones, was considerably upset by it. The coal at the mine is near the surface – the seams are horizontal and there is no gas so that the miners work with naked lights. These are very different to the usual conditions in a coal mine in England, France, Germany or America. The ride was through some interesting country and good air. We saw two trains of troops on the railway and we also passed on the road two transport trains – one drawn by water buffalo and one by wiry little horses. I am told that the army has 60,000 pairs of these buffalo for transport purposes. On the outskirts of the City, we saw the camping ground of some troops. The men look very fine muscular specimens. On the way home, we saw three unarmed Servian soldiers in uniform marching between armed Bulgarian soldiers – we heard that they were probably deserters.

I forgot to tell you of the heavy rain which followed the earthquake for an hour or so. I remember reading somewhere that this is the usual accompaniment. The weather was much cooler after the rain and we had quite a cool night – I feel much fresher after a good nights sleep in the cool air with my window wide open.

I made enquiry about an English minister and find that he is away in Philippopolis so I suppose there will be no service here today. It is very difficult to get about except by motor car when all ordinary train services are suspended.

There was no letter from you yesterday so I hope two will arrive together today. As I write this, it will be about 8.20 a.m. with you and I can picture master Fred in his bath and the other bairns in the garden. So far as I can see

237

my plans for reaching home not later than mid-July are working out alright as there seems a possibility of the re-opening of the railway from Constantinople next week.

With much love to you all, from
Burke

POST OFFICE TELEGRAPHS

Liverpool
15JU
13

Sofia 9.30   Received here at 10/41

Welbourn   Rainhill   England
Write   Varna   Post   Office   Burke

I hope we leave here
tomorrow   Grand Hotel Bulgarie Sofia
16 Juin 1913

My dearest,

I think something has gone wrong with the postal arrangements as your letter of June 10 only arrived yesterday and on Sat there was no letter at all. This morning is very beautiful and the day is also a holiday corresponding to our Whit-Monday. You remember there is 13 days difference between our reckoning of time and in the Near East? Today is June 3rd here. I am invited to play Tennis at the Club all the morning and I am to be there about 10.15. Some of these men play just about my strength[38] so that it makes good games.

I went to see the Ethnographical Museum as arranged. It is very interesting – there are a few rooms filled with cases containing wax figures on which are displayed the country costumes of the Bulgars and each case represents a district e.g. Macedonia. Another room is devoted to worked embroideries but these failed to attract or interest me – they seemed far below the Turkish standard for such things. The Curator speaks some English and he told me that probably The Studio will bring out an illustrated article on these embroideries. Then there are set scenes shewing the people at work at home industries such as spinning and weaving. The wooden implements are in some cases arranged so that they are worked by water. I saw also a machine invented by a Bulgarian many years ago for making braid – we still use largely, at Prescot and Helsby, machines of the same type.

There is a small collection of guns and pistols – some of them quite

---

[38] Welbourn was a steady player, but not very good by his childrens' standards!

ingenious – and there is wooden cannon which broke the first time it was used. There are also rugs, waist buckles, some rugs and carpets and so on. They have very few English visitors and I was requested to sign the Visitors Book which contains the name of various eminent people from the King and Queen downwards! By the way, there are two Princes (Radziwill) staying here and I fancy they are attached to the Bulgarian army. Does Fräulein know any thing of them?

The Curator is very interested in the Shakespeare–Bacon controversy and intends to write a book on it for 1916 – the tercentenary of W. S.'s death. Will you please ask Mr Swainson the name of the book which he read on the subject (author and publisher also if possible) and let me know?

Will you please explain to Miss Roby about my absence and say that the rent will be about a fortnight late in July?

I hope the children's performance at Windle St. today will be a success – I can imagine how excited they are about it – please tell them I thought about them. Toms German letter has not yet arrived and I suppose the progress is slow?

What a pity about St Helens Town Hall – it will make Mr Andrew[39] and the Borough Engineer very busy. I suppose they cannot have all straight again before the Kings visit?

With much love to you all from

Burke

Grand Hotel Bulgarie Sofia
17 Juin 1913

My dearest,

Thank you very much for your letters of June 11 and 12 which came together yesterday. I can quite imagine Fred on his best behaviour for Mrs & Miss Swainson. No doubt all the proceedings would be faithfully reported to his godfather.

Now I really am in hope that we shall get away late this afternoon either by motor car or by train. Major Hopkins arrived from England about 5.00 a.m. and I have not yet seen him. Mr Caspar is tired out – he went to the station at 2.00 a.m. to meet the train which did not however arrive until about 5.00 a.m.

Yesterday morning, being a holiday, I played tennis for nearly two hours – in the afternoon we also started to play about 4.15 but after 10 minutes or so, there was thunder followed by heavy rain and heavy hail which quite put an end to play for the day. These rolled sand courts are like mud after rain. During the storm, various cannon or bombs were let off *contre la grille* as it was

---

[39] Mr Andrew was Town Clerk of St Helens for many years.

explained to me. I wish Edith and Tom could realize how very exceeding useful a knowledge of foreign languages is. My small knowledge of French helps me a good deal. In the evening we had to dinner the president (Captain) of the Tennis Club. He is an engineer in the Government Service and has been in England for a short time but speaks no English. His French is good and fluent. He left quite early – about 9.45 – so I was able to come upstairs in good time to re-read your and Tom's letters and to read the D.T. extracts which you enclosed. Don't get worried by all the Balkan news which you read. I think things have been very critical between this country and Servia while I have been here but apparently the Czar of Russia has intervened to effect a settlement. I have had a good night's sleep and feel fit this morning to re-commence my not very arduous labours:- this was not a suitable time to come here when peoples minds are occupied with military and political matters of great importance and all the ordinary railway services are upset. *But please don't let this opinion be known locally.*

I must go to the Bank and make other preparations for departure etc.

With much love to you all

from your loving husband

Burke

Grand Hotel Bulgarie Sofia
16 Juin 1913

Please tell mother not to take too
much notice of the newspapers just now

My dear Tom,

Thank you very much for your German letter which I have received this afternoon, with two letters from mother. It is nice to hear from you when I am so far from home. I have only sent you a few picture post cards as there are not many fresh ones here.

A great deal of German and French is spoken here but very little English. I am finding my small amount of French exceedingly useful and occasionally I can even follow a little of the German which is spoken.

I have been playing tennis for two hours this morning and am so tired that I must go soon and have a nap. Tomorrow, I believe we are leaving here to go to Bourgas and Varna and then I go on to Constantinople. B and V are ports on the Black Sea which I think you can find on the map south of Constanza.

With much love to Edith, Frau and you

from

Father

I hope your play at Windle St. will be a great success today.

Hotel Continental
Bourgas
Bulgaria
June 19-1913

My dearest,

Just a line to say that we have reached here this afternoon and come all the way by motor car from Sofia. I am too tired after the long journey to tell you all about it. We got up at 3.30 a.m. yesterday, left just before 6 a.m. and got to Stara-Zagora (to sleep) about 8.00 p.m. I was called at 5.15 this morning and we left just after 6.30. We got here about 4.15 p.m. We had to come by a roundabout way and I do not know the exact distance but I think it was about 300 miles. Much of the road was very bad and bumpy – through this and all the fresh air and lack of sleep you can imagine how tired I am. I am also very red through the sun. I hope to be in Constantinople in the next few days but I have a telegram here saying that Mr Gill cannot leave London for Constantinople until June 27 or 29 so that may delay me for about a week.

There is no definite news here about the Bulgarian-Servian dispute.

With much love to you all, from your loving husband

Burke

Bourgas
Hotel Continental
June 20-1913

My dearest,

I sent you a hurried note last night to announce our safe arrival here. After 10 hours in bed last night and a further sleep this afternoon I feel a good deal more rested. It was very hot here this morning but this afternoon is cooler as there is a breeze. This morning we went down to the S.S. *Birdoswald* to see the Captain and this evening he and his wife come to dinner at 8.00. I have been busy making enquiry about means of getting from here to Constantinople but so far without any definite result. I may have to wait until Tuesday night or even Wednesday for a boat and have little or nothing to do in the meantime.

This town is a new one in the making and meantime the hotel accommodation and other things leave much to be desired. We are in fact somewhat roughing it. The accommodation is an improvement however on that obtainable in Stara-Zagora.

I hope all my letters and p.p.cs. have come through safely to you as I have been sending to you regularly? Of course, I am not hearing from you as I have moved about so much. I had some doubts about even getting letters addressed to Varna as I learn that they will have to go back to Sofia, then come here and then go to Constantinople.

241

There is news here today that Bulgaria has issued a 48 hours ultimatum to Servia and Greece and Austria a 48 hour one to Servia only. Whether there is any truth in it, I cannot say. If true, it will bring matters to a head as was much needed.

With much love to you all.

from

Burke

Constantinople College
American College for Girls
Preparatory Department

I telegraphed to you on June 21st to tell you I expect to arrive in Constantinople on Wednesday, June 25th. I hope you would get it yesterday (Sunday)

S.S. Lerano
Bourgas Bulgaria

June 21-2-3- 1913

My dearest,

I am writing this in readiness to post it tomorrow at Constanza in Roumania. I have been at Bourgas since last Thursday afternoon and have sent you two pencil notes from there but it is doubtful whether you will get them because of the censor etc. I decided not to risk any more but to send you one good letter from Constanza from where there is an excellent express service to England and you should get this on Saturday at latest. I was finished here and could have left on Friday night if there had been any way out but owing to the unsettled condition of the country, the only thing to do was to get this Austrian-Lloyd steamer to Constanza and then come south again, post here, by the Roumanian Government boat to Constantinople where I am due on Wednesday about noon. I could have waited here until Wednesday and then got a boat direct to Constantinople but I really could not stand it – i.e. the roughing. I have nearly been eaten up by live stock in the bed at the hotel, the food is anything but nice and there is nothing to do in the town except go to the cinema which is quite good but in an unbearably hot tent. We stayed at the Hotel Continental and it is very primitive. The bathing here is good and I have been in the sea swimming each day except the day of arrival when I had a warm sea bath after our long motor ride. I came on board last night and I believe that Mr Caspar and Major Hopkins are leaving for Sofia again today by motor and are travelling over the famous Shipka Pass where such severe fighting took place in the Turkish-Russian War of 1877/8.

At Bourgas, there are various signs of war. There are a good many reserve soldiers wandering about with their rifles. The promenade on one side of the

242

harbour is on a small hill and it has rifle trenches dug for the troops with dug-outs for them to sleep in. There is also an Artillery Park. The streets are very badly paved but there are some good buildings in the town. The whole place reminds me of Canadian prairie towns in the making – places like Moose Jaw and Medicine Hat. The harbour is a fine one and no doubt this will be an important port, one day. There is an English steamer here from the Tyne, bringing coals from Newcastle for Mr Caspar. We met the Captain and his wife and little girl and one day I had some English afternoon tea with them. This steamer has only a few passengers – there appears to be a young Russian married couple, another young Russian man and a grey-haired American lady who is the mathematical teacher at the above school and who has given me this letter paper. She is a much travelled and most interesting middle-aged lady who reminds me, a good deal, of Miss Way – both in voice and manner. We had a long talk last night and she told me a good deal of interesting information about the last war. In her school, she has large numbers of Bulgarian and Turkish girls and she compares the Turkish ones very unfavourably with the former. What she said about the Bulgarians generally confirmed my own impression of them as a thoroughly go-ahead nation. They recognize that they are not an educated people and so they are sending their young people abroad to be educated and are providing good schools of their own throughout their country.

Now I want to tell you more about our motor ride from Sofia to Bourgas. I am very brown and my nose is so red from the exposure to sun and wind that it is skinning. The journey was frightfully tiring, physically, and I was tired out on arrival and slept like a log for the first two nights and also had an afternoon nap. I was so tired that I also fell asleep in the motor even when it jolted along over the bumpy roads. We were to have left Sofia at 4.00 a.m. sharp last Wednesday morning (June 18) but the police stopped the car when it was coming for us so we were unable to start until just before 6.00 a.m. We made very good progress to Samokov where we had a sort of breakfast. The road was a good one mostly through the mountains and the morning air was cold so we were glad to have hot drink at Samokov. We went straight on to Phillipopolis for dinner and made a stay of fully 1½ hours. I hope my p.p.c. arrived alright from there? It is a town of about 50,000 inhabitants also in the making and with a considerable remnant of Turks and Turkish houses and shops. Before we got there, we passed through some irrigated rice fields – I had not seen before any irrigation work. It looks crude and simple. From there onwards there is little to record about the roads except that they are mostly apologies. There are good patches of road but frequently they are only cart tracks across the fields – very much like the road to Talbots Farm from opposite Mr Stones house. We had various delays through punctures and the result was that we had to stay at Stara-Zagora for the night. The smell in the hotel there was unmentionable! But we managed to survive from our arrival at 8.00 p.m. to our departure at 6.30

a.m. Owing to broken bridges, we had to make a detour between Phillipopolis and Stara-Zagora via Gezaulik (?) and via the Rose Gardens of Bulgaria. We were too late to see the fields of rose trees in bloom. This is the district where Otto of Roses is made for the whole world, I believe. We met the man who is the chief exporter – he speaks some English and he told us that, this year, the cost price to him had been nearly 25 francs for 5 grammes of it so no wonder that the scent is expensive in England!

Stara-Zagora was the headquarters of the Bulgarian War Staff at the beginning of the war and it is the place where the Press correspondents had to cool their heels instead of being allowed to go and see the fighting. One man came and spoke broken English to us and said he was attached to Bennet Burleigh the War Correspondent of the *Daily Telegraph*. Another young man came who spoke excellent American English. He had only been in the town for five days – he told us he had been in America for 12 years and is the Editor of the *Springfield Digest*, perhaps to get some copy out of us. Stara means old – the next place which we passed was Nova (or new) Zagora. I cannot remember where we lunched but it was in a primitive sort of restaurant and I know we were ravenous as we had to leave without getting any breakfast (not even coffee) and it was about 10.30 before we got food.

On one part of the ride, we passed over a sort of heath and saw numbers of tortoises and weasels. I forgot to tell you of the beautiful sight at Philippopolis. In two or three places, I saw storks nests on chimney pots. The young birds seemed to be in the principal nest and then, not far off, were two other nests for the parents. It reminded me very vividly of those lantern slides which Edith has. We also saw a good many herons both walking and in flight as well as several eagles.

The crops this year are wonderful all through the country and harvesting has begun already. I did not see a single uncultivated field despite the war and the fields seemed to have been weeded properly. The field work is being done by women, girls, boys and old men and very few young men were to be seen except in uniform.

The need of gathering in the bountiful harvest makes one realize that the great need of the Balkan States now is Peace so that the men may return to their ordinary duties. The country needs much money spending in road and railway making and in buying modern agricultural implements.

I have been much struck with one result of the war and the absence of the men folk – I do not think I have seen a dozen obviously pregnant women in the country so that doubtless the birth-rate will be low this year. I wonder whether there will be a big preponderance of male children after this war as has been noticed after other wars. Mr Herbert Rawlins first pointed it out to me.

We saw thousands of Turkish prisoners in the country – there are said to be 91000 of them and they are said to be quite well fed and cared for. The

American lady says there are only a few Bulgarian prisoners in Turkey and that they are well looked after too which is a good point in favour of the Turks.

There seem to be plenty of oxen and horses left – the country and the flocks of sheep etc seem to be abundant. We also saw a good many goats.

The business on which I have been is just about as unsatisfactory as I expected and I fear Mr Sinclair has made a mistake for once – please keep this very strictly private however. I am sick of it and it makes me weary at heart to be away on such unsatisfactory work and spending time and money which will be partly wasted. I would ten thousand times rather be at home with you and the children and forego these experiences.

I hope I shall be able to send a note from Constanza tomorrow, additional to this. Please tell the children I have only sent a few p.p.cs. as there are very few in this country to send.

With much love to you all
from your loving husband
Burke

	24 Juin 1913
Hotel & Pension	c/o Walter Seager & Co.
Carol I.	Tchinili Rihtim Han
Constanza (Roumanie)	Galata, Constantinople
	Telegraphic address:-
	Jolly Constantinople

My dearest,
After a long weary weary day I have come here to write this and then have some food before going on to the ship for Constantinople. After a not specially good night, I was called about 5.45 a.m. because the port doctor had come on board and wanted to see some or all of the passengers. He gave me some kind of a sanitary passport and said I might spend the day in the town. About 6.30, I had breakfast and then commenced by exploration etc. I had to go to the police office to have my English passport inspected and entered and I have to return about 9.00 p.m. to have something more done to it and I fancy there will be something to pay this next time! I then interviewed someone, who spoke a little English, at the office of the Captain of the Port and he very kindly found me a man to fetch my luggage from the ship, get it through the custom house and store it at the booking office until tonight when I go for my ticket. I have been quite disappointed that I could not go on the steamer until so late as I have been so weary killing time after my early rising. It has reminded me of our day in Rotterdam! I went back to the Austrian steamer for 11.00 a.m. *déjeuner* and stayed on it until about 1.00 p.m. when non-passengers had to go ashore.

I spent some time walking about the town which is another town in the making and then I came here to have some tea and try to get a bath. The former was feeble and the latter was quite beyond them. Anyway, they put me into a cab and I landed at a place where I got a decent hot sea-water bath and for which I felt better as it was nearly a week since I had had a soap down and I was getting uncomfortable. Then I sat for a long time outside a big cafe drinking *café-au-lait* and reading the latest French newspapers. I was expecting to find an English paper here but again no luck. Bourgas was about the limit, for news! They have no newspapers and live on rumours, there, it seems to me.

I have been without any letter or news of you (of necessity) for over a week and I am very much hoping to find a budget awaiting me at Constantinople when I reach there tomorrow afternoon. I have posted a long letter to you as soon as ever the Post Office here opened this morning and I hope you will get it on Friday or Saturday before leaving Rainhill and get this at Hoylake on Sunday morning. I had also sent p.p.cs. to you and the children both at home and at Hoylake.

The weather was warm here for some hours today but tonight the weather is cool with a good N.W. wind and cloudy sky but the sea looks fairly smooth. The *Imperatur Trajan* is the boat tonight and it looks a good one and quite spick and span as it is painted all white.

I hope you have received my telegram of last Saturday night, alright, telling you I expected to reach Constantinople tomorrow. I felt there was quite a possibility that you would not get it. I intend to wire again tomorrow on reaching there and I hope it will not be very long before I am able to tell you when I leave for home (do not yet know whether the railway is open through Adrianople). I am much looking forward to rejoining you and the bairns. I have been thinking today of one eventful visit to Park Grange.[40]

With much love
from your husband
Burke

POST OFFICE TELEGRAPHS

Rainhill
JU25
13

Pera Handed in at 5.5 p.m.   Received here at 4.30 p.m.
TO: Welbourn Rainhill
Arrived Constantinople today

---

[40] His wife's home when a girl in Sheffield.

c/o Walter Seager & Co.
Constantinople
June 25th 1913

My dearest,

On arriving here today, I sent you a wire to let you know it and I hope you have got it alright? Thank you very much for all your letters which were awaiting me and also for the two and a p.c. which came soon after my arrival and evidently by the same boat from Constanza. I understand that letters only leave here three times a week now as the railway is not open to Sofia yet. Please thank the children for their letters and especially Edith for her amusing verses about Fred. I hope to write to them both by next mail.

I am staying at Bobek in the furnished house which Mr & Mrs Greenwood and Mr Tenus have taken and to which they kindly invited me. It is a nice place near Mrs Binns and the Bosphorus. From the house, tonight, I have seen a number of fireflies. I saw the first one at Stara-Zagora.

I forgot to tell you of the large tumuli in Bulgaria – I believe they are both ancient and modern and are a lasting record of the many wars which have taken place in the Balkans. We went quite near to the famous Shipka Pass.

I had quite a comfortable sea journey from Constanza and got here about 1.30 this afternoon. I was fortunate enough to have a cabin to myself with a bed in it! Not an ordinary bunk. There was not much fresh air to breathe but I managed about 10 hours in bed and then had about 4 hours on deck before arrival. There were some English speaking children on board with a nurse but I do not think they were English. It was bright and sunny on arrival and the Bosphorus and the City looked at their best. Owing to the late rains, the green things still look green here. Also, the weather is not unpleasantly hot yet.

The others are talking in the room and I will try to answer your letters more thoroughly by next mail. I hope this will find you installed alright at Hoylake, quite comfortably, and I hope the weather will be fine for the benefit of the bairns so that they may get out a good deal.

With much love from
your loving husband
Burke

c/o Walter Seager & Co
Constantinople
June 27-1913

My dearest,

Since I wrote to you after reaching here on Wednesday I have had a short unpleasant experience. After a restless night, about 5.00 a.m. yesterday I started with diarrhoea followed by sickness and I had to stay in bed until tea time. Then I only forced myself to get up and it certainly did me good. Today, both have gone and I feel nearly alright again – I was *very* limp and fit for nothing yesterday.

I have been through the usual routine today – we had 7.30 breakfast and left the house before 8.00 a.m. to catch the boat to the City. I have had a quiet day and got through a good deal in the offices. It is HOT here today and I have (and am) pouring out of every pore in my body but I feel fresher after a hot bath on getting back to the house.

Mr Seager leaves for England next Tuesday and he has promised to arrange for more fig jam to be sent to us in September next. He has had a bad time in business owing to the two wars – it brought much business absolutely to a standstill. This applies equally to many of the business houses. Even now, no one knows what is going to happen here as the political situation is so uncertain. You would probably read of the public hanging of twelve of those concerned in the murder of Mahmoud Sherket Pasha. Of course, everyone is talking of it and many people went to see the result. Everyone is praising the courage with which the twelve faced their end and how they drank coffee, talked and laughed right up to the end. Some are reported to have said that 10,000 would rise up to avenge each one. There seem to be more soldiers than usual in the City – I suppose they are on hand to keep order if need be. The main army is still at Tchatabdja although the Bulgarians have gone.

The news here about the Bulgaro-Servo-Grecian disputes is much more favourable and it would seem that peace will be kept and the Czar of Russia be accepted as an arbitrator. There appears to be no prospect of the railway to Adrianople being opened and so I expect I shall come straight home via Constanza leaving here on July 8th. There is another delay – Mr Gill has sent word that he will only arrive on July 4th – a week today. He is a nuisance!! He originally intended to be here about yesterday but I fancy the Post Office-National Telephone Co. appeal case in London has detained him against his will.

Thank you for your two letters which arrived just before I left the office this afternoon. By the same post, I had from Mr Nelson the abstract of my paper from the Electrician but he omitted to send on the 'favourable comments'. I have had also a very good notice in *Engineering* which is one of the best of the technical papers.

I am glad to know that my wire from Bourgas did reach you as I have read since that the censorship has been increased in vigour in Bulgaria. My letter to Mr Bunn from Sofia only took 12 days to cover what usually takes less than 1 day!

With much love to you all
from your loving husband Burke

I hope to write to T & E later – we have much enjoyed Edith's 'POME' about Fred.

My dearest,

I am beginning this now although there is no mail out until Monday. At this hour, I expect you are installed at Hoylake and I hope you have had no misadventures in the transfer from Rainhill. I am writing a separate letter to Edith and Tom and I will also send a p.p.c. to Mr Swainson as I expect the Pew Rent collection will be on Wed. July 16th. I have telegraphed today to Mr Caspar at Sofia to say that I do not propose to go to Adrianople *now* as the railway is not open yet and so I fully *expect* to be able to leave here on July 8th and arrive at Hoylake on the 12th.

I am quite recovered, I hope, of my stomach trouble but today I waked up with a bad cold in my voice box and have not been able to speak naturally all day long. I am gargling, taking Formamint lozenges etc. and I hope soon to have it under control. It is pretty hot here but by no means unbearable. Tonight I have to go and call on Mrs James Binns, where I stayed twice last year, and offer my good wishes on her daughter's engagement to Mr Dowdney (one of our assistants here and a cousin of Mr Dowdney of Prescot).

Tomorrow I am to take afternoon tea with Mr & Mrs Walter Seager & their numerous young family. Mr S. leaves for England on Tuesday and I am to see him there again.

Tomorrow week I am to take tea with Mr & Mrs Martin with a view to admiring their No. 1 – Molly – aged 1 year.

My young hostess – Mrs Greenwood seems to be a very capable young lady and a good housekeeper. They are doing their best to entertain me and make me feel comfortable. I have been badly bitten so today she has borrowed a big mosquito net for my bed and I hope that trouble will be ended.

Sunday June 29th

I did not go to Mrs Binns last night because of my throat-cold. Instead I played some accompaniments for Bunn and Greenwood. Bunn has very little idea of singing but Greenwood sings very well when he chooses suitable songs and his is distinctly a case where money would be well spent in lessons from a good teacher. Songs like 'The Yeomen of England' and 'Off to Philadelphia' suit him splendidly. They play Bridge most nights and they are teaching me Auction Bridge which is more a 'training' game still and takes quite a lot of skill, requires a quick brain and a tenacious memory.

I am writing this before breakfast and before the heat gets so that you don't want to buck up to do anything. I can see it will be a scorcher today.

I have written direct to Mr Kitchen to arrange about his paying for those Midland debentures so you need not worry about the matter. I think that possibly you might be well advised to sell your Grand Trunk investment which pays about 3½% and invest the money in these Midland[41] 5% deb. instead. It is a Co. which is doing well by itself and has its interest and principal guaranteed by the B.I. also.

I am glad you ran down the quotation and let Doris know – none of us are likely to forget its source after such a hunt.

I fear there is not the slightest chance of my having a further week's holiday with you during the Hoylake time. I had been looking forward to being at Hoylake all the month but now I shall be exceptionally busy on my return – of necessity – clearing up my foreign business and dealing with arrears of home work.

I am glad to hear that Morris[42] and Tom get on so well and that the visit was a successful one.

June 30th

I regret to find that there is no mail leaving here until tomorrow – July 1st. I have sent in the order today for my tickets for Tuesday July 8th and I expect I shall be home with you on the following Saturday.

Yesterday morning, I wrote the reply to my paper and then went to call on Mrs Binns. In the afternoon, after a sleep, Mr Bunn and I went to tea with Mr & Mrs Seager and it *was* a climb to the top of the hill where his bungalow is. They have a wonderful view of the Bosphorus and the air is fine. The weather is quite changeable here just now. Yesterday afternoon, we had heavy rain and today is quite breezy and cool.

In the evening, at 8.15, after supper, we went to Church and heard a fairly good sermon by Mr Few – the Scotch minister who did such good work in organizing relief for the cholera-stricken soldiers of the Turkish army.

We have been very busy all the morning with the Telephone Co.'s engineers and tonight I am invited to tennis at the re-opening of the Bebek Tennis Club. On Wednesday evening, I am to go to supper at Mrs Binns and, one evening, Mrs Greenwood has friends coming in for music but of course I shall be unable to sing. My throat is a little easier today.

The afternoon mail is in and with it, two letters from Prescot but no letter yet from you – I expect about four will arrive together next mail day – i.e. Wednesday.

The British Ambassador leaves here for good tomorrow and I hope we shall see the departure from the roof of this building – it is not yet known when the new one arrives.

---

[41] Midland Electricity Co. Ltd., of which he later became a director.

[42] Morris Oppenheim, son of their solicitor. He later became Sir Duncan Oppenheim, Chairman of BAT.

Please only look for two letters after this, *at intervals*, before my arrival.
With much love to you all
from
your loving husband
Burke

c/o Walter Seager & Co.
Constantinople
July 2-1913

My dearest

Thank you for three letters and a p.c. which arrived together by last mail. This 3 mails a week business makes things awkward for everybody both in personal and business correspondence and it is strange to have three days newspapers arrive together. I do not know what Seager does with three copies of a bulky newspaper like *The Times*. I expect he does a good bit of skipping.

On Monday evening, I had a few sets at Tennis but there was no hard play. The exercise did me good and I was able to get a warm bath after getting hot. Mrs Robt Rowell whose husband is in England on business who entertained me last year, came in for Bridge and we did not get to bed until nearly midnight. She is looking into English girls schools and knew a good deal about Roedean but she fears it is too expensive. She wants particulars of an 'individual' small boarding school near Sheffield kept by Mr & Mrs Platt. She has heard a very good account of it but she cannot get the address and I said we would try to help her. I wonder if Miss Escott or Miss Tutin could supply the information?

Greenwood and I went over to see our jointers at Scutari yesterday and we had lunch at the Haidar Pacha station Restaurant – the German place. This station is the terminus of the Anatolian Railway.

I had two sets of tennis last night before dinner. Afterwards, we had a little music and some auction bridge and went to bed earlier.

Tonight, Bunn and I go to supper with Mrs Binns and the Greenwoods are to come in afterwards. They have also asked a Scotch couple who have been here only a short time with 5 bairns and their servant troubles have been very serious and they are doubting whether they should have come at all.

Yesterday, the English Colony was very interested in the departure of the British Ambassador, Sir Gerard Lowther, and his wife. There were various diplomats at the Quay to see them on board the Constanza boat.

I have been in luck as I got the very last berth on the train for Tuesday next by applying last Monday!

There have been more fires here but I have seen none of them. On Monday evening about 45 houses were burnt out in Stamboul at one spot. Bunn has an invitation from the Chaplain of the British Cruiser S. S. *Black Prince* for us to lunch on board with the officers tomorrow and see over the ship. This is the ship sent here for the protection of Britishers until all troubles are over. The other nations have similar battle-cruisers here, off the City, and they make an imposing sight.

Today, Dowdney and I are going out with the Telephone engineers to Yedi-Koule (Seven Towers). This is the old outer fortified wall of the City. It is quite cool and clouded sky after rain in the early morning.

I am writing this on the boat and we are now nearing the Bridge. I find it difficult to write either in the office or the house.

With much love to you all

from

Burke

c/o Walter Seager & Co

Constantinople

3-7-1913

My dearest,

Thank you very much for a letter from Rainhill, one and also a p.c. from Hoylake. I am glad to know that your plans worked out alright and you are safely installed there. I am glad to think that this is the last letter which I shall write to you from here as I follow by the next mail boat. The news here today about Bulgaria, Servia and Greece is very serious. Fighting seems to be general although there has been no declaration of war. We learn also that the train service from Belgrade to Sofia is entirely suspended so it is a good thing that I decided not to attempt to return to Sofia. I don't know how I shall get the luggage[43] which I left in Sofia unless Major Hopkins has taken it for me to London.

We went to lunch with the chaplain and doctor of the *Black Prince* about 1.45 today on the ship and afterwards they showed us over it. There was not time to see everything and we had to miss the torpedoes and the sick bay. It was most interesting to see what a lot of guns etc can be stowed away in such a small space. She seems to be a well-found cruiser and she carries nearly 800 men, all told. I still cannot make out where they are all stowed away. The chaplain seems to think his job is a fairly hopeless one. He is called 'padre' by his fellow officers and the doctor is P.M.O. (Principal Medical Officer). They seem to be very good friends. Bunn has known the padre in England, and they have freemasonry in common. Last night, we went to dinner with Mrs Binns.

---

[43] This turned up a year later, just after he had given up hope, and had made a claim on, and been paid by, the insurance company. He was very embarrassed at having to tell the company, but it told him to keep the money.

Afterwards she had friends in for music – some good, some very indifferent.

Tonight, Mr & Mrs Anderson are coming in here for music. He sings excellently and has a good tenor voice. She is a nice little lady and reminds me of Aunt Emily somewhat but with more vivacity. She is one of those people who have the gift of quick sympathy. I imagine she is about 40 – she has 5 bairns including a baby.

Later I am sending this on spec – I expect to arrive first. I leave here early on July 7 – via Odessa.

Much love to all from

Burke

(Editor's note. The letter which follows completes one story!)

Noel K. Bunn
31 Youell Avenue
Gorleston
Great Yarmouth
Feb 23 1962

Dear Donald,

I have a handful of letters requiring attention, but yours of the 22nd intrigues me so much that it becomes first in the queue!

I would have declared that I have a vivid recollection of the Bigland affair, but it doesn't seem to fit. I do not know when your Father paid his first visit to Constantinople. I (and Podmore) travelled with him on his second visit and, examination of my passport (which lies before me) shows that we arrived on May 2nd 1912. I know well that Bigland was engaged to marry a Miss 'Charnaw' (that is how it was pronounced). I remember spending a Sunday with your Father and Bigland at Moda but I have no recollection of it being a 'cheering up' visit. Now here is my version. I was to have been B's 'Best Man' and as such was taken to visit the family and meet the lady and her sister – the future Lady Reading – P. and I had fun as to who was to carry the one top-hat we owned between us – it was my property and I insisted that the bridegroom did not require one. Don't ask me what I was doing with a top-hat and tails – my sister had been married in April, the rig out had been provided for that occasion and I suppose I could not bear to leave it behind.

I thought that it was some months after that – say the autumn – that Bigland applied to the Telephone Co. for short leave of absence on the grounds that he was feeling unwell and wanted to go away for a change of air. Immediately after his departure he wrote to the Tele. Co. resigning his job and revealing that it was because his engagement had been broken off. That was the first hint I had had of the impending trouble and I never saw Bigland again. He went into

253

The Family in 1913.

the priesthood immediately afterwards and I always thought that he had broken off the engagement for that very purpose. I had one brief and unhappy meeting with the lady.

Bigland later went to India, became 'Monsigneur' and on rare occasions we exchanged 'oral' greetings. He died many years ago. Your Father's dated letters are obviously more reliable – I would be most interested to learn the date of the letters which tell the story. Your Father visited us later – travelling via Russia – and stayed with us, i.e. the Greenwoods and me in our house – but that must have been about the middle of 1913. Your Father was unwell during that visit and Mrs Greenwood looked after him and was scared out of her wits. The G's had a rushed wedding before joining me in Constantinople – they married May 2nd and arrived out there May 15th 1912.

Podmore did not remain long out there, I understand he married money – *that* I can understand but why money should have married him is beyond my comprehension.

What a terrible crime to keep the letters people send to you!! I don't think I have a solitary one of yours!

But send me the date of that letter and at the same time send me news of your Mother.

Yours sincerely,
Noel K. Bunn

31 Youell Avenue
Gorleston
Great Yarmouth
April 3.62

Dear Donald,
The weather is so vile that I am up to date with my correspondence! But whether I have already acknowledged your letter of the 29th ult I am not absolutely certain! At any rate I was vastly interested in it.

The only person left of all those I knew in Constantinople with whom I have any contact is a Mrs Greenwood – whose husband was my deputy on that job and, incidentally, they spent the latter part of their honeymoon in Constantinople! I have put the question to her and her reply is:

'My memory is quite good. Bigland proposed to Miss Charneau of Moda – sister of the Dowager Lady Reading – at a moonlight picnic – all excitement, as the moonlight had too much influence on the couple! Engagement broken – Bigland resigned and popped off to become a priest.'

So my memory has not played me false on this occasion. I never heard of the previous engagement or of Miss Bodenham. A moonlight picnic – usually taken on a huge barge with six or more servers – along the shores of the Bosphorous – would certainly not take place outside the summer months. I went on several such – usually about a score of people.

Well, all of this doesn't amount to a row-of-beans but it has entertained me immensely – it confirms your Father's on the spot report (if that were necessary) and it also confirms my recollections. One can only assume that Bigland decided he had made the same mistake twice and had better make sure he did not do it again!

This time 50 years ago was an eventful month for me.

April 4th initiated into Masonry;

April 5th first met the girl I married;

April 19th attended my only sister's wedding;

April 21st received instructions to go to Constantinople;

April 29th left for Constantinople with your Father.

I may be a day out on the last item – I still have my passport but cannot extract the various dates. At any rate it was an almighty rush – after meeting your Father in London and getting my orders I had no time to get back to Newcastle to collect my gear and had to get 'the office' to collect and despatch it to me.

Yours sincerely,

Noel K. Bunn

Letters written to his wife by B. Welbourn AKC, MIEE, aged 46, Contracts Manager of British Insulated Cables & Helsby Cables Ltd. (the 'BI'), when travelling on business for it in the USA in 1922.

(Editor's note: The grounds for this journey were twofold. The Weir Commission on Railway Electrification had been set up by the government, and a National Grid scheme for electrical distribution, involving high voltage overhead lines, was being discussed. Much experience in both these fields was available in the USA. On his return from the USA & Canada Welbourn wrote an immense and detailed report on what he had seen and learned. Possibly as a result of this trip, the BI obtained the first contract awarded for 66kv lines for the Grid in 1926.

For much of the journey he was accompanied by a boyhood friend, about ten years older than himself, Mr C. J. Atkinson[1], a farmer in Weston St Mary, and a Lincolnshire County Councillor.)

> Room B 3B   On Board the Cunard
> R.M.S. Scythia
> 8/6/22

My dearest,

I am not ashamed to say that I had the same lump in my throat today on saying goodbye that I had 15 years ago when I went to Canada and I want to thank you for bearing up and not making it more difficult.

Mr Atkinson had various enquiries from Mrs A. about Donald[2] and Dick which he forgot to pass on to you and she also sent a kindly message of greeting for you.

After unpacking, I promptly lost my keys and finally found them under the cushion of a settee on which I had been sitting. We have discovered only about 30 saloon passengers on the list so no wonder we were able to change our cabin. The ship is quiet and restful so far and the sea is like a mill-pond. Very

---

[1] Born 1 February 1862, died 17 June 1944.

[2] Donald, his third son, is writing this footnote. Dick, his younger brother is Emeritus Professor of Endocrine Surgery at the Royal Hammersmith Medical School.

shortly after leaving L'pool, the sky clouded over and there have been only brief spells of sunshine. Immediately after leaving the landing stage, we had to put our watches back to Greenwich Time – they don't know Summer Time here – and we lose an hour daily so that we are not due in N.Y. until Friday evening, June 16th.

We can do as we like about dressing for dinner but we are told that it is usual to do so. It is at 7.00 p.m. and the other meals are at 8.00 a.m. and 1.00 p.m. with tea at 4.00. The breakfast hour is however very elastic, I gather.

It's amusing me to see how Mr Atkinson is growing accustomed to the idea of 'staying the course'. He has just been asking me for the route which is New York, Boston, Albany for Schenectady, Pittsfield, Toronto, Chicago, San Francisco, Seattle, Chicago, Pittsburgh, Philadelphia and home.

Letters until, say, July 20th should be addressed c/o Thos. Cook & Son, 245 Broadway, New York '*Please forward*'.

I had a p.c. on board from Edith[3] and also one letter from Mr Lydall – a colleague of Mr Beard[4]. I will send E. a p.p.c. of the ship.

With much love to you all,

from Burke

Cunard R.M.S. *Scythia*
9/6/22

My dearest,

It is now 8.10 p.m. our time and about 10.40 Rainhill time and although the weather is calm there is a swell on and I am not feeling too comfortable.

I went to bed early last night and slept well until about 4.30 a.m. but the noise of the deck-washing followed by the early stoppage at Queenstown effectually waked us up. An Irishwoman with a rich brogue and with plenty of blarney came on board to sell lace and shawls and she spoke to us through our window. She told us not to be shy in our beds as she had often seen her old man like that!

After breakfast at 8.30, we took some exercise and looked at the Irish coast for a time until we passed the Fastnet Lighthouse. Then we went to sleep. I had about 20 mins but Mr A. had about an hour. The weather is cloudy tonight and not very warm but we had sunshine for a time during the day.

There are not many birds about and we have only seen part of one porpoise thus far. The ship is very quiet as there are only some 40 saloon passengers aboard. Tomorrow morning, we are to call on the chief engineer at 10.00 a.m. and I hope he will invite us to see his turbines which drive the ship. The feeding

---

[3] Welbourn's eldest child, then a Home Student at Oxford University.

[4] J.R. Beard, a partner in Merz & Maclellan, later President of the IEE.

is well done but there is far too much to choose from. The dining room is like a restaurant with its small tables instead of the old-fashioned long tables with revolving chairs.

There is to be a dance at 9.00 p.m. tonight but it does not call me and I think I shall go to bed. We are both tired with all this fresh air.

Sunday June 11th

Yesterday, we both sent home messages via wireless to the S. S. *Cameronia* which is due in Glasgow tomorrow. From there, the message will go by post and you ought to get yours on Tuesday evening at Hoylake. We began to get more into the life of the ship yesterday. In the morning, we called on Mr Bain, the chief engineer, who showed us his turbines, oil-fired boilers etc. In the afternoon, instead of going to sleep, we played various games of quoits etc and had quite a lively match against two Americans. In the evening, a white-haired old lady played very well on the small grand piano in the lounge and, by 9.30, we were so tired out that we went to bed. I had the best and longest sleep that I have had for weeks. This morning, we had Service in the lounge at 10.30. It was conducted by the Purser. Another officer read the Lessons and the hymns were accompanied by the orchestra of 5 which includes 2 violins, 1 cello and 1 double bass and the pianist. The Service was well attended by the 1st and 2rd Class passengers and the singing was hearty and was lead by a small male choir of ship officials. The Captain could not be there owing to the light fog which is causing us to lose time. The weather is clearer again just now but, this morning, there was a good deal of fog-horn blowing. Of course, with wireless aboard and a definite course to follow, the danger from fog is very much lessened.

We are much struck with the absence of all bird life and so far we have only seen part of one porpoise. This is disappointing as I had expected to see lots of porpoises and plenty of birds.

This morning, after Service, we had a long and interesting talk with an elderly American named Keith (of Scotch origin). He has been with his wife on a 2-month holiday in England and Scotland and seems to have combined pleasure with some business to his great satisfaction. Mr Atkinson is thoroughly enjoying himself and says he is feeling very fit. His alert mind is not letting much slip notice and I fancy he will return with a widened outlook. He is following my advice and intends to look into some aspects of American farming. We have scarcely read anything since we came on board.

My dear Edith and Tom[6]

I will send this to Rugby first as I do not know when it will arrive nor where E. will then be.

As we left the Landing Stage, our first surprise was that we also left Summer Time behind although this prevails in the U.S.A. There are only some 40 1st class passengers on board and I think not many more in the 2nd. We looked over the 2nd class sitting rooms this morning and find they are quite comfortable. It took quite two days to get accustomed to the ship and the routine. During that time, there was a good deal of swell on the sea and I was not feeling too comfortable about the head etc but we are in calmer waters in mid-Atlantic and I feel quite alright. We also left the sun behind in the Mersey and have seen little of it since. As we came to the Gulf Stream, we also came to light fog which has caused the ship to be slowed down at times and will delay our arrival in New York – probably until next Saturday. Meanwhile we are making the best of it and are getting as much rest and fresh air as we can. Mr Atkinson is looking fit and rested already and seems to be enjoying his novel surroundings. He intends to go to San Francisco but I do not yet know whether he will make the complete trip.

We reach Queenstown on Saturday morning before we were up and the ship waited in the Bay for fresh passengers, mails etc. While there, a voluble Irishwoman, with lots of brogue and blarney, came on board to sell lace and shawls and was carrying on just outside our window on 'B' deck. We passed Daunts Rock and the Fastnet Lighthouse and had left land behind well before dark. Since noon on Friday, our daily runs have been 381 and 386 miles. We are now moving faster and I fully expect it will be more tomorrow.

Our routine is very simple –

7.00 a.m.	Tea
7.30	Sea bath
8.30	Breakfast
11.00	Chicken broth
1.00	Lunch
4.00	Tea
7.00	Dinner
9.30	Sandwiches

In between, we read, write, play deck games and, generally, do our best to keep from getting bored stiff. I don't know what I should have done without Mr

---

[5] If Welbourn was separated from his children, he always wrote to them on Sundays if at all possible.

[6] Welbourn's eldest son, then at Rugby school.

Atkinson. In the evening, we dress for dinner and we go to bed about 10.00 p.m. because we cannot keep awake any longer in this strong air.

This morning we had Service in the lounge at 10.30. It was reverently conducted by the Purser in the absence of the Captain who had to stay on the bridge owing to fog. The ship's orchestra of 5 did the music and the singing was quite hearty.

Another surprise is that all birds have deserted us and we have only seen one porpoise. Yesterday, we sent wireless telegrams home via S. S. *Cameronia* which will post them in Glasgow probably tomorrow.

With much love from
Father

Pl. let Mother have this. I have written separately to Fred[7].

RADIO COMMUNICATION COMPANY, LIMITED
34-35 Norfolk Street, Strand, W.C.2.

O C E A N L E T T E R

'Laconia' Station   Date 12 June 1922

Handed in on board the S.S. *SCYTHIA* on 10th June 1922
for transmission and posting via S.S. *LACONIA*

To: Welbourn Rainhill Liverpool
Tenth All well   expect arrive Saturday   sea calm   forward only important letters   remember me to friends   love to you and children   hope restful time Hoylake[8] Rugby   Oxford   Welbourn

Continuation of letter on board R.M.S. *Scythia*

Monday June 12th

It is difficult to get precise information on board and I learn that we are only now in the Gulf Stream with a water temperature of about 62 deg. Fahr. This morning, we played deck games from breakfast to lunch. It has driven away the vice-like feeling in my head and all other symptoms of sea-sickness and we get up sufficient appetites but not ravenous ones.

---

[7] Welbourn's second son was in his first term at The Leas School, Hoylake, run by P.S.Dealtry & L.B. Barr.

[8] Hoylake in the Wirral, where Welbourn's wife and two youngest boys were on holiday by the sea.

We get a so-called Wireless newspaper each morning but the sum total of the fresh news is very meagre. I am writing this at 5.25 p.m. – about 9.00 p.m. Hoylake time – so I suppose the bairns are in bed and asleep now. I hope this holiday will do you all much good and that you, especially, will have as *restful* a time as possible. I wish I could have you here with nothing to do but eat, sleep, read, and re-create for the 8 days. We have again had fog and the steamer has been going slow but the sun came out a few minutes ago and the water is now beautifully green with more white horses shewing. For a few moments, this morning, we saw several porpoises and Mr Atkinson has been quite relieved and delighted to have a glimpse of one bird. A concert is being organized for Seamen's Charities on Wed. night and I shall see if I can help but my throat does not feel 'good' at present. There is a young girl on board who sings very sentimental songs and reminds me for all the world of a kitten. I suppose she will be singing.

Last night, the orchestra played some selections in the lounge for nearly an hour – the Faust pot-pourri was quite enjoyable. I am getting a very sticky feeling with the salt-water baths so I am retiring to the cabin soon for a miniature fresh water bath with the aid of the fresh water (cold) in the hand basin.

June 13th

This morning is very beautiful but there is more 'sea'. The sun is shining brightly and the water is blue with white horses. There is a considerable head wind which is quite warm and, so far, we do not need any overcoat. After breakfast, we took deck exercise in the form of shuffle-board for about 1½ hours since when we have been talking with an American and also filling in our Landing Form.

If Winter Comes has now reached me but Mr A. is actually reading it and finds the start very good. I have waked quite early again today (4.00 a.m.) and yesterday (5.00 a.m.). I cannot understand it as I am keeping off coffee in the evening and am having no afternoon sleep.

June 14th Wed.

We have had a 'painful' day. When we waked, this morning, we found a considerable sea on resulting in many casualties. I felt decidedly squeamish but managed both breakfast and lunch and am now alright or nearly so. During the morning, we had heavy rain and a change of wind and the sea has gone nearly as quiet again as it was off the Irish Coast. The sun is now shining and people are more cheerful and are out playing games on the deck once more. The result of the storm is that the concert is postponed until tomorrow night.

I have had an interesting talk this afternoon with an Englishman who lives in

New York (he is not Major W.). He was to have gone to Rugby but his father died when he was 12 so he could not go and he went with a scholarship to Tavistock instead. He is now in New York.

I have read some more of *If Winter Comes*. It is well written but the foundation is wrong – I think. The author starts by setting up a ninepin which makes a big draw on one's knowledge of human nature and then proceeds to build resulting trouble thereon. Mr Atkinson continues to enjoy himself and he is spending the afternoon playing games and getting hot, preparatory to having a hot bath before dressing.

Owing to the head wind, we had a bad run in the 24 hours ending at noon and only did 325 miles – about 60 miles below the best day's run. No one knows when we will get to N.Y. but there seems to be a hope that we shall arrive on Sat. morning.

Today, we have actually seen two other ships and one is now overhauling us and is believed to be the *Berengaria* – one of the biggest Cunarders. Please tell the boys that we saw 3 flying fish today but there are still no birds. Also, I have not seen a single fly in the ship.

June 15th

I saw one solitary fly this morning, on deck before breakfast. We have also seen a few birds again. During the morning, we had sunshine and at times a very blue sea. The morning began dully, however, and has reverted to that this afternoon. We have had a quiet day and have only played deck games a little. I have been reading *If Winter Comes* and am not entranced yet and I am getting well towards the end. There is a white-haired old lady on board who is very musical and who still plays Mozart etc very well indeed. Her fingers are wonderfully supple. She is to accompany my song at the concert tonight so we had a very brief practice this afternoon. My throat feels strained after it and I am aware that I must not yet use my voice much. It is something however that it is improving. The ship's run was only 365 miles but there still seems hope that we may get to land on Saturday morning. I will tell you about the Concert tomorrow.

June 16th Friday

The Concert was more enjoyable than I expected it to be and the collection for the N.Y. and L'pool Seamen's Charities realized £18. 7s. 9d. I will send the programme etc in a separate envelope. You will see that the *Wireless News* contains little wireless news, as I expected. We get very little news on board but we have heard by wireless that you have had abundant rain, whereat Mr A. is very pleased.

We have fog again today and the horn is going regularly. Rumour is rife as to when we shall get to N.Y. and places it between 6.00 a.m. and afternoon, tomorrow. It is evident that I shall get no start on work until Monday after this loss of time through fog and head-wind. Today is much cooler so we hope not to be frizzled in N.Y.

I have been wondering what causes the curious sense of detachment which comes to one on board – no real news – rather a monotonous existence – dread of a rolling and pitching ship and sea-sickness. The first two days, my head felt as though in a vice – due, I think, to the motion of the ship.

It's a violent up-rooting of one's regular routine and wrenching from one's home-life and environment. I shall be quite glad now to get to grips with the work which I have come out to do and then to see my way to getting back home to you and the bairns with the least possible delay. Before you get this, you will have been to Rugby and Oxford with Donald and I hope you will have come back rested and refreshed both in body and mind.

I am getting this into the post on board so that will explain the English stamp.
With much love to you all from
Burke

It is 9.00 p.m. here and your watch tells me it is 1.30 a.m. Sunday with you. The watch seems to have behaved perfectly since I brought it away!!

The Wolcott   Thirty-first Street by Fifth Avenue
                                               New York
                                               Sat. 17/6/22

My dearest
We got here, at last, about 11.15 this morning. The fact that we passed the Nantucket lightship about 4.15 yesterday would, no doubt, be recorded in the *Liverpool Post*, this morning, and Mrs Atkinson would also see it in *The Times* or *Yorkshire Post*.

We had to get up about 6.00 this morning so we are tired tonight and I expect we shall retire early after writing a few letters. As we came up, we passed the new 55,000-ton Cunarder, the S.S. *Berengaria* at anchor, waiting for her turn to come in. We had to pass the U.S. doctor and Immigration officer on board and then we had no real trouble in passing through the Customs. We sent our luggage by the Express Co. and it came in less than an hour after our arrival by tram.

We have one room with two single beds and with a combined bathroom and lavatory attached and the charge is $7.00 per day, i.e. $3.50 each. The dollar is now worth about 4*s.* 5¼*d.*

Rain greeted our arrival and this evening, there has again been heavy rain with lightning and thunder. In consequence, the air is fairly cool but our appetite has departed with the sea air.

Immediately on arrival, I got two people on the telephone and got busy. One of them came to lunch with us and stayed until 3.00 p.m. The other is seeing me about 9.45 a.m. on Monday and then things should begin to hum. We met some very nice American people named Keith on board and, to our great surprise, they invited us to stay next Sat. night with them at Poughkeepsie. This is likely to fit in well with our plans as it is near Albany and Schenectady where I have to go. Mr Keith himself lives in Albany at the Ten Eyck Hotel during the week and will motor us up there on Sunday evening when he goes. They said they had received so much kindness in England that they desire to take this way of repaying it! He is about 58 and is of Scotch extraction while she is, I should think, about 55 and she was born in India.

After Mr Cratwicke had gone this afternoon, we wanted fresh air and we got the cheapest thing that has come our way since we left – about ¾ hours ride on the top of a *fast* motor bus for 10 cents. We went right along Vth Avenue to the Hudson Riverside past the Central Park in which the grass is looking very green. In another 6 weeks, I expect it will be all scorched. The heavy rain came while we were still about 200 yards from here and we had to shelter for a time in a shop doorway. The thing that impresses me most as having changed in the past 15 years is the *enormous* increase in the motor traffic – there seems an unending stream of cars, motor buses etc along Vth Avenue.

Lots of the ladies are wearing a kind of light weight black mantilla cloak with a long fringe round the bottom. This hotel is very quiet and I suppose it is reasonable for N.Y. but our simple lunch cost $2.00 each including the tip.

Mr Atkinson sends his greetings and is anxious to know whether you have had a good parcel of vegetables from Weston. He is much bothered by the American money but I suppose he will soon get used to it. On Monday, he will try to set the wheels in motion here for seeing some agricultural implement works in Chicago.

I hope you are keeping as cheerful as possible and not worrying too much over my absence. I intend to get home as soon as I can.

People are still pouring out of here to Europe. 8,000 have gone today and, of these, 2,000 were on the S.S. *Majestic*.

The Wolcott   Thirty-first Street by Fifth Avenue
                                                         New York
                                                         17/6/1922
My dear Edith and Tom,
I have managed a very memorable performance in going to sea for nearly 9 whole days without suffering from mal-de-mer. My head felt as though in a vice

for the first two days out from Liverpool. On Wednesday, we had rough going through a storm for several hours but heavy rain came and beat down the waves.

Life on board was becoming monotonous. We played shuffle-board, deck quoits etc., sometimes music and a game of Australian Whist or Patience in the evening and so on. It was so warm that we only wore overcoats once for about 10 minutes. The star evening was on Thursday when we had a concert for N.Y. and L'pool Seamen's Charities and raised over £18. The Chief Steward sang awfully well and in good style. Another official did some Dickens scenes. The portraying of Uriah Heep was especially good.

There were some 'characters' on board – one was a man in the 'Moving Pictures' business and he was priceless.

After getting up about 6.00, this morning, and passing the U.S.A. doctor and immigration inspection, we actually landed about 10.00 and then had to find our luggage and get it passed by the Customs House proper. We finally got here about 11.15 and our baggage came by the Express Delivery Co. pretty quickly afterwards. We have a room with 2 single beds with a bathroom etc attached so we are self-contained. Our room is on the 12th floor and you may imagine that we use the lift. The hotel is quiet and is not one of the costly palace hotels.

Next Saturday, we are hoping to travel by the Hudson River to Poughkeepsie to spend Sat afternoon and night with some American people whom we met on board. They say that they have received so much kindness from English people while in our country that they want to entertain us to repay it! On Sunday evening, Mr Keith will be motoring to Albany where I have to go and will take us with him.

The greatest change that I see in N.Y. in 15 years is the colossal growth of the motor traffic – so far, I have only seen about 4 horses.

It was raining on our arrival, this morning, and this evening there was quite a heavy thunderstorm with much rain so that the air is fairly cool and fresh.

With much love from Daddy

Mr Atkinson is very puzzled over the American money!!
Tom Pl. send on to Edith.

The Wolcott
Thirty First Street   Sunday June 18th 1922
By Fifth Avenue
New York

My Dearest,
The weather is so humid and lifeless here, as yet, and we have no appetites since we left the ship. It is a very similar feeling to that which I had in Petrograd.

This morning began the same and we felt that we *must* get some fresh air with the result that the Hotel people advised going to Long Beach on Long Island. We did this and found a miniature Blackpool with miles of promenade, abundant fresh air and not many houses but lots of motor-cars. (It has just struck 7.00 p.m. and your watch is 11.35 p.m.). The bathing is the great feature and we have never seen anything like it before. There were few people on the Promenade but whole families were spending the day on the beach in thousands. Most of the people were adults and were in bathing costumes. Obviously, some of them were only for show and not for bathing but most of the people were bathing too and having their meals on the shore. Underneath the Promenade, there were open rather primitive restaurants where people could eat and get provisions. Many of the men must be spending their holidays there and be living in bathing costume judging by their brown skins. Many of them have arms and shoulders which look painfully red after peeling. Some of the men were the finest physical specimens that I have ever seen. Two in particular might have been used as models of Greek athletes. I was not impressed with the women folk beyond the fact that there was no immodesty. The absence of horse-play was very noticeable – also there was very little sand-castling by the children. Many of the adults played catching balls on coming out of the water. The surf was splendid and reminded me of Hoylake on a rough day.

We had lunch at a restaurant on the front that had an abundant supply of sea air in it. We were attracted to it by the novel way in which the joints were being cooked in full view of the front window. They were slowly turned on bars in front of a very hot iron plate which was heated from behind by gas. It all seemed very clean and good.

I am hoping this will go by the *Berengaria* on Tuesday morning and it should reach you on June 28th when I rather expect to be on my way to Toronto.

We have no letters yet as Cooks closed at noon yesterday but we both hope to find home letters there tomorrow morning.

With much love to you and to the bairns. I have written to E & T and will write a note to Fred.

Burke

The Wolcott   19/6/22
Thirty First Street
By Fifth Avenue
New York

My dearest,

Many thank yous for your letter of June 8th received today. It has relieved me to know that you are easy in your mind and are determined to get rested before my return as I did not leave with an easy mind.

I have been out all day at work from 9.10 a.m. until 5.45 p.m. After a bath and change, we went to the roof garden of the Pennsylvania R. Hotel* for dinner and had a simple meal by an open window where we could hear the band playing dance music and see the people get up from their tables to have a dance and then return to their meal. Only one man was in evening dress and all the men danced in their boots. We left there about 9.00 p.m. and walked along the street for 1/2 miles or so to see the extra-ordinary electric signs. It's like Fairyland. I had heard of it before but did not realize what modern advertising had come to.

Mr Atkinson is only disappointed that he has no home letter yet. He is thoroughly entering into the job of seeing as much as he can and he has had a busy day, on his own. He went up the 50-storey Woolworth Building, went on the Tube and generally explored. He wants to go up in an aeroplane but I won't take any responsibility and I think he won't go!

Here's my washing bill $2.22. $1.00 = 4s. 5¼d!! Isn't it appalling? Fortunately, some things are cheap such as the local trains and trams. For long distances, apparently, one can ride in the Elevated Railroad trains all day for 5 cents – it is a uniform fare for any distance so that the short-distance people really pay for the long distance ones.

The weather still keeps cloudy and showery but warm.

*This P.R. Hotel claims to have 2,200 rooms each with a bath.

I am just finishing this off before breakfast (June 20th) and hope it will catch the outgoing mail. I don't think I shall be able to see Miss Way yet.

With much love from

Burke

The Wolcott
Thirty First Street   21/6/1922
By Fifth Avenue
New York

Dearest,

I have been out of town today and so I have been unable to go to Cook's for letters. There were none when I called yesterday and they did not expect another English mail until today. I expect to go down there tomorrow morning.

I had a full day yesterday seeing people and some engineering work. In the evening, after a hurried meal, I took Mr A. to hear Marconi lecture to the American Inst. of Electrical Engineers on 'Radio Developments'. The house was full – ½ an hour before he began and the N.Y. papers are full of it, this morning.

Today, I had breakfast at 7.00 a.m. and only got back from the country at 3.30 without having had any food. I had some afternoon tea at a shop on 4th Avenue and then went to keep another appointment. It is now 5.45 and I await Mr A. – I don't know where he is but he seems to be having a very interesting time in his sight-seeing. I have got for him a letter of introduction so that he may see the Long Island Experimental Farms tomorrow and he is mightily pleased. I don't suppose he will want to do anything very exciting tonight. He suffers from corns[9] rather badly and his feet get very tired.

I am much struck with the change in the shape of American boots and shoes. They are now very similar to English shapes except that the large majority of the ladies wear low heels similar to those which you have on your 'nurse's' home shoes.

It's been wet here again today and rather humid so that I need another bath.

With much love to you all.

Burke

The Wolcott   22/6/1922
Thirty First Street
By Fifth Avenue
New York

Dearest,
It is 9.50 p.m. and I am tired and sleepy and am getting to bed but, before doing so, I want to send you my daily note. Your letters No. 1 and 2 have arrived but no further mail is due until after we have left on Saturday for Albany. We are to stay on Sat. night with the Keiths at Poughkeepsie and then go with Mr K. to Albany on Sunday night in his motor. I hope to get to Toronto (King Edward Hotel) somehow on June 28th and to attend the American Instn. of Ele. Engineers Meeting at Niagara Falls on the following day and possibly I shall have to speak. *Quite roughly* I think our programme will be as follows:-

Arrive Chicago	July 5 – University Club
Leave Chicago	July 8
Arr. California	July 13 – Cliff Hotel, San Francisco
Leave California	July 20
Arr. Seattle	July 22
Arr. Chicago	July 29 – University Club
Arr. Pittsburgh	July 31 – William Penn Hotel probably

---

[9] The state of people's corns was a constant topic of conversation in the 1920s!

| Arr. Philadelphia | Aug 2 |
| Arr. N.Y. | Aug 3 – c/o Thos. Cook, 245 Broadway |

Leave for home as soon after this as I can get a boat. I shall probably be able to write you definitely about this from Chicago and to book our passage while there. I had hoped to get the Laconia from N.Y. on Aug. 3rd but I think it will be very hard going to do it. I think Mr A., under pressure, from home, is making up his mind to go right through with me. Meanwhile, he is having a full time of sightseeing and he seems to be absorbing a good deal of permanent interest, e.g. he visits the Law Courts, the Zoo, etc. etc. I am having a strenuous time now that work has really begun in earnest and I have seen and heard much of real engineering interest. I don't want to get over-tired so I am going to bed now.

Please give my love to the bairns and thank Dick and Donald for their messages.

With much love to you from

Burke

The Wolcott
Thirty First Avenue   23/6/1922
By Fifth Avenue
New York

Dearest,

I heard from Tom today about the curtailment of Speech Day due to the epidemics. I hope we will escape and that you and Donald won't get anything infectious.

We have both had a full and tiring day – I intended to go early to bed but some Americans came and interrupted our writing and kept us standing and talking for ages! and it is now 10.40 p.m. and Mr A. still has to pack so that our luggage can go at 7.00 a.m. tomorrow. I hope we shall be able to rest on the River steamer on the way to Poughkeepsie (pronounced Po-keepsie). Edith will possibly know of it as the place where Vassar College is.

Goodnight and much love to all.

Burke

I don't expect to receive any more letters until June 29/30 at Toronto.

Hudson River Day Liner
24/6/1922
We are getting near to West Point where
the U.S.A. equivalent of Sandhurst is.
The river is v. calm. The boat is not over-
crowded and the people are quiet.
I am glad to have a few quiet hours as I
am v. tired this morning after 3 short nights
and the rush in the humid atmosphere of
N.Y. I think W.J.A. has at last decided
to stay the course with me. He does not
like the idea of sharing a cabin with a
stranger on the ship. BW

Mrs Welbourn
Rainhill
Lancashire
England

The Ten Eyck
Albany, N.Y.
25/6/22

Dearest

We arrived here about 7.30 tonight after a motor ride of 75/80 miles from Poughkeepsie with Mr Keith in his open car and now, after dinner and a stroll, I am very tired and ready for sleep. The Keiths met us on the arrival yesterday of the N.Y. River boat, motored us to their wooden house and made us feel thoroughly welcome. After light lunch, they took us for about 2 hours motor ride and I had great difficulty in keeping awake in the evening after so much fresh air. This morning, we went to the Episcopal Church and heard a good broad-minded sermon. The music was fairly good from a mixed choir of ladies, men and boys. The service is modelled on that of our Church.

Tomorrow, I go out to the General Electric Works at Schenectady and I expect to go to their Pittsfield Works on Tuesday and that we shall reach Buffalo sometime on Wednesday evening, be at the Convention at Niagara on Thursday and get to Toronto in the evening.

It's quite cool here tonight but I expect we shall be in heat in a few days time.
With much love from
Burke

Pl. tell Donald that we could see today the Catskill Mountains – the home of Rip van Winkle – but it was too hazy to see them really clearly.

Edith should be home when this arrives so I have not written to her separately. I have written to Tom – will write to Fred.

POST CARD

Maplewood Hotel
Pittsfield, Mass 26/6/22

Quite unexpectedly I am here alone for
this night in a delightful country hotel –
large, quiet, well-furnished, nice people
and an air of culture which is refreshing
after N.Y. I have had a bad headache
all day and am off to bed quite early to be
ready for the fray again tomorrow. I expect
little rest from now on until I leave for home.
The Shakers are a curious community of 300
people about whom I must tell you later.
Much love, Burke

Mrs Welbourn
Rainhill
Lancashire
England

The Ten Eyck
Albany, N.Y.
27/6/22

Dearest,

I hope you got my p.p.c. from Pittsfield? It was such a nice quiet refined
hotel – after I got to bed last night, a telephone message was brought to me
from Mr A. to say that he would come over to lunch today. It rather upset my
plans but we arranged to meet and then to make the return journey at 4.00 p.m.
by road in the public char-a-banc and we enjoyed the 38 mile drive – most of it
being through quite nice hilly country. The ride took about 1 hour 50 mins and
cost $1.50. Mr Keith is still here and he has his son, daughter-in-law and baby
girl of 4½ tonight on their return journey to their home in the Middle West.
The son has given Mr A. a letter of introduction to Ford's Motor Works at
Detroit.

We had dinner at a quiet restaurant tonight and have now come in to write
our letters etc before going to bed. My bad headache of yesterday has gone but
I can still feel that it has been there. There is thunder tonight with heavy rain
and it will perhaps clear the air which is cool again. Last night, I was quite cool
in bed and was glad to have a warm bath on rising. People are complaining of
the lack of sun and the backwardness of the crops.

We leave here for Buffalo and Niagara about noon tomorrow and expect to
reach Toronto on June 29th. While there, we expect to learn whether the U.S.
Railwaymen go on strike on July 1st and whether we have to re-arrange our
plans.

I have just finished two busy days and now have my notes on them to write up while they are fresh in mind.

With much love to you all.

Burke

POST CARD
(New York State Education Building)

The Ten Eyck Hotel
Albany, N.Y. 28/6/22
Leaving soon for Toronto. The building shown
looks v. fine and is close to this hotel.
The country around here is beautiful –
v. much like Derbyshire and Central Wales.
There are small communities near here called
'Shakers' – something like Quakers but they
have all things in common. This is a busy town
and the hotel always seems to be full of people.
Wireless 'Broadcasting' is very popular
and everyone was agog to hear Marconi
talk on Monday evening.
Much love, Burke

Mrs Welbourn
Rainhill
Lancashire
England

POST CARD

The Prospect House
Niagara Falls
29/6/22 N.Y.
Arrived last night in time to see the American
side Falls illuminated. Mr A. *very* much
impressed. He has gone off to see it in detail
today. We go to Toronto tonight and expect
to arrive about 10.00 p.m. Fine morning –
Love from
Burke

Mrs Welbourn
Rainhill
Lancashire
England

Dearest

I have had to spoil ·my resolution of writing to you *every* day while away. I went out yesterday at 9.00 a.m. after arriving here about midnight from Niagara and I did not get back here until about 1.00 a.m. this morning.

I had a good reception on Thursday morning, as a Britisher, when I spoke at the Elec. Convention at Niagara Falls and various people came and introduced themselves afterwards. One of them was Mr Lynne of Chicago to whom I have a letter of introduction and whom I am to see there next week. Another was A. E. Davison one of the Government engineers of this province who took me in hand, motored us round to see some of their prize work which I had come to see, devoted all yesterday to me and motored us back 150 miles arriving back here at 1.00 a.m. and again gave me all day until 6.00 p.m. today. He has been tremendously kind and helpful and he has saved me much time and trouble.

We crossed from Niagara on Thursday by the boat across Lake Ontario, had dinner on board and then sat on the deck until we got here. I think Mr A. had one of the days of his life at Niagara !! He thoroughly enjoyed the Falls, Gorge etc, had no conception of what he would really see and we are going over again tomorrow. He has already come to the conclusion that he ought to have got away from England earlier in his life and he seems very grateful to me for taking him round and making travel easy for him. There is very little to see in Toronto so he's going on to the Ford Works at Detroit on Monday and is to re-join me at Chicago next week. He has had a restful day, today, and has written shoals of letters telling of his experiences at Niagara etc and recommending 'Prohibition' to all and sundry.

Thank you for your letters from Rugby and Oxford received at 1.00 a.m. today. I hope all went well and that you got back refreshed in body and mind. Apart from the change, I am getting no mental rest and, in addition, I am missing my typist[10] very much as I have a good deal of writing to the Works to do. I am having a great deal of constipation trouble and have had to take medicine regularly since I left home despite an abundance of fruit, lettuce etc. I have been writing a lot tonight, it is now about 11.30 p.m. and I really must go to bed – I hope this will catch Tuesday's boat from New York.

I am waiting to hear whether you got my wireless message from the *Scythia*

---

[10] Miss Nancy Webber, who came to him about 1916 and remained with him until 1942. The loss of a million men in World War One and emigration due to the agricultural depression before it, meant that many women like her never married.

on June 10th alright – Mr A. has had no acknowledgement of his either. You shd have got it at Rainhill by June 14th.

I hope this will just reach you in time to convey my love and birthday greetings. About one month later, I hope to be with you again.

With my best love to you and the bairns.

Burke

I have not seen my unusual brooch yet for Joan.

King Edward Hotel
Toronto, Canada
3/7/22

My dearest,

You asked in a recent letter if I had seen any wild flowers. I have seen just a few only. We have been *much* struck by the absence of flowers both in the U.S.A. and here. In the big Central Park in N.Y. Mr A. only found flowers in a large glasshouse. Yesterday, near the Niagara Falls we found a delightful garden in the Victoria Park. In it, there were lots of roses and herbaceous flowering plants besides a considerable variety of trees. While there, Mr A. did the last remaining thing and went down into a Tunnel which leads down behind the Falls so that you can see the water tumbling over. The Horse-shoe Fall on the Canadian side is wearing away the bed of the river at the rate of 6 feet per annum i.e. 90 feet since I first saw it and it certainly seems to me to be a more pronounced horse-shoe now. Alas, at the American end of the shoe, I think less water is coming over – possibly this is due to the greater use of water for electrical purposes.

Please tell the children that Mr A. (who's an energetic sight-seer) went over the Shredded Wheat Factory near the Falls. He was much impressed with the extreme cleanliness. There are numerous needle baths and *every* employee has to strip and have a bath before starting the day's work. It seems to be on all breakfast menus here but 'Force' is seldom given. 'Shredded Wheat' is called 'Bundled Hay' by some Americans!

Toronto is much improved since I was here previously. The streets are much better paved and there seems to be a good tram service. Taxis are, however, appalling in their charges and are to be avoided. One engineer here, A. E. Davison, of the Ontario Govt. Hydro-Electric Commission has been exceedingly kind to me. He was expecting me and introduced himself at Niagara. He has devoted about 3 whole days to me and my wants and has given me shoals of useful information. This afternoon, I began an interview with some other people and aim to resume at 9.00 a.m. tomorrow. It may lead to good business in the future.

I am glad to hear you have had rain. There has been a lot in America and Canada during the past fortnight and now they are wanting sunshine. I hope our lawn is recovering and that the grass is growing again, on it. You appear to have had a full time at Rugby and I do hope you and Donald have escaped all contagion. I am glad, too, that you have had such a favourable report on Edith's work. I hope she will get a reasonably good Degree in 1924.

Please tell Dick he is quite right. The only lions in the N. Continent are in Zoos and I have not been there to see them. Mr Atkinson has gone to Detroit, this afternoon, and I go to Chicago tomorrow night on the sleeper. He is to rejoin me there on Wed. or Thursday. I shall be glad to get away from this flat, enervating place. It seems so unnatural to have no appetite and to feel more or less listless nearly all the time.

I am *not* looking forward to the 3/4 days across from Chicago to Los Angeles. I am deliberately cutting out the Grand Canyon trip for myself as I am trying hard to get back to you by the Aug. 3rd boat from N.Y. I am not certain enough of it, however, to book my berth yet. I am afraid I cannot write again until July 5th at Chicago.

With much love from
Burke

University Club
Chicago, Ill.
6-7-1922

Dearest,

It is now 12.15 a.m. but I am beginning this to let you know I am here now and expect to leave again on July 8th for Los Angeles etc. Mr Atkinson left Toronto on Monday for Detroit and I expected him here yesterday. On arrival I had a wire from him dated July 4 – 5.45 p.m. from Detroit which mystified me as follows: 'Will be tomorrow night late *if I reach there*. Atkinson'. I have stayed up until now and the last train is in but he has not come. I am wondering whether he has decided to cut out the rest of the trip and go home – If he has, he gave no hint of it on leaving Toronto.

After arriving here off the long night journey and having a bath, writing the remainder of my Toronto letters and having lunch, I went out to pay my first call and I did not arrive back until after 11.00 p.m. Two men dined me and then took me to a play 'Lightnin'' which has been running for 3 years and is very good. It depends on the acting and the scenery is exceedingly simple. I have seen little of Chicago so far but it contains the usual high buildings and 3,000,000 people.
8.00 a.m.

It's a cloudy morning but warm. From my bedroom window, I can see an uninteresting bit of the Lake (?Michigan) with 2 dredgers and also a number of motor cars 'parked' in the foreground.

Nearly opposite is the Art Museum and further along the Marshall Field N. H. Museum – a huge place and said to be splendidly equipped.

This Club is at the corner of Michigan Avenue – a very fine straight street – and Monroe St. My room overlooks the Avenue and is much too noisy so I shall try to get it changed tonight.

Its now breakfast time and I have a full day before me.

Much love to you all.

Burke

University Club   July 6th 1922
Chicago

Dearest

I have now heard from Mr Atkinson that he has been delayed in Detroit by the July 4th 'Day of Independence' holiday and that he will be here tomorrow morning. I hope then to get our tickets for San Francisco and to arrange things so that we get back to this City about July 28th and get to N.Y. on Aug. 2nd. I am hoping we shall be able to arrange through Cook's here, for berths on the *Laconia* on Aug. 3rd but I expect they will have to wire to N.Y. before being able to fix us up. I have had no letters for some days from you but I hope some will arrive before we leave. When we come back I expect we shall spend overnight at a Hotel – probably the Blackstone where I dined last night as a guest before going to the Theatre.

Today has been a very full one for me and I have spent most of it out of the City visiting Electricity Stations etc. I can see my time fully occupied until I leave. I have seen very little of the City itself but I have seen miles and miles of suburbs from the train and taxi.

The city is low-lying and nearly at lake level and I find it enervating and I have no particular appetite. I shall be glad to get away to the West but I expect it will be a hot 3-day ride by the Santa Fé route to Los Angeles and San Francisco.

I am having a quiet evening and intend to go to bed early – I hope I shall be able to sleep as my room is both hot and noisy and there are no bedrooms on a quiet side of the Club.

July 7th 8.30 a.m.

I was in bed at 9.40 last night, slept well and got up at 7.00 this morning for early breakfast etc. so as to be ready for Mr Atkinson who is due to arrive at 6.55 a.m. After all this, I have just realized that the Railway Time here is Sun

277

time and not Daylight Saving Time. It is very confusing all the time. The trains are running late so I may have to go out before he arrives and order up the tickets without consulting him further.

It's quite an overcast morning here and it may remain so all day so far as I am concerned if it will only keep the heat down. I am sitting in a cool spot to write this and yet I am freely perspiring.

6.00 p.m.

Mr A. arrived and full of his experiences at Ford's Works etc. We have got our tickets for San Francisco etc and are awaiting a reply from N.Y. about our passage to England. We expect to know before 1.00 p.m. tomorrow.

Your letter No. 8 has just arrived and thank you for it as I had had no news for days. No. 7 has gone astray somewhere, I fear.

We have just seen a Water-plane rise from the Lake Michigan. Its a fine evening and fairly cool so we are going down to eat at the Lake side and see if it is less enervating there.

Please thank Dick for his message. I'm sure there will be a good welcome for me when I get home.

With much love to you and to the bairns from
your loving husband
Burke

I expect we shall reach the King Edward Hotel, Toronto about June 29th and leave again about July 3rd for the University Club, Chicago. We are to be guests there.

University Club
Chicago
July 8th 1922

My dearest,

Just before Thos. Cook & Sons closed at 1.00 today, we got our return passage booked for Aug. 3rd from N. Y. by the S. S. *Laconia* and I feel inclined to say 'The Lord be thanked'. The cabin, C.88, is almost identical with the one which we first had on the *Scythia* so that we shall be alright even if we do not get moved to deck B after we start. I expect we shall get to Liverpool on the evening of Friday Aug. 11th – an absence of 64 days from you! I can only do it by cutting out some of the things that I wanted to see at and near Pittsburgh; Boston will also have to go and I shall have to miss Miss Way unless she comes to N.Y. She has written telling me to see some people in San Francisco.

We leave after dinner tonight for the Pacific Coast and part company on

Monday at Williams where Mr A. breaks off to go to the Grand Cañon while I go to Los Angeles where I arrive on the afternoon of the 11th. We join up again at San Francisco – probably on the 15th and arrive at the New Washington Hotel, Seattle on the 20th and leave there on the 22nd for Chicago. We shall probably break the journey at one or two places in the Mountains so that I may examine the electrification work in detail. We expect to be back in Chicago on the 28th where the address *for one night only* will be: c/o Sargent & Lundy, 1412 Edison Building, Chicago.

Pittsburgh – arrive Sunday July 30th.

Philadelphia – arrive Tuesday or Wed.

New York – arrive Aug. 2nd at night probably and stay at the Wolcott Hotel as before. I do not think it will be safe for you to post to me after July 23rd.

If we only arrive in L'pool on the evening of the arrival day, Mr Atkinson will be unable to get home. Do you think we can offer him a bed at Rainhill or shall we be too fully tenanted already? If you would post to me the page out of *Benson*[11] which gives the L'pool–Spalding trains, Mr A. would be grateful.

I have sent no p.p.cs. from here – partly because I have been very busy and partly because I have seen none. I am intending to get some in California and send to various people.

With much love to you all and with many anticipations of returning from my wanderings.

Your loving husband,

Burke

The California Limited
Santa Fe

July 10/1922
en route

Dearest,

I have sent you a p.c. today to let you know I have remembered your birthday. As you will see, it is difficult to write in this shaky train – the shaking and heat together are very tiring. The temp. in the train has been about 87 deg.F today but I felt the heat more still, yesterday.

Most of yesterday, we rode through a great corn-growning belt in Kansas, but otherwise there was nothing notable. In the evening, there was a wonderful lightning storm – both sheet and fork – in 3 quarters of the sky at once. We ran out of it and only got a little rain. I slept well and got up at 7.00 a.m.

We have ridden all day through barren, sandy country for the most part, on a plateau in the mountains. There are lots of prairie dogs – like squirrels.

---

[11] The pocket railway guide which everyone had in the house.

I must stop as it (the shaking) is making me feel quite sick.
With much love
Burke

Hotel Van Nuys
Los Angeles, Cal.
Room 613
July 12th, 1922

My dearest,

I arrived here about 5.00 p.m. yesterday the train being 2 hours late. I soon had a welcome bath and a meal and was in bed by 7.45 p.m. too exhausted even to write. I got up at 6.30 this morning and, after a cold bath, I feel somewhat better and am sending you this before breakfast. The experience of riding for 3 days from Chicago to Los Angeles in the summer is one which I hope I may never have to repeat. The first day through Kansas was alright but the other two were dreadful through the sun-blasted country and the desert of New Mexico. The temp. in the train yesterday was 90 deg.F and the air coming in through the windows was like a hot blast.

Some of the scenery is good and much of it is interesting. Pl. tell the children that we passed close to an extinct volcano yesterday. The lava all round it was quite plain and it is now cold.

There was a complete change after we passed through the mountain range out of the desert about 100 miles from here. The last 2 hours' ride was through orange and almond groves etc. and there were pepper trees, palms, cactus and lovely hydrangeas.

The houses of the people in the desert region are mostly built of earth (*pisé de terre*, I think the French call it) and they look like pictures out of a travel-book. The Red Indians with their wares at railway stations were very picturesque as were also the Mexicans with their dark skins and large sombrero hats.

From the little I have seen of this place, I am very unimpressed with it. Mr Atkinson left me on Monday night to go to the Grand Cañon for a few days and is to rejoin at San Francisco on Sat. He is an indefatigable sight-seer. I hope to find some letters at San F. on Sat.

With much love to all,
Burke

Hotel Van Nuys
Los Angeles, Cal.
12/7/1922

My dearest,

Just a line before going to bed – you will see that I am beginning and ending the day with you. I feel a lot better tonight after my long rest of last night although I have had a rather full day in the heat – which is however a dry one and not a humid one like that in Chicago and Toronto. This morning, after a search, I found a p.p.c. shop and have sent 15 off to the children and others including Margaret Thorpe[12]. I want to send a few more while here to your mother etc.

The people here are making electrical history at a great rate – it is most interesting to me and will be valuable in the future in my work. Tomorrow evening, I am probably dining out with the Telephone Manager and his wife and I have accepted an invitation to an Engineers' Club luncheon and this may mean a speech. Altogether it is to be a busy day. I am booking a sleeping berth for San Francisco for Friday night.

Did I tell you what a nice place the University Club at Chicago is? The large dining hall is like a College dining hall with carved wooden and vaulted roof, stone walls, stained-glass windows etc. There is a large reading room with the Times and other English papers so that I have some home news as late as June 23rd including the Prince of Wales' home-coming. Here the Irish news looms very small – there will be a paragraph of possibly 7/8 lines while there will be over a column about the defeat of Mrs Mallory at Wimbledon By Mdlle. Langlen.

I wonder if it makes us see the Irish difficulty in their correct perspective. Everyone here is talking about the prospective collapse of Germany's finances and I fear it will affect trade at home and in Europe and delay its recovery. I have not heard from the Works – do you know if they are busier, yet?

With much love – I am getting homesick.

Burke

Hotel Van Nuys
Los Angeles, Cal.
July 13 – 1922

My dearest

The kindness of the engineers here is great. They have already furnished me with much valuable information and have promised to send more to me in England. The use of the telephone here is extra-ordinary. With a pop. of 700,000, there are 167,000 telephones and the end is not yet. The automatic telephone is used like the one[13] at the Prescot works and the older manual sets are being converted to the new system.

I have not seen gas here at all – in fact, I have only seen one gas jet since arriving in the country. The use of gas seems relegated to cooking while electric

---

[12] Daughter of Greenall, Whitley's brewer. My constant companion at that time.

[13] Strowger.

cooking, heating, washing machines, toasters, irons etc are making great headway. This morning, I had my first experience of a wireless telephone and overheard a business conversation between the mainland and the Island of Catalina. So far, there is no privacy. Some people are motoring me out to dinner tonight as their guest and I hope they won't keep me late as I did not sleep well last night. I hope they will get me away from the heat.

I must go now.

With much love from

Burke

Clift Hotel
San Francisco
July 15th 1922
11.00 p.m.

Dearest,

Thank you very much for letters 9 and 10 received through Cook's, tonight, on my return from the Oaklands and Newark country. I left Los Angeles at 8.00 last night on the train called 'The Lark' and got up here about 9.45 a.m. to find Mr Atkinson already here and full of enthusiasm about his visit to the Grand Cañon. I bathed and went out about 10.30 and have only returned late to find that he has gone to see the play 'Abraham Lincoln'.

Mr Powell of the Pac. Gas and Elec. Co. gave up the whole of Sat. afternoon to motoring me out to see their Newark and Clarement Sub-stations and afterwards we called for his wife and took her to dinner. Then they put me on an electric car which took me to the Ferry Boat for San F. Our bedroom here was so noisy that we have changed into another which is a shade less noisy. The heat here is not so trying as at Los Angeles but, all the same, it was broiling in the sun in the country this afternoon in the open country. The views were quite spoilt today by the haze over the sea and the mountains.

This is also a wonderful place in the electrical sense – electric light, power, trains, trams, telephones and wireless. I am resting tomorrow (Sunday) from my labours which are making me tired in this heat and on Monday, I am being taken for a longish day in the country to see more overhead lines etc. On Tuesday, we leave for Seattle and arrive there on Thursday and then I think we shall begin the long homeward trail about July 22nd. I don't quite like the Railroad Strike situation but I hope it will not interfere with our arrangements.

My trunk has not yet arrived from L.A. and it is very awkward as I have no clean collars, etc.

Much love to you all

Burke

Dearest

The enclosed will show you how we have been spending Sunday. The solo was quite good and I should imagine that the lady had had an English training, judging by her pronunciation. The sermon was excellent and lasted about 40 minutes. The man was very voluble and forceful and never at a loss for a word.

We went on to look at a very large new R.C. church which Mr A. had noticed on the previous day and then we had quite a decent lunch at a somewhat primitive restaurant, near by. We then went to the park opposite and listened to the band which was very fair and we looked into the Museum and a small Japanese Garden.

The day is quite cool with overcast sky and enough mist to veil the sea so that I have not been able to see the Golden Gate.

I leave here about 7.30 a.m. tomorrow for a long day in the country and expect to be taken about 150 miles by motor. We breakfast on the Ferry Boat on which the first part of the journey will be made. I could usefully spend a whole week here but I cannot spare the time.

The life here is envious. Numbers of picture theatres appear to be open today but I do not know if the ordinary theatres open. There are lots of people in the streets and there were many in the park. These people can depend on 3 months' weather now without rain so they can dress and plan accordingly.

I have only seen one woman smoke, so far, since we landed but I am told that a good many do it, in private. The way that many of them paint their lips and powder their faces is deplorable. They do it in public, quite openly, and Mr A. wonders what some bridegrooms think when they see their wives' real faces for the first time!

I have been much struck with the better manners on the Pacific Coast. Both at this hotel and at Los Angeles, I have been made to feel at home or, rather, welcome and not just somebody from whom money is to be extracted. At L.A., I left word that I wanted to be called at 7.00 a.m. At the hour, the telephone bell rang and I was greeted as follows:- 'Good morning, Mr Welbourn – It's seven o'clock'. Here, my trunk went astray and the partners etc took endless trouble to find it and finally get it to my room.

This morning, before Church, I went to call on Miss Way's friends but found they had gone away so I have that off my mind and I have written to her to say I am returning home and shall be unable to pay her a visit. I regret this as I shall probably never see her again.

Mr Atkinson hopes you have had a good holiday and says I am to tell you that I am taking good care of him. As a matter of fact, he was much bothered over the coinage here for some time but he has about settled down on it. He had a most enjoyable time at the Cañon – some of the things that he did were rather perilous for a man of his age but he has come through it alright. He is much impressed with the opportunities in this country, for young men, and I should not be at all surprised if he encouraged one or more of his sons to come out here to farm, on modern methods.

Unless this railroad strike spreads and interferes with our plans, we are both calculating today that we shall be in our homes once more by 4 weeks today.[14] I am looking forward to a week's rest on the ship as I shall need it – so I am hoping the sea will be kind to me!

I am a little vague about the relative time as between here and England. Some of these cities have Summer Time and some do not. I have not discovered what they do here but I assume that we are 8 hours behind you so that 6.50 p.m. here is 2.50 a.m. Monday with you.

I have not taken many photographs yet. I got 2/3 of Niagara Falls and a few at Los Angeles and about 9 here yesterday. This week and next, I expect to get some dozens if the weather is only fine enough. One difficulty here is to hold the camera sufficiently steady as the heart beats so much quicker in the heat. I think it is about 10 beats to the minute, faster, and that explains why people have to work less in the hot climates unless they want to have a shorter useful life.

You mention the cold nights – it is acceptably cooler here but at L.A. one sheet only was very ample. I had a very nice letter from Tom enclosing 3 snapshots including the excellent one of you. Your letter No. 7 has still not turned up but I have your letters telling of Edith's arrival at Hoylake and of the bad weather there and of your arrival home. I hope the good rains have made our back garden grass recover? I was getting very concerned about it.

The fuchsia and geraniums, hydrangeas grow here profusely but so many people neglect to have any flowers in their gardens. I am glad to hear that Miss Neathan is promising well – I hadn't heard that you had engaged her so I suppose the news was in No. 7.

With much love to you and the children (big and little).

Your loving husband,

Burke

---

[14] At about this time I have a clear picture of myself in my parents' bedroom at Craven Lodge, while Mother reads a letter from Father, and counts the days until his return.

POST CARD
(Lobby, Clift Hotel, San Francisco) 16/7/22

Dear Donald

This shows the entrance lobby of the Hotel   D. B. Welbourn
where we are staying and the other one for Dick   Rainhill
shows the outside. It is one of the quiet hotels   Lancashire
and aims at comfort instead of luxury. I saw a   England
Humming Bird today for the first time but I
didn't hear any hum. It is however very small.
With love from
Daddy
I hope you like the new kitten.

> Clift Hotel
> San Francisco
> July 18/1922

Dearest,

It's now 8.5 a.m. and I have breakfasted and returned to the bedroom to wake up Mr A. who is suitably surprised. I had a very tiring day yesterday – about 150 miles in a motor. It was very hot inland and then very cold getting home. The climb up the motor road through the mountain was somewhat thrilling and they asked me if I was scared at the ravine below and the twists and bends in the road. The sun has parched up all the grass and the hills look weird with green trees standing out from a light background of burnt-up grass.

I am getting useful experience here and today I am finishing up my investigation of Transmission Lines. We leave for Seattle this afternoon, and have to face a further 2 nights in the train. There, I am going into the Railway Elect. work and expect to have 3/4 days on it and to get to Chicago on the 27th or 28th. It's about 4 days in the train from S. to C. I believe but we may break the journey at one point. I am rather dreading the heat in Chicago etc after the cooler evenings here. We have had no home letters since Sat ? but we hope for more before we leave today.

With much love and looking forward to getting home.
Burke

> New Washington Hotel, Seattle
> July 20 – 1922

Dearest,

Arrived about 6.30 a.m. today after 2 nights in the train and was delighted to find 3 letters from you.

It was *very* hot again in the train and I slept very badly the first night out from San Francisco but I had quite a fair night on the second. I have to go out now and may be away all day so I just wanted to send my love and to let you know we are getting along on our journeyings. I hope to turn East on Saturday.

With much love to you and the bairns from

Burke

I hope I shall find your elbow much improved when I get home.

I am wondering whether I can telegraph to you from Queenstown to let you know the probable time of arrival at L'pool.

New Washington Hotel
Seattle
July 20/1922

My dearest,

I think the children may be interested in the enclosed which describes one of the great holiday trips. It is about 2 days' journey from here and is supposed to be somewhat inferior to the Grand Cañon of Arizona which Mr A. took 3 days to see. He had great adventures there and was glad to get back alive. I expect it was safe enough really and that it was the strangeness of riding at an angle of 45 deg. on a mule and of hanging over awful precipices for the first time that rather scared him.

He writes multitudes of letters and has done so again today while I have been out, in addition to going for two drives. He says it is the finest City which he has seen here yet but, so far, I have scarcely seen anything because of the mist and the smoke from the big forest fires. We ought to be able to see the snow-clad Cascade Mts. from here and Puget Sound.

My visit here is a little inopportune as the railway officials are all upset by the strike and are having to work to keep trains running. Despite this, I had 3½ hours today with the chief elec. eng. of the Chicago, Milwaukee and St Paul Rly. He has the biggest Rly. electn. in the world under his control. Tomorrow, he is arranging for me to go with a Japanese engineer for about 250 miles on the Rly. and I shall be away for about 12 hours. Also on Sat. night, I am going off to Deer Lodge Mountain about 700 miles on the way to Chicago – and am to stay there 2 nights to see more of the work. The man himself is also to be there – his name is Beeuwkes, pronounced Bukas. He is a good fellow like many of the other engineers whom I have met. In fact, I have seen little or none of the cock-sureness which so many people associate with Americans. Most of these engineers are feeling their way through their problems and frankly admit it.

I had my hair cut today and the barber has overdone it! I might have told him to shave my temples and the back but, fortunately, I stopped him in time and he has left plenty on the top.

We get to Chicago one day ahead of schedule so I hope to get to Pittsburgh for July 29th – our wedding day – and have a Sunday free from travel.

I hope to see there a young English couple from Manchester – Mr & Mrs Crosby, whom I met at Niagara. Mr C. is an engineer who is now stationed at Pittsburgh.

With much love to you all,
Burke

New Washington Hotel
Seattle
July 21st 1922

Dearest,

I have just been re-reading your three letters and enclosures. It is very sweet of Dick to be so affectionate and for Donald to comfort you. His remarks are very quaint and remind me of Toms at the same stage.

Fred has evidently attracted attention to himself in the ½ term exams at the Leas. I wonder if he is to have a faculty for displaying his knowledge in them instead of having nerves?

I'm glad to hear you are likely to get holiday arrangements fixed up for the beginning of September. I have sent Miss Roby a p.p.c. to cheer her up in her illness – I had already sent her one (from Niagara, I think). I sent about 20 from L.A. last week and have sent about 12 more since so I hope no one will feel neglected. I couldn't find your mothers address so I sent hers to Claygate to be forwarded. You might mention it when you write to her, please, in case it does not arrive.

The Rly. Strike has not troubled us in travelling so far but I think things are developing and I shall be pleased if we get back to N.Y. without any hitch. The Coal Strike is evidently by no means over and, as you will see, Pres. Harding is taking drastic steps to get the coal mines working again.

Mr A. went off about 7.45 a.m. for his days trip in a motor – to Mt. Rainier – 17,408 feet and he expects to be back about 8.00 p.m. I am going off, in a few minutes, for the day on Rly. Electr. and expect to be back by 9.00 p.m.

It's a quite cool, misty morning but I expect I shall find it hot inland – the mountains cut off the sea breezes and the valleys are swelteringly hot. I don't mind that as the air is dry. It's the confinement in the trains combined with the heat and all the hours of jolting that knock me up so much. We had a good nights rest but I have not fully recovered yet from the trip from San F.

With much love,
Burke

New Washington Hotel
Seattle
July 22nd 1922

My dearest,

This is just a note before leaving here on the night train for Deer Lodge. I left early again today for Tacoma to see the Railway Shops and Stores of the C.M. & St P. Rly and got back about 4.30 – very weary. Mr A. got in from another ride in the country just after I did. We had a cup of tea, I have had a bath, paid the bill and cleared up and when we have had a meal we shall be off on the homeward trail at last and, I hope, be actually home within 3 weeks. I don't like the look of the Rly situation – it seems possible that the clerks will come out on strike on July 29th on which day I expect we shall reach Pittsburgh. Its about 12 hours from there to New York and if the worst happened I expect motors would be run so that we should get there by Aug. 3rd, somehow.

There are no more letters here from home so I hope we shall get another batch in Chicago next week. There are a lot of forest fires about here and the visit is absolutely spoilt from the sight-seeing point of view owing to the pall of smoke over the country-side. I have not seen the snow-covered Cascade Mts. which ought to be plainly visible from here*.

Some American battleships have arrived so there are festivities and sailors are on leave in the City.

* Deer Lodge is about 4,500 feet up and I hope we shall get away from the smoke there so that I can get a few photographs.

I am glad Fred has done so well in his ½-term exam. Mr Dealtry[15] will evidently believe me, about F's ability! Tom did send the snapshot of you and I suggested to him that it would enlarge but I don't think it will stand considerable enlargement. Its very stuffy here and I am going for some air.

With much love to you and the children
Burke

Hotel Deer Lodge
Deer Lodge, Montana
July 27th 1922

Dearest,

We arrived here last night to find a somewhat primitive town of 7,000 people. We were tired and were in bed by 10.00 p.m. and slept soundly in this good crisp mountain air – about 4,500 feet up. Today, I have been electric railroading again and Mr A. has gone off farming. I only got a very few photographs

---

[15] P.S. Dealtry, Headmaster of The Leas School, Meols Drive, Hoylake, the preparatory school to which all Welbourn's sons were sent.

owing to thunder, lightning and clouds although very little rain came.

I am now waiting for the man who has had me in hand as I have asked him to drive. Everything is upset here owing to the Strike so I am disappointed to some extent. I cannot however expect much when I find the heads of departments in overalls working on repairs to keep trains running.

I look forward to another good night and do *not* look forward to another two days and nights in the train to Chicago as it will get hotter and stuffier and dustier as we go East.

I have had to buy a hair-brush today as I left my pair in the train yesterday.

Must go now – much love,

Burke

The Blackstone
Chicago
July 28th 1922
12.30 a.m.

My dearest,

Thank you very much for 3 letters and various enclosures and also for a letter from Tom who wants permission to go ahead and make a wireless telephone set. Please tell him to do so and to have the tools etc. as our birthday present. It will cost some pounds so tell him not to expect anything else. It will help him a good deal in his engineering training on the weak current side and it should keep him (and us) *au courant* when broadcasting starts.

We got here today from Deer Lodge after 48 hours journey which was pretty wearisome altho not so hot as expected. One night, we had rain and a wonderful lightning display. The scenery in the Rocky Mts. is fine but I do not consider it so fine as in the Canadian Rockies and this is, I believe, the general opinion. (I find it very difficult to write as Mr A. *will* keep interrupting me to talk about cattle being imported from Canada to England etc. etc., following on 13 letters and 1 Radiogram which he got, on arrival).

I have had a full time since getting here and tomorrow evening we go on to Pittsburgh where I spend the week-end while Mr A. goes straight through to Philadelphia to see some friends of the Revd P. L. Houson with whom I was at school at Moulton[16]. Mr Quayle of the Auto. Telephone Co. came to spend the evening with us and, after dinner, he took us to the theatre – Lightnin Bill Jones, which was well worth seeing again, for the acting.

Jack Atkinson˙has been meeting Mr Best in Sheffield – Mr B. has made various suggestions to him about getting employment.

---

[16] Moulton Grammar School was about 4 miles north of Weston St Mary where Mr Atkinson lived. Welbourn went there at the age of 6, and stayed until he went to Framlingham.

This is an expensive hotel and it is a good job we are only here for one night – the charge is $12.00 for the room. It is a set-off to the Deer Lodge primitive hotel where the charge was $6.00 for 2 nights for both of us.

The Railway Electr. from Tacoma to Othello and then from Albany to Harlowton was most instructive and the information gained on it will be valuable to the B.I. and others. Tomorrow, I intend to try to borrow some lantern slides from the Rly. Co. here for my address to the Lpool Engineers in October or November[17].

I think the Railroad shopmen's strike shows signs of collapsing – the train drivers, guards, track maintenance men and clerks are not out. It is the maintenance men in the shops who are out and, of course, the trains cannot run fully for long if they are not properly repaired etc. The Miners strike is the more serious, I think, and I see that coal is to come from England and Australia. We get scarcely any English news as none of the hotels take the home newspapers. Such a lot of the papers in this country are rubbishy to us as they have so much sensational news about murders etc. etc. I think we are going to make N.Y. alright to get our *Laconia* on Aug. 3rd – I shall be glad to get away for home and I look forward to the welcome home.

I hope I shall get exercise on the boat as I am pretty liverish with all this travelling and heat. Its not possible to take much active exercise here because it sets the heart beating too violently.

With much love to you all.
Burke

William Penn Hotel
Pittsburgh
July 29th 1922

My dear Wife,

I have remembered many times during a full day that it is our 21st Wedding Day. As I write it must be after midnight at home and I hope you are safe and sound asleep! All being well, it will not be long before I am with you.

I reached here from Chicago about 7.45 a.m. today after a bad night in the train and after being awake from 5.30 a.m. After a hurried bath and breakfast, I had to rush off to East Pittsburgh and have only just returned about 7.00 p.m. After dinner I want to write up some of my notes which are nearly 4 weeks in arrears – I simply couldn't keep pace with them and one cannot work in the shaky, noisy, hot trains. Mr A. went straight on to Philadelphia to see some friends of Revd. Houson and is to await me there on Tuesday – I expect that the night journey there on Monday night will be my 12th and last. I am very sick of

---

[17] Chairman's Address to the Liverpool Sub-Centre of the IEE, delivered on 6 November 1922.

this night journeying as you may well imagine.

I am wondering about your elbow. If it isn't better soon, what do you say about our having a week at Matlock or Buxton for treatment?

I hope you and the 3 youngest got your Chicago p.p.cs. alright? Perhaps I will get some more tomorrow for E and T. Mr & Mrs Crossley are coming here to see me tomorrow night. She's Belgian and they have been married less than a year.

With much love to you all.

Burke

POST CARD (Pittsburgh)
29.7.1922

This town reminds me of Manchester
on account of the smoke and works.
It is largely run on Natural Gas
out of the earth. The places where it
is tapped look like the wooden erections
over oil wells. I am wondering which
day you break up. Love from
Father

J. T. B. Welbourn Esq.
c/o Mrs Evers-Swindell
Sunnyside
Pedmore
nr. Stourbridge

William Penn Hotel
Pittsburgh
July 30th 1922

My dearest

Today, we were at Kew and saw the 3 old ladies and we were getting ready for the departure tomorrow for Dieppe and Paris[18]. The recollection of it all is still very vivid.

This morning, the enclosed card was brought to me and I set off about 10 to 11 for the Church. After walking in the blazing sun and humid atmosphere for ½ hour and still not finding it, I gave up the search when I came to a public garden with some fine flowers in it.

I went into the Conservatory and saw a magnificent Victoria Regia from Brazil and other flowering water-lilies. The Regia had six leaves like tables with turned up edges. The largest would be about 6' 0" across and the root going to it looked like a rope.

In the entrance, there was a fossil fish said to be at least 1,000,000 years old

---

[18] On their honeymoon.

and brought from the country which is now the Mohave Desert where I found the heat so trying in the trains on the way to Los Angeles. Apparently, there was once a big inland sea which divided N. America into two parts.

I walked back here and have been nearly asleep resting after the heat which made my head go funny.

Last night, just as I was starting work, about 8.45, I had a call from a newspaper reporter from the Pittsburgh Post and he stayed until 11.00 p.m. I got no work done but I had a most informing talk with him. He is a Canadian-turned American and a fervid admirer of ex- President Woodrow Wilson. Consequently, he was not pleased with Lloyd George & Co.

How much of the talk will appear in the paper tomorrow remains to be seen. He didn't take any notes and our talk ranged over a wide range of subjects. Incidentally, he did most of the talking and I felt that I was really the interviewer!

Dick and Donald would have been much interested today in a Pet Shop. One window was jammed full of baby chickens. At the wire door of the shop were two puppies and a mother terrier.

I had a fine sleep last night and did not get up until 8.45. I propose to have a quiet afternoon in this bedroom which is cool and on the shady side of the hotel.

With much love to all from
Burke

(Editor's note: The letters stop here. Welbourn returned home with a blue-print giving the circuit of the very latest ideas for a 3-valve wireless receiver. This was built by Tom, and we were the first family for many miles around to have a wireless receiver. It required an aerial strung across the front garden; most of the components were war-surplus from Woolworths, except for the variable condenser, a very large affair in a glass case, bought from the BI. The earphones were split, so that two visitors could listen simultaneously.

Welbourn also returned with incredible travellers tales of how charwomen ('dailies') were wealthy enough to come to work in their Tin-Lizzies, the first Fords.

Mr Atkinson saw white lines on the roads for the first time, and introduced the idea to England on the roads of Lincolnshire.)

These three letters, written by B. Welbourn AKC, Contracts Manager of the British Insulated and Helsby Cables Ltd. are the only ones of his regular letters to his wife, other than those from his travels, which survive.

To Mrs B. Welbourn
Rigg Hall Farm
Staintondale
Cloughton S O
near Scarborough

Craven Lodge
Rainhill
August 13th 1910

My dearest,

Thank you so much for your letters. I did not get one at the Club[1] yesterday as I expected. I asked finally at 3.45 before I left for Liverpool.

Here, I have had a break of 1¼ hours and much excitement. Outside, I heard a noise and discovered two boys at the apple tree. I jumped through the window and caught one – named Arthur Morris who lives at the toffee shop next to Miss Hoskins' – the other's face I did not see but he is named, I am told, Jimmy Howard. The boy I caught is a born actor. He feigned a coming fit, told me lies very glibly as to his name and where he lived and I only got what he called 'God's Truth' when I threatened to march him off to the police station. I took him home and left him to be dealt with there. I suspected that he is Roman Catholic and he said he is. He said he has no parents living. The Hayes family *seemed* very indignant when I took him home but I am not sure how genuine it was.

Anyway, I am warning the police again without mentioning names.

I am very sorry you have not had a letter from me on one day this week. I am quite sure I have written daily but probably Maggie[2] missed posting by 8.00 p.m. one night. I fancied she was cutting things rather fine. Did you get two letters together one day?

You are right about the East Coast air. The climate here is much more

---

[1] The Constitutional Club, Northumberland Avenue, London.

[2] Mrs Margaret Townley, who came in to do mending.

fatiguing just now. I do not feel anything like so fit since I got back and added to this, I have been unable to sleep properly on a single night. I have slept until about 2 or 3 o'clock and then have had quite a disturbed time for the rest of the night. I seem to have had a very full week and it seems ages since I left you last Monday. I did want you, yesterday, coming up in the train alone from London but I do not mean to be selfish and recall you from your holiday. I have been wondering whether you would stay on until the Tuesday or Wednesday if I could join you next Saturday afternoon? I want to go to Newcastle and could go straight on, on the Monday morning, via Whitby and Middlesborough but let me know as soon as possible if this suits you and also Mrs Ripley.

Mr Gull has been in to ask me to read the lessons for him tomorrow both morning and evening and to go to them for supper. Mr White read for him last Sunday but Mr Gull prefers me to do it!!!

Mr Challinor continues the organ duties until the end of September but takes up his new work at Horwich near Bolton before then. The applicant-organist played at the choir practice on Thursday night and Mr Buchanan thought he shaped very well.

I enjoyed my 50-minute chat with Mrs Gray[3] and her sister last night. Mrs Gray seemed so very pleased to see me and was in very good form. She asked after you particularly and sent you very cordial messages. She says they intend to come again in 2 years' time and to land at Queenstown, do Ireland and then do the Trossachs, the English Lakes and the East Coast. This time they have spent most of their time in Rome, Venice, Munich and Paris and only had a few days in the Lake District. They very thoroughly enjoyed the Passion Play at Ober-Ammergau – chiefly, I think, because of its religious value.

There was not time to talk about many things, of course, but I felt my visit had given real pleasure. Miss Way is possibly going on a visit to Vancouver. She has had whooping cough very severely and is much annoyed, at her age!

I have experienced a few really pleasant things this week.
1. Revd W. Gilmoure's personal simplicity, and earnestness for his work, freedom from all religious cant.
2. The playing of the military Band at the Exhibition and especially a long cornet solo. The man seemed to me to be better and more artistic than Howard Reynolds who used to perform on the cornet at London Concerts about 14 year ago.
3. The beauty of the trees and country generally from London to Crewe yesterday. There were also some wonderful cumulus clouds with curious lighting effects on them towards sunset.
4. Tonight, Geoff Taylor[4] has given some splendid calls on his bugle.

Tomorrow, I am going to tea at Mrs Marsh's. They asked me to dinner also

---

[3] He had stayed with the Grays in the USA in 1907.

[4] A neighbour in the Territorial Army.

but I have declined. I have not had time to see the Nash's but am going down after writing this. It is now 8.45 p.m. and I will break off.

I have not had time to see the Chamberlains and do not know whether there is tennis afoot or not. I think it is very likely that I shall go to Chesterfield on Tuesday or Wednesday, and on to London but I cannot say until I have been to Prescot. I have been away since Wed. morning. Already, this is quite a long letter for me – my thoughts are flowing unusually well. Layton is in trouble again. About 2 months ago, he went to the Isle of Wight for his own health and took his wife with him. On the night of arrival, she had a miscarriage, was in bed for three weeks and was then moved to London to be operated on for womb displacement. She cannot be moved home for about another 3 weeks!

Sunday – Aug. 14th

Last night, there was a light upstairs at the Nash's but I could get no answer to my two rings so I went to the Collingwood's and found that Mr Nash does not return until today. Mrs Nash and the children are back.

Mrs Collingwood started to tell me of the specialist's visit to Mr C. and of the serious thing he had found out and then Mr C. came into the room and we had to change the subject. I do not know yet what the trouble is but Mr C. certainly looks thin and grey. Mrs C. looked very well and was most pleased with the letters from you and Fräulein.

After I got home last night, I had to cut the grass although I had had Rainford here to do it on Thursday. I really think his eyesight is defective. I got very hot and then had a bath before supper. It was than that Mr Gull came so he had to wait.

Thank you very much, dearest, for two letters this morning. One of them is the one destined to arrive tomorrow morning.

The reason for not going to Peterboro' is that I cannot get away. I had to be at Winsford yesterday instead of London and only got home at 4.45. Also I *must* be at Prescot at 9.00 a.m. tomorrow.

I had ¾ hour to wait in Liverpool yesterday for my train to Rainhill. At Lime St, Edward Tracey came and made himself known to me. He was Secretary of the B.I. before Kerfoot, and left about 8 years ago and went to Australia. He is down-at-heel and I took him to the James and gave him a good tea. He did not ask for money. I never knew him well nor had I very great respect for him personally nor his ability.

I intend to send Marjorie[5] a birthday letter. I think her birthday is on Aug. 16th, isn't it?

I am glad you are able to see so much of your mother and the girls. If I get to Scarboro' next Saturday perhaps you could meet me and we could go up to see

---

[5] Marjorie Appleyard, his wife's youngest sister.

some Tennis Finals? I told Aunt Emily[6] about Tommy's 'Do you mean the mountains on the horizon?' and she said it reminded her of Doris who was not then 2-year old saying 'Are we going to the photographer's?' Mr & Mrs C. were also much amused at the big words.

There is a receipt from the Bank for your £25 cheque.

It was very nice of Mr Nash to send you such an appreciative letter. I am just going down to the Post Office with this and to make another attempt see the Nash babies before Church. Also I want fresh air to clear my head.

Much love to you and the babes

from your loving husband

Burke

(Editor's note: The next letter was written at his mother's home shortly after the birth of their son Fred on 12 October 1912.)

13 November 1912   Carr Dyke,
                                                             Peakirk

My dearest,

Thank you very much for your welcome letter, which came before I was up this morning.

I left the Atkinson's[7] yesterday evening after a most enjoyable visit. The motor-cycle stopped in Weston Hills but I got it away again. Near Cowbit station it stopped altogether, & I had about 4 hours work at the roadside pulling it to pieces to try & make it go. Finally I had to go by the 2.00 pm train with it to Spalding. There were 4 oddments which could not be done on the road single-handed. I have been to Spalding again today to see about it but did not bring it away owing to the heavy rain.

I called to see Mr Munro at the Bank and had a short chat.

I sent you a ppc to Rainhill & I hope this will actually await you at Rhos[8]. I think that I have remembered the address correctly. My intention is to leave here tomorrow morning and, if fine, to ride home possibly via Sheffield. If wet, I fear I must use the train so that I may join you on Friday or Saturday.

I have been buying apples today, 1½ stones of eaters and 4½ of cookers. They have been packed and sent off home, *carriage paid*. The eaters were 1*s*. 3*d*. the stone, the cookers 1*s*. 0*d*. a stone. Carriage on the lot was 1*s*. 11*d*. I thought it was a bargain not to be lost.

---

[6] Emily Gregory, widow of Henry Gregory. Doris, the youngest child, became Lady Jephcot, whose husband was chairman of Glazo.

[7] Mr Atkinson of Weston Hills near Spalding travelled with him to the USA in 1922.

[8] His wife had gone to stay there with the baby.

My Father on his motor-cycle, circa 1912.

I intend to go to Peterborough on the next train to see Mary Able[9] & get back here for tea at 5.00 pm. The sun is shining, & I hope it (the weather) will remain fine for the rest of the afternoon. Last evening & night the wind and rain were very heavy.

I am sending a ppc to the children to cheer them after you have gone to Rhos. With much love from
your loving husband
Burke

(Editor's note: The following letter is written in the indelible pencil which Welbourn always carried on him. The address is that of Walter Appleyard, the younger brother of Welbourn's deceased father-in-law. Both of them were executors of his estate. Walter Appleyard, chairman of Johnson and Appleyards Ltd., and also of Bassetts Sweets, became Lord Mayor of Sheffield in 1916.)

14 November 1912 Endcliffe Crescent, Sheffield

My dearest,

Thank you very much for your p.c. this morning. The weather was so unsatisfactory & the roads were so bad that I decided to come on to Sheffield & do some Trustee work. There are a good many important points to discuss including that of finding some additional capital for J & A Ltd. They do not seem likely to do anything good until they have more working capital & can take advantage of trade discounts & get free of the bank overdraft incubus.

Your uncle and aunt very kindly asked me to stay tonight, and I have accepted their invitation. Your uncle has a very bad cold & is confined to the house.

They are very interested in Fred & his photograph & have made kind enquiries about you.

I found all well & rather more prosperous than I expected at Peakirk. They have a nice new cosy little home. The house is rent free with coals + 15/-per week.

My intention is to go home tomorrow, get the side car, deal with the accumulated letters and make an early start on Saturday morning for Rhos. If there is anything you want bringing (not too bulky) I could bring it in the car in addition to my own luggage.

Nickolls is waiting to go to the post with this.

With very much love from
Burke.

---

[9] A distant relative.